Changes in Contemporary Ireland

Changes in Contemporary Ireland: Texts and Contexts

Edited by

Catherine Rees

CAMBRIDGE SCHOLARS PUBLISHING

Changes in Contemporary Ireland: Texts and Contexts,
Edited by Catherine Rees

This book first published 2013

Cambridge Scholars Publishing

12 Back Chapman Street, Newcastle upon Tyne, NE6 2XX, UK

British Library Cataloguing in Publication Data
A catalogue record for this book is available from the British Library

ISBN (10): 1-4438-4472-1, ISBN (13): 978-1-4438-4472-7

TABLE OF CONTENTS

LIST OF ILLUSTRATIONS

LIST OF TABLES

ACKNOWLEDGEMENTS

With grateful thanks to Daniel Sage for all his advice, help and encouragement.

Thanks also to my colleague at Loughborough University, Deirdre O'Byrne, who co-organised the *Changes in Contemporary Ireland* conference this book was inspired by, and so helped bring some of these contributors initially together.

INTRODUCTION

CATHERINE REES

The title of this book focuses on the word "change". All the essays enclosed within this volume discuss how much life has changed in Ireland in recent years. Whether it be in political, social or cultural fields, life for many in Ireland has undergone significant change in recent decades, and the aim of this book is to discuss some of the ways in which these changes are reflected in Irish and Northern Irish society. However, while it might be common-place to speak of these fundamental changes, it's crucial to also analyse and explore the term "change" and to ask some supplementary important questions. What has changed? For whom? How can we measure it? At what cost? And can we ever meaningfully speak of complex social and political factors moving together as one in a single and forceful move in one direction? For every "change" is there not another parallel story of compromise, reversion and concession?

The narrative of change in Ireland is well established and clearly there have been numerous important shifts in everyday experience for people living in both the Republic and Northern Ireland. Many critics have pointed to significant social changes in both political policy and social attitudes in the 1960s as an instigator of change for the Republic. As Neil Hegarty explains, "The introduction in 1967 of free secondary education, combined with increasing links to Europe and to modern media and the growth of the women's movement, all contributed to the development of a more progressive and liberal civil society" (2011: 330). Developments within global communications and the mass media are often cited as the driving forces of social change and public opinion. Martin McLoone argues that "Television encouraged a more questioning attitude to all kinds of authority" (2008: 115), highlighting "the Irish diaspora; economic prosperity and social changes in Celtic Tiger Ireland [and] the peace process in Northern Ireland" as key factors that have "greatly influenced the ways in which Irish culture and identity is both articulated and understood today" (8). Christopher Morash's study of media over the twentieth century in Ireland claims that through engagement with new modes of media a "new spaceless geography" (2010: 4) has been created and therefore eroded notions of Ireland as a single or bounded nation.

In Northern Ireland, change has been even more tangible. Brian M. Walker begins his study of Irish politics in the twentieth century with the claim "Recently we have witnessed significant change in Northern Ireland" (2012: x) and later refers again to "recent dramatic change to identity amongst so many people and communities" (xiv). Morash cites the Good Friday Agreement as evidence of "something [having] shifted radically in Irish culture" (220) and Patrick Joseph Haynes and Jim Campbell's extensive study of Post-Traumatic Stress Disorder after Bloody Sunday refers to the 1994 ceasefire and subsequent signing of the Belfast Agreement (known as the Good Friday Agreement) as "a watershed" (2005: 35).

The language of "change" is thus evident; social and economic factors in the Republic have driven huge cultural developments and political upheavals in the North have paved the way for historical changes in establishing a peaceful society following decades of violence. But to speak of such a complex entity as a nation moving forward in a single direction is necessarily reductive. Although we can clearly measure policies, events and moments that seem to signify change, we must also interrogate claims that suggest that "Ireland" is experiencing any single or simple momentum. As Colin Graham has pointed out, "'Ireland' is a future which is always posited and never attained…Ireland becomes 'Ireland', a 'cited', quoted version of itself which is both excessive and phantasmal" (2001: ix). As such, any attempt to describe a nation, particularly one as historically complex as Ireland, is impossible, as competing forces struggle to map their own account of the country onto a multiple and multifocal series of attitudes, beliefs, values and experiences. In this way, it is important to remember that when we speak of "change", we cannot speak for every citizen and every event. While some may experience profound change and upheaval, others may encounter little difference in their everyday lives. For every political development there are other, less well publicised, failures and losses. Crucially, "change" is often mediated through external channels, and so how people encounter this narrative of change may be not first hand, but through the media or political discourse. The media is responsible for not merely reporting events but also creating memories, both individual and cultural. Graham Dawson has describes how "media memories [have] contributed to the formation of personal memories" (2010: 240) in major events such as Bloody Sunday. Indeed, Greg McLaughlin and Stephen Barker have argued that the media smoothed over cracks in the Northern Irish peace process (2010: 25) and Haynes and

Campbell suggest that the media can conversely exacerbate the violence by "fuelling speculation about whom to blame and influence people's responses, particularly a desire for retaliation" (2005: 54). McLoone argues that films set in Belfast and focusing on sectarian images of the city in decay serve to "prolong Belfast's pariah status and to obfuscate considerably the underlying politics of Northern Ireland" (2008: 53). In this way, we can see that the images and reports we receive about a nation, and events within it, are not uncontested and are not always simple or straightforward. Narratives are always competing and often the most newsworthy is the most prominent, and conflicting or complicating reports are thus often neglected.

Nevertheless, and with this caveat in mind, it is possible to speak meaningfully about developments in Irish society, so long as we remember that "change" is often partial or fractional. The term "change" is in itself charged, stimulating images of forward momentum, positive development and future planning. Those who feel disempowered and disenfranchised in society may find it hard to buy into this narrative of progression. There are also stark differences between experiences in the Republic and Northern Ireland. In the 1960s, when social changes were becoming notable for those south of the border, 1968 saw the beginning of the Troubles in Northern Ireland, bringing decades of violence, trauma, political stalemate and economic depression. Although this book studies "Ireland" as an island, and looks equally at both countries, it's important to remember that they remain divided nations, and change impacts on them in different ways at different times. With that in mind, turning first to the Republic, we can chart some significant and important upheavals in the past few decades, and these events create a narrative of globalisation, mass media development, economic boom and bust, scandal and radical shifts in public attitudes.

Change in the Republic: Tigers, Televisions and Transition

Changes in the Republic of Ireland in the past few decades seem to highlight the position of the country in global terms. As social attitudes, political policies and mass media networks reach outwards, Ireland has apparently lost some insularity and has now become part of a global community. Morash tells us that in 2004 Ireland was deemed "the most globalised country in the world" (2010: 1) ahead of more obvious contenders Singapore, the United States and the United Kingdom.

Morash argues that mass media has played a significant role in widening Ireland's position on the global stage. He suggests that as Ireland adopted its own televisual identity in the 1950s and 60s, and began making and showing programmes based on Irish experience and life, Irish society became accustomed to reflecting on and debating long-held values and beliefs. An oft-quoted example of this is the ground breaking *The Late Late Show* which gave guests the opportunity to debate openly and freely, and outside the strictures of the otherwise all-encompassing Catholic Church. Morash argues that a new authority became important, that of information, and that this "was superior to the authority of office–whether of church or state" (2010: 180). Scandals in the Catholic Church, largely related to the uncovering of years of sexual abuse of young children by priests, which was suppressed by the wider Catholic community, also helped erode this authority. Whilst *The Late Late Show* "shaped public opinion" (Morash, 2010: 241) and helped to question the traditional values of early twentieth century Ireland, another factor was equally important in exposing Irish audiences to global products and programming. Satellite television was enormously popular in Ireland and helped the nation define its television viewing in terms of global rather than national boundaries. Access to, amongst other things, pornography, circumvented a national culture of censorship "which had been one of the defining features of Irish life since the 1920s, and which had contributed so much to the sense of Irish insularity" (Morash, 2010: 215).

The Irish economy did not grow as quickly as its media industry, suffering recessions throughout the 1970s and 80s. However, an enormous economic upturn in the 1990s, described as the so-called Celtic Tiger, helped place Ireland even more firmly on the global market. Entry into the European Union, and adoption of the euro, (1973 and 1999 respectively) was also politically significant and "served to further undermine much of the economic, social and moral isolation under which the country had suffered […], and which had been linked to restrictive identities" (Walker, 2012: 133). Mary Robinson was elected to the presidency in 1990 and challenged several traditionally restrictive laws including the ban on artificial contraception and homosexuality (Hegarty, 2012: 331). In 1997 Mary McAleese was elected as president and helped yet further to challenge patriarchal views of women in power, "symbolising the new role of women in modern Ireland" (Walker, 2012: 138). The visit of Queen Elizabeth II in 2011 was also charged with political significance and suggested that "a line had been drawn under the past" (Hegarty, 2012: 340). New access to economic prosperity reinvigorated Irish cultural life too, with literature and theatre especially thriving in the urban centres and also rural areas. The Irish film industry was also doing well and tourism was a major factor in economic revenue, with global visitors frequently arriving in the country. In fact, a 2003 Irish guide book, *Culture Smart! Ireland*, designed to offer advice on "customs and etiquette" to mainly American tourists declared that "the Irish economy is performing exceptionally well and seems likely to continue doing so" (Scotney, 2003: 67).

Of course, we know now that this prediction was too optimistic and reading these words seems deeply ironic at the time of writing this introduction in 2012. Economic prosperity did not continue in Ireland and economic ruin was only narrowly averted in 2008. As Ireland became more and more connected to global markets, the international financial crisis of 2007 impacted on Ireland particularly hard, and a property bubble in Dublin, based on excessive bank lending, burst spectacularly, and left many Dubliners stranded in homes stripped of value and thus unsellable.

This tale of economic boom and bust tells us that the narrative of change and progression in Ireland is far from straightforward. Neil Hegarty suggests that Ireland was hit particularly hard in the economic recession because "The history of Ireland had propagated a sense of failure and of inferiority" but that the Celtic Tiger offered an opportunity to "put this traumatic history firmly in the past" (2012: 334-335). In this account we can detect a sense of failure and pessimism underpinning the success story of the 1994 Celtic Tiger phenomenon. Whilst great and important changes were being felt in Irish society, culture and politics, it's crucial to remember that these changes were not only one-way, and that other, complicating and more ambiguous processes were also occurring at the same time, or underpinning this narrative of forward momentum and change. For example, Hegarty points out that while sexual abuse in the Catholic Church was being uncovered through the 1990s and early 2000s, a report into the scandal detailed abuse taking place as late as 2009 (Hegarty, 2012: 339), a time when perhaps many felt that this particular problem had been exposed and ended. Writing in the present collection, Sharon Leahy argues that RTE and *The Late Late Show*, so crucial in helping to question traditional values and attitudes, is also guilty of perpetuating racist images of immigrants into Ireland. McLoone suggests that global images of Ireland, so important in selling the country to foreign tourists, consist primarily of "kitsch paddywhackery [and] the cult of alcohol" (2008: 5). He goes on to argues that global Ireland has no choice but to trade on historical tragedies and traumas (2008: 5) in order to sell Irish identity and experience across the globe. These disabling and tragic images of Irish identity are clearly sentimental and based on old colonial prejudices yet, McLoone suggests, they form a crucial role in commodifying Ireland on the global market. If Ireland must compete in these markets, it perhaps does so at the expense of establishing more positive images of national identity.

While the narrative of "change" is clearly important and evident for the Republic in the 1990s and beyond, we cannot see it as a simply one directional process. As Ireland develops its identity within international markets and travel, it is also bound by more unsettling images of economic recession, the covering up of abuse and the tourist kitsch of sentimentality. However, while change in the Republic was largely progressing well, life for those in Northern Ireland was much more clearly marked by violence and upheaval.

Change in Northern Ireland: Troubles, Trauma and Truce

To move forward and embrace change it is often necessary to accept and agree upon shared views of history. In Northern Ireland, this is notoriously difficult where "there is no consensus about the past" (McLaughlin and Barker, 2010: 37). If there is no agreed upon version of the past, it becomes hard to see where change in the future can develop. In many ways the history of Northern Ireland in the 1970s and 80s is an anathema to the idea of change and transition; it is looking backwards to previous traumas and battles rather than facing forwards to develop new ways of living. Although Northern Ireland was also affected by the global changes of the 1960s and onwards I've charted in the Republic, the historical narrative of Northern Ireland in this time is primarily dominated by the Troubles. Generally understood to begin in 1968, the Troubles describe a period of sectarian warfare across Northern Ireland, although largely focused on the urban centres of Belfast and (London)Derry, in which British armed forces were deployed in the country and the devolved government was replaced in 1972 by Direct Rule from London, giving British politicians the power to administer changes to Northern Irish society and politics.

One way to view the events of the Troubles is through the lens of trauma studies. Haynes and Campbell have reviewed Bloody Sunday through the study of Post-Traumatic Stress Disorder (PTSD) and make some observations that can be applied more widely. On 30th January 1972 fourteen men[1] were shot dead by British security forces during a civil rights march in Derry, in an event which came to be known as Bloody Sunday. These men were killed by their own state, which is a shocking and unusual occurrence in the United Kingdom. Initial inquiries into the shootings were flawed; they supported the actions of the British forces and suggested that the victims had been likely terrorists. However, subsequent inquires (namely the Saville inquiry which culminated in 2010) dismissed these claims, and concluded that the fourteen dead had been unlawfully murdered. This event is emblematic of the Troubles; it caused widespread hatred and fear of the security services and questioned their role in Northern Ireland as well as representing the tragic loss of innocent life associated with the violence of this period. It has been referred to as a "seminal event of the Troubles" (Dawson, 2010: 230) of "totemic stature" (Conway, 2010: 2).

Many of the families of those killed are, according to Haynes and Campbell, suffering from PTSD. This psychological disorder describes symptoms of anxiety and depression following a traumatic event, usually one threatening the life of the sufferer or that of a loved one. The effect of the trauma is often most acutely felt when the event has been created and perpetuated by humans; "If the trauma stems from a natural phenomenon, it is a disaster; if created by humankind, it is an atrocity" (Haynes and Campbell, 2005: 41). They go on to make a comparison between an abusive family environment and the actions of the security services: "The abusive caretaker in this case [...] is the British government, which in family members' perceptions, has blamed the victim, distorted the facts, and continued to perpetuate the abuse. As with child victims, the Bloody Sunday families had no recourse but to suffer in silence" (2005: 176). Within the framework of trauma studies, "change" can be figured as "working through", a process whereby victims confront their trauma and attempt to "gain critical distance" (LaCapra, 2001: 143) by accepting past events and allowing their lives to move forward. This can be seen within the overall discussion of "change"; in Northern Ireland change can be a psychological process as much as a political or cultural one. Indeed, Haynes and Campbell suggest that even after political change has been achieved, some find it "difficult [...] to adjust to the notion that suddenly, there is peace" (2005: 130).

Within the context of Northern Ireland we can see that the concept of "working through" might have some relevance to our discussion of

[1] Thirteen were shot and killed on the day or soon after and a further one died four months later from his injuries. Seven of the victims were teenagers.

"change". For those who lived through the Troubles, "change" came to be mobilised though the Good Friday Agreement (GFA) which, following an IRA ceasefire in 1994, paved the way for the end of hostilities and allowed for power to transfer back to Stormont, the Northern Irish government, with newly elected officials. Inevitably, change here did come at a cost. Haynes and Campbell's research found families of Bloody Sunday victims who felt justice would never be done because the GFA forced compromise (2005: 169). They also point out that traditional sources of support, such as religion and political beliefs, might be the very factors that "retard the development of political solutions" (1995: 52). In Northern Ireland it can be difficult to establish any real differences between victim and perpetrator, as both sides can record traumas and grievances. Crucially, "change" and "working through" does not call for these events to be forgiven or necessarily forgotten: "working out does not mean avoidance, harmonization, simply forgetting the past, or submerging oneself in the present. It means coming to terms with the trauma" (LaCapra, 2001: 144). In this context, change is very much related to compromise and discussion, and it would be too simplistic to see these changes as fully completed or over. Nevertheless, there has been significant development in the political stalemate in Northern Ireland and a renewed and rejuvenated interest in its geographical space and future in global economies. Perhaps the "working through" of past traumas is starting to take effect.

Change or no change?

It is clear that "change" has been a watch-word in studies of Irish history in recent years. In many ways it would be churlish to deny the fundamental and significant changes that have occurred in Irish society over a relatively short period of time; great economic development (and then sudden recession) in the Republic accompanied by radical shifts in public opinion, and the political developments in the North are truly momentous and illustrate great fortitude in the people both making the political history and those living with it.

But, as we have seen, "change" cannot be understood as merely one directional and it is not felt by all people equally at the same time. Walker notes in his discussion of the GFA, for example, that "changes must not be exaggerated… many on each side had only partially embraced these changes and there remained a lack of trust" (2012: 148). Hegarty agrees, and points out that life in Northern Ireland remains, for many, still segregated (2012: 329) and so-called "peace lines" still divide Belfast and carve up the cityscape isolating the nationalists and unionists in ghettoised areas. Similarly, the Celtic Tiger may have brought prosperity and success to many in Dublin, but it brought with it global problems such as "racism, high levels of alcoholism [and] inner-city crime" revealing the Tiger to be "multifarious [and] contradictory" (McLoone, 2008: 6). Global success has a price, underpinning positive change with darker and more troubling images.

Ultimately, any discussion of change can never be completed, because change does not simply "end" or reach a final conclusion. As we saw with the success story of the Celtic Tiger, the subsequent recession undermined the narrative of positive economic rejuvenation in Ireland. Bloody Sunday was a low point in the violence of the Troubles, but only a couple of decades later, peace talks were underway. The GFA brought hope and some tranquillity but recent rioting in the streets of Belfast again complicates this story of reconciliation and harmony. Hegarty points out that "history can never be wished to a conclusion" (2012: 340) and this is an important lesson to remember. Change can only ever be seen as part of a process in which we are all constantly moving and one in which we can only ever really look backwards and reflect on what has already passed. Throughout, changes in experience and identity are a constant process. Irish identity is perhaps particularly "malleable" (Hegarty, 2012: 342). While we can undoubtedly agree that Ireland (both North and South) is now prominent on the global stage, we must also remember that it remains impossible to offer a single or simple account of any nation, especially one with such a complex and contested history (and present). We should also be distrustful of attempts to describe any images of the nation as final, authentic or complete. As Baudrillard tells us,

> When the real is no longer what it used to be, nostalgia assumes its full meaning. There is a proliferation of myths or origin and signs of reality; of second-hand truth, objectivity and authenticity (1983, 12).

About this book

This book is divided into four sections, "Landscape, Memory and Religion", "Lifestyle and Entertainment", "Media and Film" and "Drama and Literature". Each section deals with specific case studies, and these studies help explore and discuss the subject of change within what we can loosely call "contemporary" Ireland. An exact time frame has not been strictly applied, but generally these chapters address the sorts of changes I've outlined in this introduction and they refer to recent events within both the Republic and Northern Ireland. I have deliberately not divided the chapters into those that deal with the two geographical areas separately;

rather the hope is that the thematic order will be most interesting and useful for the reader. The volume also takes a mutli-disciplinary approach, and the volume has been largely ordered by topic rather than academic discipline.

The first section covers a diverse series of topics; the sexual scandal in the Catholic Church and the resulting loss of faith for many in Ireland, a public art sculpture in the centre of Belfast and artefacts dealing with trauma and memory in post ceasefire Belfast. Peter Guy's "The Casey Effect" provides a fascinating account of recent troubles in the Catholic Church and reflects upon the future for a nation so defined by its association with Catholicism as that influence declines dramatically. This secularisation of Irish society is, Guy suggests, part of wider social and economic shifts in recent times and he argues that the church must now offer what he terms a "postmodern approach to religion" to appeal to new, perhaps more sceptical and certainly more media savvy, church members. Joana Etchart's chapter looks at a piece of public art, the RISE sculpture in Belfast. She argues that although this project was designed to reflect and engage with the local community, the public's voices were not heard in the planning of the art work. Although the sculpture was designed to reflect a peaceful and contemporary view of the city, Etchart's research finds that the inner workings of local governance within Belfast are still too fragmented and contested to properly manage and execute these large-scale, high profile artistic events. Staying in Belfast, Shane Alcobia-Murphy's chapter explores trauma and memory in artefacts produced within the city, including poetry and photography. He suggests that the city must remember the past, and not simply forget past traumas. This recalls the discussion earlier in this introduction which explored the peace process in Northern Ireland through the lens of trauma narratives. Moreover, we can see through Alcobia-Murphy's study that "the political and ethical meanings of memory cannot be viewed as separable from the particular rhetorical, narrative and visual conventions that give it shape" (Burke and Faulkner, 2010: 13); trauma is manifest in artistic artefacts through a conscious and deliberate evocation of memory.

The 'Lifestyle and Entertainment' section of this book includes the exploration of two separate but related cultural signifiers of Irish culture; sport and Guinness. Kathleen Heininge's "Guinness Go Leor" examines the global phenomenon of the Irish pub. Although the image of the Irish as habitual bar room enthusiasts is a stereotypical and disabling colonial myth, the "Irish bar" has spread globally and each establishment tries to emulate "authentic" Irish pubs as much as possible. Of course, as Heininge points out, attempts to "authentically" recreate Irish experience frequently involves recycling sentimental and partial myths but, interestingly, Heininge's paper argues that as these bars dominate a global image of Ireland, actual pubs in Ireland are forced to change and modify to be more in keeping with the "real" global pubs they are supposed to have inspired. In this way, globalisation creates a homogenised international experience which undermines national distinctiveness. Two chapters go on to explore football and sport in both the Republic and Northern Ireland. David Storey looks at the ways in which Irish society and identity are bound up and mediated through sport. He explores the relationship between identity and globalisation through the increasingly internationalisation of professional sports, and on the identities of professional sports men and women from across the globe, playing in modern Ireland. The chapter also reflects upon the relationship and controversies surrounding sports in Northern Ireland and the Republic, and reflects upon how cross-border migration causes some level of tension but also perhaps serves as a symbol of peaceful north-south relations. However, at its heart, sport relies on a very literal relationship with geographical space, and contested territories make sport in Ireland a heated and often controversial subject. Alan Bairner also looks at football, and takes a more unusual approach, comparing poet John Hewitt and the Northern Irish football team to examine questions of politics and identity within the sport. His argument is that, as long as "Northern Ireland" refers to a process of partition, it is impossible to de-politicise the team, and the choices individual players make as to which team to play for. Bairner uses Hewitt's interest in establishing and discussing a distinct regional identity for Ulster and for the six counties of Northern Ireland to explore the tensions in the terms used to describe these regions, and for the problems associated with assuming a specific and distinct sporting national identity.

The "Media and Film" section of the book is the longest, and encompasses film, television, and on-line technologies. In the first chapter in this section, Sarah Martindale and I look at Martin McDonagh's film *In Bruges* (2008) and compare it to his brother's, John Michael McDonagh, debut movie *The Guard* (2011). The brothers occupy an interestingly liminal space in terms of their Irish identity; they were born in London to Irish immigrant parents but both have set the majority of their work in Irish locations. They are therefore engaging with Irish imagery and experience in a potentially controversial manner. We use an interview with the former chief executive of the Irish Film Board, Simon Perry, to examine the role of national film, and to problematise and critique the limits of national borders in making and understanding movies, particularly as the images of the Irish we are presented with in both films are potentially troubling. Sharon Leahy's chapter offers a critique of a staple of Irish televisual identity–RTE–and argues that she has uncovered a number of instances of racial prejudice inherent in its programming. She points out that in an era of globalised televisual experience, national identities can be constructed through portrayal in the media and that, in various cases, there are worrying images of ethnic minorities in some of RTE's outputs. As this broadcaster is in many ways held responsible for shaping and moulding Irish national identity and for helping to shift public attitudes towards more liberal and secular thinking, this research is startling, and forces us to question how much power we give television to shape national consciousness. Robert Busby and Paddy Hoey use their chapter to chart the significance of the virtual sphere to politics and political campaigning. They use the example of éirígí, a republican splinter group, to examine their use of the internet to broaden their campaign and public profile. Interestingly, although their politics were primarily of local significance, the medium of the internet positioned their dialogues within a global framework, and their appeal is in combining issues important to a Northern Irish heritage with international debates. This modern approach to political debate perhaps transcends more traditional methods, but the importance of the media more widely in ensuring and creating political presence in the public consciousness is always felt. We return to televisual analysis for Fiona Fearon's chapter, which compares three recent tragic events in Ireland and the way in which the accompanying funerals were depicted in the world of 24 hour rolling news. She charts the history of funerals in Ireland, from events of great significance where mourning is almost celebrated as a signifier of national character, and then more recently as a more private activity. Her chapter suggests that the intrusion of the media into the ritual of the funeral makes mourning a public performance again and that the grief is then, perhaps partially, constructed by the media as they cover the event. She also looks at how fandom and celebrity help fuel the public's fascination with the deceased, perhaps at the expense of more private, meaningful grief. Finally, Fiona Coffey looks at so-called Troubles films, and makes a distinction between "open and "closed" forms of film; those which provide finished narratives and deny alternative endings, and those which defer closure and prefer a more open-ended understanding of the complex political dynamics in Northern Ireland. She also identifies films that present a rather stereotypical binary in their depiction of nationalist or loyalist characters, and whom they suggest we as an audience should sympathise with. Her conclusion is that as the political landscape shifted so radically in the 1990s, so films had to accommodate these changes by offering more reflective and nuanced filmic depictions of the Troubles. As the peace process unfolded, so too in film did the restrictive and binaried depictions of entrenched political opinions the GFA was attempting to overturn.

The final section explores the ways in which the issues outlined here are addressed in fictional depictions of Ireland–in literature and in drama. We begin with Catriona Ryan's essay on the playwright Tom Mac Intyre and his 2009 play *Only an Apple*. The play deals with a fictional politician (but largely based on disgraced Taoiseach Charles Haughey) and explores, through the use of two fantasy historical figures, the place of Ireland within contemporary European contexts. Adopting a psychoanalytical approach, Ryan describes Irish national identity in the late twentieth century as emerging from a colonial heritage and into a new European framework. She explores the play's use of language to describe deconstructed political and national identities, and she coins her own phrase to describe Mac Intrye's engagement with his national past balanced with the modern-"Paleo-postmodern". This term is used to describe the relationship between the traditional and the new. Cary Shay's study of the female Doppelgänger opens the discussion up to contemporary literature. Also taking a psychoanalytic approach, Shay uses novelist Anne Enright and playwright Marina Carr to explore the splitting of the female subject as a response to the social conditions for women in Ireland. Her focus on feminine identity, and particularly that of the mother, leads her to conclude that despite the significant changes promised by the Celtic Tiger, equality has not been afforded to women, especially in the areas of reproduction and maternity. The volume concludes with Eammon Jordan's chapter on perhaps Ireland's most successful and famous playwright of the 1990s and 2000s–Martin McDonagh. Although he is London-born, McDonagh's plays are based in Ireland and offer audiences comic, yet also sometimes touching, vignettes of life for some economically deprived inhabitants of the rural West. His 1997 play *The Lonesome West* is Jordan's focus here, and he uses the increasingly popular field of masculinity studies to examine McDonagh's depiction of men alienated from hegemonic masculinity's assumed position of power. Jordan argues that these images offer inversions of idealised pastoral Ireland, and he also looks at funerary traditions within Ireland (as we have also seen in Fiona Fearon's chapter in this volume) to comment upon McDonagh's satiric approach to religion and the priesthood.

Some concluding thoughts

At the time of writing this introduction a news story concerning Ireland is featuring heavily in newspapers and television news reports. Savita Halappanavar, a pregnant woman in Galway, recently died after beginning to miscarry. As the doctors could detect a heartbeat, an abortion was denied, despite pleas from the family to act. After the baby miscarried, the woman suffered septicaemia and died. When her husband asked for his wife's pregnancy to be terminated, he was reportedly told "This is a Catholic country" (BBC News, 14th November 2012) and this request was repeatedly refused. The woman in question was Hindu. Abortion remains illegal in Ireland.

It is difficult not to feel shocked when we hear about this story. The continuing relationship between church and state in Ireland, and the conflation suggested here between nation and religion whereby one is defined in terms of the other, is becoming a more and more contested issue, and the intervention here of the Catholic Church over a woman's body and health, particularly when she was not a practising Catholic herself, does make narratives of "change" and "progress" feel rather overstated. There has been fairly universal condemnation of this story in Britain and in Ireland this death is the subject of two separate inquires. However, for as long as the teachings and practices of the church direct government policies, it is difficult to see where change can spring from. Indeed, in Northern Ireland, a private abortion clinic has been the centre of protests in recent months, suggesting that abortion remains a contentious issue both sides of the border, with the law somewhat unclear in Northern Ireland, and one that provokes strong feelings on both sides. Twenty years on from the "X case"[2] this issue is still complex and controversial, suggesting little real development in the law, although it is less clear whether public opinion is still supportive of Catholic views on this issue.

---

[2] In 1992, a fourteen year old girl became pregnant as the result of rape by a neighbour. She was suicidal, and her parents decided to travel to England for an abortion. They asked the Garda if evidence from the aborted foetus should be kept to enable prosecution against the man who had attacked her. An injunction was subsequently taken out against the girl, preventing her from travelling. This was overturned on appeal but the girl in question (known only as "X") miscarried before an abortion could be carried out. The case remains an oft-quoted example of Ireland's tangled legal position on abortion although, crucially, it did establish the right to an abortion for a woman if her life was deemed to be in danger should the pregnancy continue.

On the other hand, and on the other side of the border, travel guide *Lonely Planet* recently named Londonderry/Derry as one of their top 10 global cities to visit. As the city claims the title of UK City of Culture 2013, *Lonely Planet* suggests that "this vibrant, historic walled city is undergoing a renaissance" (www.lonely planet.com, 2012). This focus on change and regeneration strikes many of the chords this introduction has set out to explore–that Ireland is a place of radical and dynamic change, moving from a place of troubles and trauma to one of renovation and rebirth. This narrative is one that has many subscribers, and it is clearly true that many significant and important changes have taken place in modern Ireland. These two news stories tell us, however, that progress on the island of Ireland is never over, and that change and development is constantly in a state of negotiation and flux–some things change, and others remain tangled in the complex wrangling of Irish political, social and cultural history.

Bibliography

Baudrillard, Jean. *Simulations*. Massachusetts: MIP Press, 1983.

BBC News website. "Women dies after abortion request 'refused' at Galway hospital". http://www.bbc.co.uk/news/world-20325659. Accessed 14th November 2012.

Burke, Lucy and Simon Faulkner. "Memory is Ordinary" in *The Politics of Cultural Memory*, edited by Lucy Burke and Simon Faulkner. Newcastle: Cambridge Scholars Press, 2010.

Conway, Brian. *Commemoration and Bloody Sunday*. Basingstoke: Palgrave Macmillan, 2010.

Dawson, Graham. "Father Daly's White Hanky: Survivor Memories, Collective Memory, and the Postmemory of Bloody Sunday in the Irish Troubles" in *The Politics of Cultural Memory* edited by Lucy Burke and Simon Faulkner. Newcastle: Cambridge Scholars Press, 2010.

Graham, Colin. *Deconstructing Ireland: Identity, Theory, Culture.* Edinburgh: Edinburgh University Press, 2001.

Haynes, Patrick Joseph and Jim Campbell. *Bloody Sunday: Trauma, Pain and Politics*. London et al: Pluto. 2005

Hegarty, Neil. *The Story of Ireland.* London: BBC Books, 2011.

La Capra, Dominick. *Writing History, Writing Trauma.* Baltimore and London: The John Hopkins Press, 2001.

Lonely Planet website. "Best in Travel 2013-Top 10 Cities". http://www.lonelyplanet.com/themes/best-in-travel-2013/top-10-cities/. Accessed 23rd October 2010.

McLaughlin, Greg and Stephen Barker. *The Propaganda of Peace: The Role of the Media and Culture in the Northern Ireland Peace Process.* Bristol: Intellect, 2010.

McLoone, Martin. *Film, Media and Popular Culture in Ireland: Cityscapes, Landscapes, Soundscapes*. Dublin and Portland: Irish Academic Press, 2008.

Morash, Christopher. *A History of the Media in Ireland*. Cambridge: Cambridge University Press, 2010

Scotney, John. *Culture Smart! Ireland*. New York: Random House, 2007

Walker, Brian M. *A Political History of the Two Irelands: From Partition to Peace*. Basingstoke: Palgrave. 2012.

PART I:

LANDSCAPE, MEMORY AND RELIGION

CHAPTER ONE

THE CASEY EFFECT: THE COLLAPSE OF CATHOLICISM IN IRELAND

PETER GUY

> "We had a conference at *The Irish Times* where we were discussing who we would put on Nelson's Pillar if it were to be re-erected. I suggested Bishop Casey. He caused the whole collapse…" (Kenny, 2000: 329)
> —John Banville

On May 2nd 2012, an hour-long documentary titled "This World–The Shame of the Catholic Church" was aired on BBC television. It sought to demonstrate the culpability of the Primate of All-Ireland, Cardinal Sean Brady, in the Fr Brendan Smyth child-abuse saga. Smyth was a prolific paedophile who used his position of trust to rape and sexually assault dozens of young children over a forty year period. When one of Smyth's victims, Brendan Boland, made a complaint in 1975 Cardinal Brady, then a canon-lawyer and rising star of the Irish Church, sat in on the inquiry–in his words-as a "notary". Boland, then a fourteen year old altar boy, gave the names of five other victims who had been abused by Smyth, only one of whom were subsequently contacted. Neither the parents nor the authorities were informed but Brady argued that he did his job in accordance to the letter of his remit–he conducted what appears to be a token investigation and passed on the information to his superiors and took no further part in the inquiry. Smyth, after an initial censure, continued his spectacularly successful career as a child molester where his activities were only curtailed some sixteen years later. The day after the program was aired Cardinal Brady, seeking some form of damage limitation, made two particularly noteworthy comments as a part-explanation for his role in the affair. One, he argued that, "In 1975 no State or Church guidelines existed in the Republic of Ireland to assist those responding to an allegation of abuse against a minor" (*The Irish Times*, May 3rd 2012: online). Second, he stated, "I didn't have the awareness I now have of the impact that that behaviour was having on those children" (*The Irish Examiner*, May 3rd 2012: online). To fully comprehend the collapse of Church authority in the 1990s, there can be no better illustration then in these two demonstrative statements.

I

It wasn't always thus. The Church had occupied a special position in Irish life since the inception of the State. When the Irish constitution of 1937 enshrined these terms into the letter of the law it provided, in the words of Brian Girvin, the "synthesis between Catholic, nationalist and democratic values in a way that provided a stable basis for constitutional continuity for the next forty years" (Girvin, 2002: 82). Irish Catholics, who had long endured religious discrimination under the Anglican ascendency, readily embraced this program for renewal and purification, the creation in effect of a spiritual Empire in opposition to more liberal-minded "foreign" trends. The fledgling Irish State was "narrow-minded, and for its own survival it felt that it needed to be" (Kenny, 2000: 117). Thus, the alliance between Church and State was borne out of a mutual need for legitimation and cohesion, "The Church offered the State continuity and stability and in return sought its support for continuity and stability in its own work" (Nic Ghiolla Phadraig, 1995: 609). As late as 1990, it could be claimed that 85% of the adult population of Ireland attended Church once weekly–a 6% decline since 1974 but still the highest in the world (Greeley, 1994: 137). Twenty years on, with mass attendance in Dublin falling to 13% and the harried Primate of All-Ireland facing a singularly hostile "trial by media", how did it come to this?

Part of the reason can be explained through de Tocqueville's maxim that the most dangerous time for a bad government is when it starts to reform itself. The indivisible link between Catholicism and Nationalism had held firm right up to the early sixties. The policy of isolationism may have worked in Ireland's favour during the 1930s but by the 1950s, the Irish economy was stagnant and the servile relationship between Church and State retarded much-needed reform in the field of education and health. The most celebrated instance, the Mother and Child Scheme, serves as exemplar. In 1950, when the then Minister for Health Dr Noel Browne decided to introduce a free maternity scheme for all expectant mothers and healthcare for children under sixteen, his proposal was met with vehement opposition by the Irish hierarchy who regarded the proposal as encroaching on one of their private domains. His fellow cabinet ministers offered no support, for "there was no electoral dividend to be gained from appearing to stand up to the Bishops" and the Minister was forced to resign (Whyte, 1971: 4).

As for education, the Dublin Diocesan regulations stated, "In the education of Catholics, every branch of human training is subject to the guidance of the Church" (Whyte, 1971: 306). As Tony Fahey states, "The primary purpose of social service provision for the Catholic Church was to disseminate and safeguard the faith, not to combat social inequality or reform society" (Fahey, 1998: 147). By 1960, the number who could afford to go on to second level represented only about 16% of those enrolled in National Schools. When an appraisal of the secondary school curriculum was undertaken by the Council for Education in 1954, it took six years to complete its deliberations and then merely returned the opinion that the dominant purpose of the schools was the inculcation of religious ideas and values (Coolahan, 1981: 80). Coupled with such prevalent social inequality there was also the factor of the effect religiosity had upon Ireland's laggard economic performance, "Even if people were ambitious and successful, they had to deny continually they had done so deliberately", thus, the Church was able to "educate and legitimate the position and possessions of the rich, and discipline and compensate the poor for their lack of possessions" (Inglis, 1998: 253-258).

By the nineteen-fifties, the Catholic Church in Ireland had reached its apex. At that point, "Ireland was producing so many priests and nuns that between one-third and half of them went on the missions" (McGarry, 2006: 32). Perhaps it was ironic then that the first stirrings for reform came not from within Irish society but amongst the Catholic intellectuals. The Jesuit priest, Fr John Kelly, wrote in the influential religious magazine *The Furrow,* "Too many people in Ireland today are trying to make do with a peasant religion when they are no longer peasants any more… we must have a religion to fit our needs" (Fuller, 2004: 61). The Vatican, of all places, appeared to be susceptible to the zeitgeist of the times. The accession of Pope John 23rd heralded a new direction and redefinition of Church practice culminating in the calling of the second Vatican Council in 1962. The Council would produce a new liturgy, *Sacrosanctum Concilliium,* which put a far greater emphasis on the notion of salvation and the love of God whilst the 1965 decree *Dignitatis Humanae* stressed the rights of the individual. The Irish hierarchy, led by the authoritarian Archbishop of Dublin, Charles McQuaid, were steadfastly against such liberalising notions though the rank and file clergy were largely (and appreciatively) enthusiastic.

II

The years leading up to 1990 were accurately ascribed by Tom Ryan as the "tension management years" (Fogarty, 1984: 102). In the political sphere, the departure of the Fianna Fail leader Eamon De Valera in 1959 could be seen as a signpost for change and his successor, Sean Lemass, though of De Valera's generation, was a man more in tune with economic and social realities. By shifting from protectionism to free trade, through the encouragement of foreign investment and with a greater emphasis on industry rather that export-orientated agriculture, G.P.A. increased from a one per cent average between 1950 and 1958 to a four per cent average between 1959 and 1973 (Walsh, 1979: 33). With economic expansion came significant social change. A reversal in emigration and a rise of about fifty per cent in material living standards helped towards a rise in the population from 2.82 million in 1961 to 2.98 million in 1971 (Lee, 1990: 360).

With growth came the increased realisation of the importance of education. By 1967, the then Minister of Education Donogh O'Malley was confident enough to announce free education at second level with the result that between 1966 and 1969 the number of secondary school pupils rose from 104,000 to 144,000, or as much as in the previous ten years (Breen, 1990: 132). Vatican II's new emphasis on the centrality of parents' roles in the school system was formally, albeit grudgingly, accepted by the hierarchy in 1969 and from 1975 new-style boards of management appeared in most national schools. Concomitant with the rising increase in numbers in the school system was the perilous decline in ordinations–between 1970 and 1995 the total number of religious in Ireland decreased by over a third (Foster, 2007: 57). As vocations dwindled, the Church was slowly forced, effectively, into a policy of retrenchment and while the Church, 'may have been able to maintain the religious ethos of its schools… it has not been able to prevent an erosion of the religious atmosphere' (Inglis, 1998: 223).

During this period, the Catholic Church remained vociferously opposed to the staple concerns of contraception, divorce and abortion. However, this was set against Irish sexual behaviour, both within and outside marriage, which became markedly more liberal; many rights denied to women–such as the right to work in the civil service after marriage–were restored. While inroads were being made into bringing some form of equality into the public and private sector, the next great battle for women was over control of their own bodies. The right of married couples to use contraceptives as an aspect of family planning had been upheld by the Supreme Court in 1973, but in the teeth of conservative opinion the sale of contraceptives became farcical–they could only be purchased by a married couple on prescription from their GP. In 1983, a bitterly acrimonious debate on abortion was held in which the conservatives won something of a Pyrrhic victory and three years later, a similarly divisive referendum on rescinding the ban on divorce was defeated, illustrating that the dominancy of the Catholic Church remained battered but ultimately resolute.

The early sixties coincided with the creation of the first Irish television channel, RTE, in 1961. Tom Inglis made the point that "television… was an important factor in the second stage of Irish modernisation", for it brought about the end to De Valera's quixotic image of firesides being the "forum of serene old age" (Inglis, 1998: 93). The "Bishop and the Nightie" episode of RTE's *Late Late Show* is held up as exemplar in which an audience member jocularly implied that she hadn't worn a nightdress on her wedding night. However, this innocuous statement so infuriated the Bishop of Clonfert Thomas Ryan that he condemned the show from the pulpit causing a slew of headlines the following day. As Mary Kenny states, "(…) intuitively, the Bishop grasped the point that TV would challenge and eventually replace the Church as the teaching authority in manners and morals, as indeed it has done" (1997:267). There were other celebrated incidents from the show not least when in 1966 a young student, Brian Trevaskis, called the Bishop of Galway a moron. As Tom Inglis concludes, "It was the media that broke the tradition of not criticizing the Church… that forced [it] into giving a public account of itself… and brought to an end the long nineteenth century of Irish Catholicism" (Inglis, 1998: 93).

III

The visit of Pope John II to Ireland in 1979 was a remarkable demonstration of Catholic fervour though ultimately overplayed in the context of its lasting significance. More than a million people attended a mass in the Phoenix Park and while the Pope had spoken repeatedly about the end to IRA violence, he also chastised Irish Bishops for failing to identify with the poor in Ireland. By the late eighties, a clear majority of the people were better educated, housed and cared for than ever before. Yet there were nearly three hundred thousand people unemployed and one in three lived below the official poverty line (McSharry, 2000: 26ff). The sixties revival was checked in the mid-seventies by an international recession, fluctuating oil prices and increased competition through our involvement with the EEC. Borrowing to make up the shortfall led the Irish economy into a morass, exacerbated by political upheaval and the spectre of the Northern troubles. The lack of employment, high taxation and a burgeoning debt crisis induced many young people to leave the country and emigration soon began to reach chronic proportions. This culminated in "[t]he terrible waste of energy and resources and enthusiasm" of what Conor Brady termed "The Geldof generation" (17th July 1985). It seemed clear that new political, social and cultural changes were needed to give voice to the transformation which occurred during the intervening thirty years. In 1990, Mary Robinson, a feminist and civil rights lawyer, defeated two male candidates in the Presidential Election on a platform that focused on attempting to bring fresh perspectives to bear on traditional concerns. Her victory, as Carol Coulter explains: "[w]as widely welcomed as a triumph for those who supported a modernising, liberal agenda for Ireland, and as a defeat for those associated with nationalism and Catholic traditionalism" (Coulter, 1993: 1). Shortly after her ascendancy to the Presidency, the Catholic Bishop of Galway, Eamon Casey, resigned in disgrace after it was discovered both that he had fathered a child with an American divorcee and that he had embezzled diocesan funds to pay for her silence.

Many have come to see the Bishop Casey scandal, like Robinson's election as President, as a watershed in Irish life. This would imply a lack of precedent in both instances and by implication they are vested with a far greater signification than they deserve. Robinson's performance as President, restricted as she was by her constitutional role, brought around little in the way of innovation. Nor was Casey the first member of the clergy to be exposed by the media for his indiscretions–indeed, far worse had already been reported but with indifferent effect. Some two years prior to the Casey scandal a priest in the Ferns diocese in Wexford, Father James Doyle, was convicted of having sexually assaulted a young male. A local newspaper, *The Wexford People*, covered the story closely but in this instance, the public refrained from directing their anger towards the perpetrator but rather towards the newspaper itself. A number of the complainants were primary school teachers who, according to one group, "felt it was unnecessary to expose Doyle in such an undignified manner… the coverage was gutter press reaction to a man who had done so much good for the community". Other reactions described the coverage as "ill-judged and irresponsible", "discriminatory" while one lamented the fact that the media did not exercise a "little discretion" (Mooney, 2011: 60-61).

Though Doyle might well have been the first cleric to have been convicted in an Irish court (to which he received a derisory three month suspended sentence) he was by no means the first to come to public attention for his actions. Part of the responsibility lay with the Vatican itself who insisted that canon law take precedence over criminal law in such cases as clerical sexual abuse. With ultimate authority resting in Rome, regional Bishops acted largely as disempowered employees, shuffling errant clerics from parish to parish and suppressing reports of abuse as best they could. That isn't to say that such reports didn't enter into the public domain from time. The same year as Fr James Doyle was being convicted of assault upon a minor, a namesake, Patrick Doyle, published a memoir of his life within the Industrial School system. As the Irish journalist Bruce Arnold states, the Industrial Schools were, "places of shame in the communities where they were located and they were shameful places". Arnold continues: "the majority of the prisons were known as industrial schools; a tiny minority of parallel institutions… were reformatories. Together with certain other establishments… these institutions in reality constituted an 'Irish Gulag'" (2009: 2). *The God Squad*, as the memoir was titled, was part of a cumulative exposé of the horrors of these schools, run by religious orders that appeared to act with utter impunity. As Doyle states in the opening chapter, "Lives have been ruined by the tyrannical rule and lack of love in such places. People have been scarred for life" (1988: 10). Two years later Patrick Touher published a memoir titled *Fear of the Collar* which recounted the physical and sexual abuses exacted on the boys of Artane Industrial School and their persistent sense of fear, shame and confusion.

Throughout the nineties, other such revelations from past inmates unquestionably contributed to the collapse in religious authority, culminating in the RTE produced documentary, *States of Fear*, first televised on April 27th 1999. "What emerged was an unremitting catalogue of cruelty, neglect and abuse, with witness after witness recalling the most dreadful beatings and unwarranted punishments inflicted on helpless children" (Kenny, 2000: 314). Perhaps most devastating of all were the cinematic treatments of the schools and institutions run by the Irish religious orders, in movies such as *Sinners* (2001), *The Magdalene Sisters* (2002) and *Song for a Raggy Boy* (2003). *The Magdalene Sisters* is based on the historical fate of over 30,000 young women who were disowned by their families for various reasons and were despatched into the care of nuns. The film didactically explores how such religious authorities progressed to criminally abusing the weakest and most vulnerable in society. Such movies impacted upon a larger, mainstream audience, causing a further (though somewhat hypocritical) backlash. I say hypocritical as these disclosures were hardly novel. On April 23rd 1954, a question was posed to the Minister for Education concerning a boy at Artane Industrial School who was beaten repeatedly with a leather strap before having his arm broken by one of the brothers. The Minister retorted, "I cannot conceive any sadism emanating from men who were trained to a life of sacrifice and of austerity", dismissed the matter as an "isolated incident" and finished by stating his reassurance to the boy's parents "that nothing of the like will happen again" (Dail Debates, April 23rd 1954: online). In 1968, when the then Minister for Education, Brian Lenihan, visited Artane and was informed of weekly beatings his response was somewhat less diplomatic: "Get me out of this fucking place" (Raftery and O'Sullivan, 1999: 380).

If the media had chosen to overlook such indiscretions in the past, the Casey scandal appeared to portend a brave new approach for Irish journalism. This isn't strictly accurate. When Casey's erstwhile lover, Anne Murphy, contacted the *The Irish Times* in January 1992 the newspaper dithered and then sat on the story for some four months. On Thursday 1st May, *Phoenix* magazine ran a short story on an unnamed leading cleric about to be involved in a scandal. *The Irish Times* still didn't publish, but the story was by then an open secret amongst the media. On the 5th of May, Casey presented his resignation to the Congregation of Bishops at the Vatican before absconding, first to the US, then to missionary work in Ecuador. On 7th May, *The Irish Times* front page revealed some details of Casey's payments "to a woman in Connecticut" while paying tribute to Casey as "the embodiment of Catholicism's human face" (May 7th 1992: online). Such was the fashion in which the Irish media finally found its social conscience. The public mood was described by Mary Kenny as "flabbergasted, breathless, appalled and disbelieving" (2000: 296). It quickly turned to anger and the media promptly followed suit.

In the years immediately prior to Eamon Casey's resignation, most dioceses in Ireland had taken out insurance policies against claims arising from child sexual abuse by priests. Kevin McNamara, then Archbishop of Dublin, had first taken out a policy for the Dublin diocese with Church and General in 1987. Concomitantly, the Bishop of Ferns, Brendan Comiskey, found himself having to deal with repeated complaints of sex abuse made against two other notorious priests, namely Sean Fortune and James Grennan. In Dublin, a canonical trial was in process against Fr Tony Walsh while in Armagh, Cathal Daly, then bishop of Down and Connor, had been made aware of allegations made against Brendan Smyth in West Belfast, but, as with the Boland case, deferred these to the superior of Smyth's order. When compared to the abuse committed by such individuals, Casey's brief consensual affair and his borrowing of money to pay for his son's maintenance were trivial. However, the Casey scandal may be construed as a test case and soon the media were confident enough to "declare open season on priests" (Ferriter, 2005: 734) leading one West of Ireland cleric to complain that the media now seemed to present all and sundry as "closet sexual deviants" (Tanner, 2001: 387).

The Irish Church, as Tom Inglis presciently observed, had been "unable to operate with the language and structures of the news media… bishops are not used to preparing immediate responses to developing stories" (1998: 236). From 1992 onwards, the Irish Church appears to have abnegated their role as confessor, a role thereafter assumed by a "plethora of media gurus" (Inglis, 1998: 326). The sudden shift in the public mood could be part-attributed to genuine anger or a reaction to the hypocrisy of certain clerics–one could argue that *schadenfreude* was also a factor. "These are the fellows who were telling *us* how to behave… who were quizzing us, in Confession, as to whether we had entertained bad thoughts. No, no, no" (Kenny, 2000: 296). Another hostage to fortune occurred just prior to the Casey scandal when the cleric, Michael Cleary, spoke out on his radio show about the X-Case, suggesting that it was a fabrication of the liberal left. The X-Case involved a fourteen year old girl (named only as "X" in the courts and the media to protect her identity) who had been raped by a neighbour and became pregnant. As the girl was suicidal, the family attempted to travel to Britain for an abortion but the High Court ordered an injunction preventing them from doing so, as per the earlier 1983 constitutional amendment. Cleary was perhaps the most high profile rank-and-file cleric in the country and his insinuation was bad enough in itself. However, when he died less than a year later it was revealed that his live-in housekeeper was also his lover and mother of his two children, one of whom he placed in adoptive care. Further revelations appeared with almost monotonous regularity. In November 1994, the Brendan Smyth case managed to bring down the Irish government when it was revealed that his case file had sat on a shelf in the Attorney General's office for eighteen months thus preventing his extradition to Northern Ireland. In that same month alone, the following stories were reported in the media: Father Daniel Curran was jailed for seven years for abusing children in Belfast; an anonymous Galway priest was convicted for sexually assaulting a young man; another anonymous priest had been given a 15-month suspended sentence by the Dublin Circuit Criminal Court for sexually assaulting a male hitchhiker; a priest had been charged for molesting a thirteen year-old boy in a hotel bathroom after a funeral and then there was the story of Fr Liam Cosgrove who died in a gay sauna in Dublin. According to the club's owner, "Two other priests gave him the last rites… priests made up a significant number of the club's membership" (*The Irish Independent*, January 5th 2009: online). It was a near-relentless indictment.

The Church had once offered status of sorts to the people and in such a class-conscious society, pious supplications to the faith were the norm. What is apparent then is that a bargain of sorts was struck between most priests and the mercantile classes–each side served their own purposes. The clergy could be called on to perform such onerous tasks for a price, to perform the rituals that perpetuated the *status quo* in return for comparative benefits. This arrangement helped perpetuate the social order up to the early nineties but each side was obliged to keep up a façade of sorts. Propriety was absolute and any such transgressions of desire were pounced upon and denounced. It was a self-defeating relationship but with the deluge of scandals in the nineties the Church could no longer perform in this role. By the late 1990s there was no social capital to be gained from declaring yourself a devout Catholic. Young people, who had come out in record numbers to welcome the Pope to Ireland in 1979, departed in droves and ordinations to the priesthood subsequently collapsed. They were utterly discredited and the mercantile classes found that they could operate well enough without them anyhow, turning their attention to the vulgar accruement of commodities instead.

The economic boom of the nineties further enhanced the secularization of Irish society. The "Celtic Tiger" economy was built upon a series of grants and loans from the EU to facilitate Ireland's entrance into the euro and thereafter, on cheap credit from lending institutions. Ireland rapidly developed a series of connections with foreign cultural influences-partly through foreign investment but also in such areas as the burgeoning hospitality industry and by access to the financial markets. Affordable travel and the phenomenon of economic immigration also helped contribute to Ireland's move from defining itself as a peripheral, essentially moral community to a modern, liberal and ultimately secular society. By 2001, the influential US magazine *Foreign Policy* would vote Ireland as "the most globalized country of the year" (Coulter 2003: 110). This era of the ego, where greed was good and hyper-individualism tolerated, even applauded, masked a widening gap between rich and poor. While Ireland was ranked as the fourth richest country in the world in 2002, a United Nations Developed Program report observed that Ireland was one of the most unequal among western countries with the richest 10 per cent of the population 11 times wealthier than the poorest 10 per cent (*The Irish Times*, 24th July 2002: online). As such, there were actually more people with an income level below the poverty line than there had been in the late eighties, a time of recession.

One thing was clear though-calling oneself an "Irish Catholic" had stopped being a "badge of honour" but rather "an embarrassment to be reluctantly admitted". Indeed, "Modern Ireland is the nation of the Celtic Tiger rather than the land of Saints and Scholars. Gone are the days when there were no weddings and dances during Lent. Vocations to the priesthood and religious life are nearly non-existent" (Twomey 2003: 29). Yet the Irish were reluctant to sever all ties to the Church and if there is to be a redefinition of its role in Irish society, there are certain statistics which point towards a possible starting point. In 1995 Brian Girvin noted that 80 percent of Catholics believed their personal faith had not been affected by the scandals (Girvin, 1996: 607). A 2011 social survey report showed that 52 percent went to mass at least once a week and the numbers attending mass even on a monthly basis is around the 70 percent mark (*Irish Catholic Bishops Conference*, 2011: online). While the numbers attending weekly mass have declined dramatically it is still much higher than in other Western, traditionally Catholic countries such as France where weekly attendance is around the 5 percent mark (*The Christian Telegraph*, 2012: online). In Celtic Tiger Ireland, Catholic identity became individualized and therefore plural. What was once a vertical regulation of faith, (that is, from the top down) has become horizontally regulated with people following extremely variable modes of Catholic expression. In the aforementioned poll 50 percent state that they pray "everyday" and as many as 85 percent believe in God. Thus, those who engage in Catholic worship do so now, not because of some moral stricture but through a more punctual connection which has come about in part because of the change of locus in Celtic Tiger Ireland: that is, from the rural to the global network.

This redefinition of Catholicism is progressing not so much on account of the Church but rather in spite of it–what was once an natural appendage to Irish identity is now irrevocably associated with the worst excesses of triumphantism and intransigence. Those who stand by the Church today do so without disregarding the awful abuses that were perpetuated under a cloak of convenience. They do so, rather, because the Church means more than the people who run it and has always done so. It is an organic institution which has seemingly abandoned its core values and retreated behind a cloak of dogmatism–it now appears that its followers in turn have become increasing diffuse in their postmodern approach to religion. Ultimately, it is up to the Church to follow suit, to abandon its obsession with sexual morality and individual salvation and to "embrace an ecological ethic of global responsibility" (Inglis, 1998: 259). How this plays out in post Celtic Tiger Ireland remains to be seen.

Bibliography

Arnold, B. *The Irish Gulag–How the State Betrayed its Innocent Children.* Dublin: Gill & Macmillan, 2009

Brady, C. "The lost potential of Geldoff's generation", in *The Irish Times*, 17 July 1985.

Breen, R. *Understanding Contemporary Ireland–State, Class and Development in the Republic of Ireland.* Dublin: Gill and Macmillan, 1990.

Coolahan, J. *Irish Education: History and Structure*. Dublin: Institute of Public Administration, 1981

Coulter, C. *The Hidden Tradition: Feminism, Women and Nationalism in Ireland.* Cork: Cork University Press, 1993

Coulter, C. and Coleman, S. *The End of Irish History? Critical Reflections on the Celtic Tiger*. Manchester: Manchester University Press, 2003

Dail Debates. "Adjournment Debate–Industrial Schoolboy" April 23rd, from: http://historical-debates.oireachtas.ie/D/0145/D.0145.19540423 0005.html,1954

Doyle, P. *The God Squad*. Dublin: Raven Arts Press, 1989.

Fahey, T. "The Church and Social Policy" in *Social Policy in Ireland:Principals, Practice and Problems* edited by Healy, S., and Reynolds B. Dublin: Oak Tree Press, 1998

Ferriter, D. *The Transformation of Ireland 1900-2000*. London: Profile Books, 2005.

Fogarty, M., Ryan, L., & Lee, J. *Irish Values and Attitudes*. Dublin: Dominican Publications, 1984.

Foster, R.F. *Luck and the Irish: A Brief History of Change, 1970–2000*. London: Penguin, 2008.

Fuller, L. *Irish Catholicism since 1950: The Undoing of a Culture*. Dublin: Gill & Macmillan, 2004.

Girvin, B. *From Union to Union. Nationalism, Democracy and Religion in Ireland–Act of Union to EU*. Dublin: Gill & Macmillan, 2002.

—. "Church, State and the Irish Constitution: The Secularization of Irish Politics?" in *Parliamentary Affairs*, 49:4 (1996) pp. 599-615.

Greeley, A. "Are the Irish Really Losing their Faith", *Doctrine and Life*, 44.3 (1994), p.132-143.

Inglis, T. *Moral Monopoly: The Rise and Fall of the Catholic Church in Modern Ireland*. Dublin: UCD Press, 1998

Irish Catholic Bishops Conference "Practice and Belief Amongst Irish Catholics" from:
http://www.catholicbishops.ie/wp-content/uploads/2012/01/Practice-and-Belief-among-Catholics-in-the-Republic of-Ireland.pdf, 2011

Kenny, M. *Goodbye to Catholic Ireland*. Dublin: New Island, 2000.

Lee, J.J. *Ireland 1912–1985* Cambridge: Cambridge University Press, 1990.

McGarry, P. "The Rise and Fall of Catholicism in Ireland" in *Irish and Catholic? Towards an Understanding of Identity* edited by Fuller, L., Littleton, J., and Maher, E. Dublin: The Columba Press, (2006) pp. 31-46.

McSharry, R. and White, P.A. (eds.) *The Making of the Celtic Tiger–The Inside Story of Ireland's Boom Economy* Cork: Mercier, 2000

Mooney, T. *All the Bishops Men–Clerical Abuse in an Irish Diocese* Cork: Collins Press, 2011.

NicGhiolla Phadraigh, M. "The Power of the Catholic Church in the Republic of Ireland" in *Irish Society:*
Sociological Perspectives edited by Clancy, P., Drudy, S., Lynch, K. and O' Dowds, L. Dublin: Institute of Public Administration, 1995, pp. 593-619.

Raftery, M. & Sullivan, E. O' *Suffer the Little Children: The Inside Story of Ireland's Industrial Schools*. Dublin: Gill & Macmillan, 1999.

Tanner, M. *Ireland's Holy War: The Struggle for a Nation's Soul 1500–2000* New Haven: Yale University Press, 2001.

The Christian Telegraph. "Liberalism Killing French Catholic Church–Traditionalists Taking Over". Retrieved May 4th 2012 from:
http://www.christiantelegraph.com/issue8258.html

The Irish Examiner "Clerical cover-up–Cardinals' position is untenable". May 3rd, Retrieved May 7th 2012 from:
http://www.irishexaminer.com/archives/2012/0503/opinion/clerical-abuse-cover-up--cardinals-position-is-untenable-192584.html

The Irish Independent "A Priest who walks tall while the bishop lies low", January 5th Retrieved May 8th from:
http://www.independent.ie/opinion/analysis/a-priest-who-walks-tall-while-the-bishop-lies-low-1592017.html, 2009

The Irish Times "Dr Casey resigns as Bishop of Galway" May 7th, Retrieved May 7th 2012 from:
http://www.irishtimes.com/150/articles/print-and-be-damned.html,1992.

—. "Who We Are" 24th July, retrieved May 4th 2012 from:
http://www.irishtimes.com/timeseye/whoweare/p4bottom.htm , 2002.

—. "Cardinal Brady's Statement" May 3rd, Retrieved May 7th 2012 from: http://www.irishtimes.com/newspaper/ireland/2012/0503/1224315512518.html

Twomey, V. *The End of Irish Catholicism?* Dublin: Veritas, 2003.

Walsh, B.M., "Economic Growth & Development, 1945-1970" in *Ireland 194 –1970* edited by Lee, J.J., Dublin: Gill & Macmillan, 1979, p.29-45.

Whyte, J. *Church and State in Modern Ireland, 1923-1970* Dublin: Gill & Macmillan, 1971.

CHAPTER TWO

BELFAST RENEWED: A SIGN OF CHANGE?

JOANA ETCHART

Introduction

Belfast has changed considerably since 1998, when the Good Friday Agreement was signed between warring sides in Northern Ireland. As peace developed[1], so did urban regeneration plans aiming at giving a new face to the city[2]. Undoubtedly, the architectural outlook of the city has changed as places with a cosmopolitan dimension[3] developed. This can be best exemplified by the creation of Quarters, such as the Cathedral Quarter, which has attracted a significant number of arts and culture-based organisations. Some examples include Belfast Exposed Photography (a gallery for contemporary photography) and Nv Tv (Northern Visions Television, a local community television station). Belfast's new MAC arts venue (Metropolitan Arts Centre) is also located in that area. Such changes

---

[1] A power-sharing Assembly was formed in May 2007 and the main paramilitary groups decommissioned successfully in 2005 and 2009-10. Despite these achievements, peace remains fragile as there have been continued sectarian disturbances. Dissident paramilitary groups have also carried several attacks.

[2] Although it has been noted by Neill that plans aiming at improving the image of the city have existed since the late 1970s, as shown by a document issued by the Northern Ireland Information Service in 1978, entitled *Nine Point Package to Spell the Rebirth of Belfast*. See Neill, 2010: 307-8.

[3] Gaffikin and Morrissey (2011: 102-3) argue that there are four types of space in Belfast nowadays: ethnic space (segregated catholic/nationalist or protestant/unionist communities, mainly residential neighbourhoods with contentious interface areas) ; neutral-and safe-space (mainly in the city centre and the waterfront) ; shared space where people from both communities actually interact (potentially in the Queen's University campus); and cosmopolitan space with little reference to local identities and a focus on the international.

offer new, attractive mappings for the city. In addition, the waterfront area has undergone radical changes: a multimillion pound project transformed this formerly industrial site into a new, multifunctional place comprising a museum, residences, offices and shops. This new place called the Titanic Quarter was built on the former Harland and Wolff site on Queen's Island and takes inspiration from its industrial heritage. In the 2000s, the built environment has gradually offered new perspectives literally, as well as figuratively, as new places now generally aim at becoming "shared"[4]. Spatial "sharedness" is meant to counteract the traditionally divided geography of Belfast, which has been characterised by residential segregation between unionists and nationalists in the wards[5] (i.e. the mainly residential neighbourhoods surrounding the city centre).

Belfast now shows many of the features identified by culture and urban studies specialist Malcolm Miles as fundamental to designate a culturally-led urban regeneration, such as "a flagship cultural institution in a post-industrial zone, often a waterfront site" and "the designation of a neighbourhood as a cultural industries quarter for small–and medium–size businesses in the arts, media and leisure" (Miles, 2005: 893). This chapter offers to look at a culturally-led project in Belfast, the 2011 RISE sculpture, and aims to analyse why and how this came to be built. It is assumed that this example will corroborate the assumption that change is undeniably underway in Belfast.

The RISE sculpture as a sign of change

The RISE sculpture, designed by artist Wolfgang Buttress, was inaugurated in September 2011 in Belfast. It is located on one of the busiest roundabouts in Belfast called the Broadway Junction. The area surrounding the roundabout takes in four electoral wards (Beechmount, Falls, Falls Park and Blackstaff), as shown in the following map.

---

[4] Creating "shared space" emerged as a policy objective in the 2000s as a response to the social fragmentation. However, researchers have noted that this notion remains vague. See for instance Komarova, 2008. See also the author's critical assessment of the discourses surrounding the Titanic Quarter (Etchart, 2008).

[5] The proportion of catholic/nationalist and protestant/unionist population varies in each ward. A map was drawn following the 1991 census, giving a general idea of how communities were distributed in each ward:
http://cain.ulst.ac.uk/images/maps/belfast_religion.gif

Fig 2.1: Belfast Ward Boundaries (Green boundaries) and Broadway Junction area (Red dot)

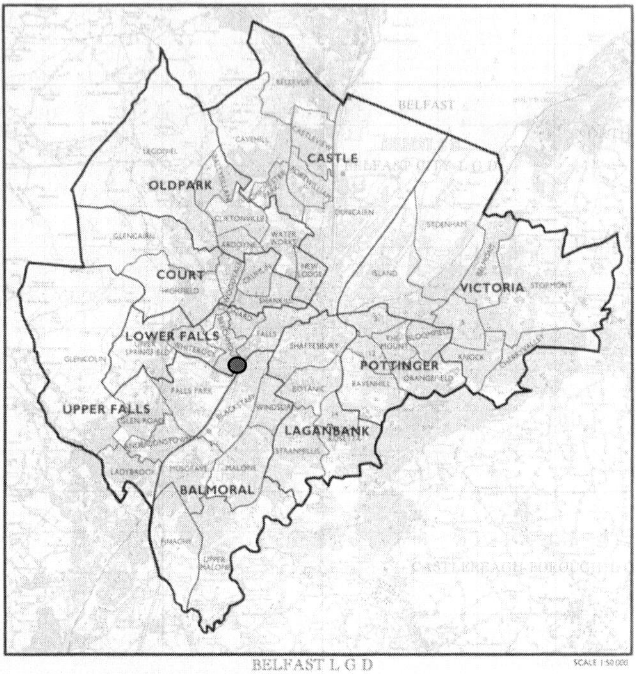

Source: Land and Property Services, 1992

The RISE landmark piece of art is oddly located outside the conventional comfort zone[6] of the city centre, framed in white in the following map issued by the BCC.

[6] Most culturally-led renewal projects devised by statutory bodies have been developed in the city centre area. The reasons for this are varied but, mainly, development and regeneration policies have tended to focus on the city centre given that invisible barriers have separated it from its peripheral neighbourhoods fragmented into nationalist and unionist areas. Possibly then, locating a new piece of art in the "neutral" city centre has been an easier venture, as opposed to doing it in areas where place marking practices are still vividly used to enhance one's identity.

Fig. 2.2: Belfast City Council map showing location of RISE sculpture.

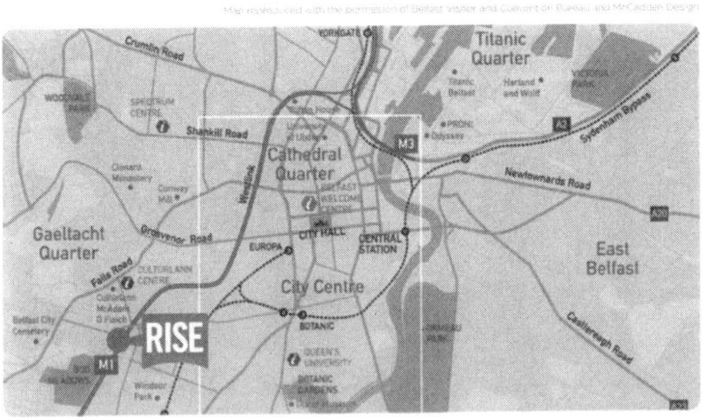

Source: BCC Tourism, Culture and Arts Unit, 2012

The peripheral setting of the RISE sculpture might mean that some of the invisible barriers separating the city centre from the wards are gradually falling. Moreover, the sculpture sits in the middle of two antagonistic areas–the republican Falls (Beechmount, Falls, Falls Park wards) and the loyalist Village (Blackstaff ward). The Broadway Junction–a formerly lush roundabout–and the busy M1/Westlink both stood as a "natural" separation line[7] between the two communities. The erection of a piece of art in a place accessible to all–as it is now used as a footpath–tends to imply that community relations have improved in the area and that former lines of separation may now be transformed into places offering more connectivity.

All this reinforces the assumption that positive changes are taking place, all the more so as the RISE sculpture has not become a focal point for trouble despite it being described as "a flashpoint area for sectarian violence to erupt" by Community Crime Prevention Officer for West Belfast (BCC, 2005).

---

[7] The Broadway Junction area is an interface area separating two antagonistic communities (catholic/nationalist and protestant/unionist). Some communities are separated by so-called peacelines–gates, fences and walls–which were built to prevent sectarian interface rioting. Sometimes parks and roads may also function as separation lines, as in the Broadway Junction area. The Belfast Interface Project identified 41 peacelines in Belfast in 2005 (Jarman, 2005). Details available at: http://www.belfastinterfaceproject.org

In terms of architectural landscaping, the sculpture RISE truly offers new scenery in an area dominated by advertising boards, graffiti and murals.

Fig 2.3: Rise sculpture with footpath underneath (marked by low fence)

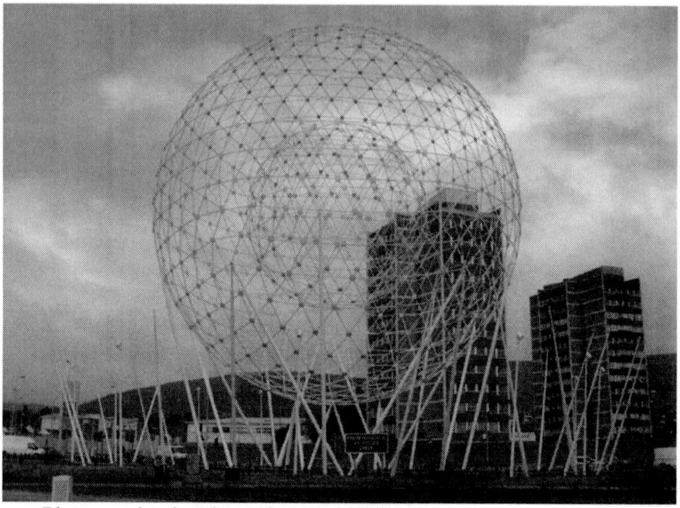

Source: Photograph taken by author (April 2012)

Fig. 2.4: RISE sculpture seen from Donegall road (Village area)

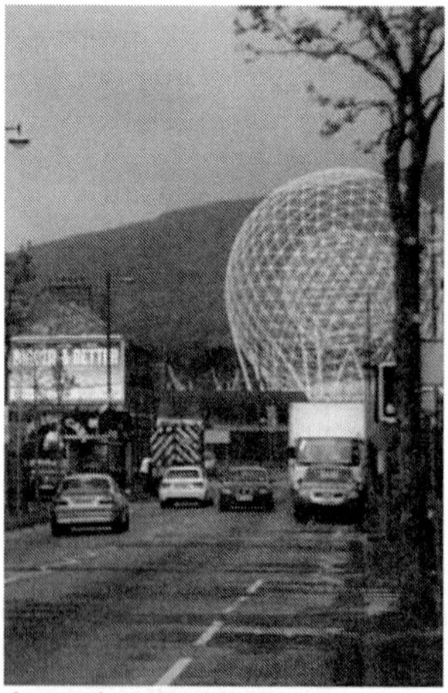

Source: Photograph taken by author (April 2012)

The Belfast Junction is typically what could be called a non-place (Augé, 1995) where people are in transit-either travelling on the M1/Westlink junction or walking across the roundabout. Most of the adjoining areas are access roads, commercial premises or empty plots of land. All such spaces only offer the possibility for people to be passing on them and barely allow longer activities such as visiting, working or lingering away. The new RISE sculpture, however, brings in new, fresh perspectives into the built environment through the use of light materials (white, silver steel) and round shapes (two globes, one inside the other). More importantly, it contributes to putting people back in the frame by becoming a place to visit.

Fig. 2.5: Fenced up vacant land near the RISE sculpture (Seen from Donegall road)

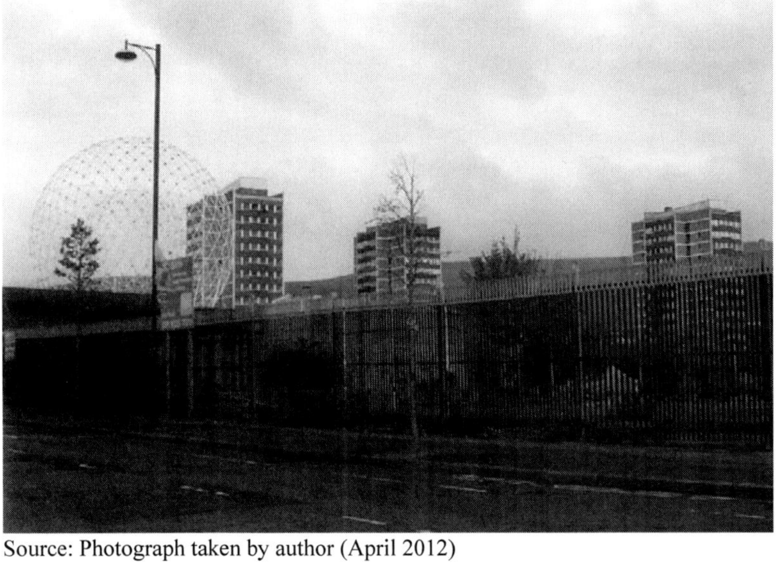

Source: Photograph taken by author (April 2012)

Moreover, the piece of art is a "cultural" item–in the general sense of the word–as it goes with a message enhancing harmony and promising a bright future. According to the Nottingham artist who designed the sculpture, Wolfgang Buttress, RISE is in the shape of two globes and is lit up at night to symbolise the rising of the sun (BBC News, 2011). He explains: "Before there were people on this spot, there were reeds and marsh and I wanted to make a connection to the land, and something universal" (UTV News, 2011). The bog meadows are reflected in the reeds that sit below the balls. Buttress thus adds meaning to the piece of art and creates a connection with the spot where it stands, by linking it to Belfast's past ("before there were people") and by referring to original, natural elements such as reeds and marsh. He focuses on universal value. Interestingly, so do the BCC in their 2012 leaflet, where they claim that RISE "symbolises a new era for Belfast and hope for the city's future" (BCC Tourism, Culture and Arts Unit, 2012). Those universal, somehow vague, references to peace and harmony also appear in other Belfast art pieces mainly located in the city centre, such as the 2007 Beacon of Hope and the 2009 Spirit of Belfast. The lack of reference to recent history, be it related to the Troubles or to the division between antagonistic communities, and the importance laid on universal values and symbols–typically exemplified by the rising of the sun–point to the cosmopolitan character that has been attached to the sculpture. This is related to the belief that urban development, and particularly culturally-led regeneration with a cosmopolitan character, may contribute to reinforcing peace building efforts.[8]

Research questions

This assumption, however, disregards the fact that the "cultural improvements" derived from urban regeneration may also give rise to unforeseen tensions. For instance, the new places may become gentrified, thus widening socially marked discrepancies[9]. Big-scale renewal projects in general may also be perceived as serving the interests of capitalist drivers, thus giving rise to tensions between defendants of private and public interests. Finally, tensions may also arise between decision-makers

---

[8] For instance, Scott Bollens (2012) believes that urban development may lead away from violence, as in the case of Bilbao in the Basque region. He claims that: "The Guggenheim and other cultural improvements have moved the region towards a more cosmopolitan character with a closer relationship and openness to contemporary culture, a quality conducive to advancing a moderate and non-violent Basque identity agenda" (Bollens, 2012: 87). The assumption is that identity disputes become incongruous in places that have been renewed and that now represent "modernism", as opposed to "old" nationalist discourses and cultures. It is believed that cosmopolitanism may render the causes of the conflict obsolete, hence the importance of cities, where cosmopolitan cultures are likely to develop, and of architecture which conveys an ideology of universalism. On the sociological impact of architecture, see Jones, 2011.

[9] See Murtagh's description of Belfast as a "twin speed city" (Murtagh, 2008).

and local residents if the latter have not been consulted adequately. In other words, the way in which the place-making process is led matters when trying to determine if it is indeed beneficial.

In theory, many participants could be integrated in the process. Toby Dennett, Director of the Sculptors' Society of Ireland, mentions "commissioners, funders, administrators, consultants, curators, planners, politicians and communities" (Dennett, 2005: 8). Thus, culture-led projects entail a collaborative process generally involving a whole range of individuals, organisations and interests in its conception, creation and delivery. Urban planning specialists Gaffikin and Morrissey (2011) have enhanced the value of collaborative planning in divided cities, insisting that collaborative work should be seen as a new, beneficial approach in order to address segregation. This could be even more relevant in interface areas, where "participative" decision-making, with "meaningful consultation" would be relevant (Goldie and Ruddy, 2010: 14). Taking all that into account, the question then is not what is built in times of peace, but: How are decisions made? Who is involved? Are urban development plans seen as a tool for developing collaborative work, through which communities and maybe former enemies are led to discuss projects together and to make decisions together? In other words, this study will not ask itself whether or not regeneration, and more specifically culture-led regeneration (through public art), contributes to peace building. However, its aim will be to examine the decision-making processes that lead to the creation of new places in order to assess if and how collaborative practices are emerging. Thus, can the new elements of Belfast's built environment–in this case the RISE sculpture–be seen as symptoms of change or are they a mere façade?

Origins of the Broadway public art project

The RISE project emerged in 2004 when the Roads Services (Department for Regional Development, DRD) and the Development Committee of the Belfast City Council (BCC) worked jointly to submit a case requesting funds to produce a landmark public art at Broadway Junction. Two sets of driving forces led to this.

On the one hand, the Roads Services issued a new scheme in 2004 to improve the M1/Westlink, which is the strategic route that connects the M1 to the M2 and M3 motorways within Belfast, and which also provides access to Belfast City Centre. The new scheme aimed at widening the M1 motorway to three lanes. Under the scheme, the Broadway roundabout was to be reconstructed. The Roads Services' intention was to reduce congestion issues on the Westlink (Roads Services, 2006). On the other hand, in the early 2000s, public art strategies were being increasingly endorsed by local authorities in Northern Ireland as part of regeneration schemes[10]. Funding programmes were available from the European Union and the National Lottery through the regional partner of the Arts Council of Northern Ireland (ACNI).[11] This action was further promoted by the New Labour government, who endorsed an ambitious urban policy framework following Lord Rogers' 1999 Urban Task Force report. This led to the creation of an agency specifically working on the built environment and insisting on notions such as good design, functionality and sustainability. The agency, called Commission for Architecture and the Built Environment (CABE), believed that the built environment could have a positive impact on the community (Better Public Buildings Group, 2000: 5). In 2004, a steering group was also established in Northern Ireland to work on the issue of the built environment along the same lines. Public art appeared as a central element, as explained by the report that followed in 2006. Objective 5 specified that:

> Art can play a vital and inspirational role in transforming spaces. Through multidisciplinary and collaborative practice, artists can help architects and designers create imaginative environments that reflect local identity, meet communities' needs and enhance their functionality (Department of Culture, Arts and Leisure, 2006: 25)

Although the beneficial outcomes of public art were enhanced, there was no mention of the specific context of Northern Ireland as a segregated society in a post-conflict situation. Perhaps the only hint at it appeared when the report mentioned that public art had a "Therapeutic benefit" (Department of Culture, Arts and Leisure, 2006: 25). Such a positive and compelling view, however vague, explains why local authorities developed public art schemes in the 2000s and why the BCC was keen on engaging on a public art venture on the Broadway Junction. However, concerning the RISE sculpture, there has been no thinking made on the accuracy of having a public art project in this specific place, which also functions as a separation line between the republican communities in the

---

[10] For example, a new programme was launched in February 2004 called Arts of Regeneration, aimed at local authorities, for the development and implementation of a Public Art programme (Development Committee, 7th April 2004)

[11] In Northern Ireland, Lottery funding for arts is distributed by the Arts Council of Northern Ireland. For more details on the development of arts in Northern Ireland see Arts Council of NI, 2005.

Falls and the loyalists in the Village. Although the question was raised by local Community Crime Prevention Officer in 2005 as to whether this new place would become "a contested space" (BCC, 2005: 6) as a consequence of the clearing of the formerly lush roundabout, there is no evidence that this issue was further debated or talked through as part of the project.

Moreover, the original hybridisation of two strategies is quite perplexing. The M1/Westlink improvement scheme aims at widening the road, while the public art project is meant to improve the living environment. This could be seen as paradoxical, particularly in the 2000s when the European "compact city" is being promoted elsewhere with urban plans taking into account the need to switch from all cars cities to more pedestrians/cycling/public transport friendly places. A Belfast-based group of architects and planners called Forum for Alternative Belfast has highlighted that traffic priority in Belfast has had negative implications for the living environment. They note that: "Car access for commuters is favoured over the ability to walk and cycle through good city streets and neighbourhoods–which were largely divided and blighted in the process of building these roads" (Forum for Alternative Belfast, 2011)[12].

Thus the original planning strategy appeared complex and challenging. Being so, it required collaborative work at many levels, not only between the two promoters, but also between them and potential partners from the local communities and professionals (architects, planners, academics). My research shows, however, that collaborative work was not on the agenda. More interestingly, this study will highlight that the decision-making process happened in a rather irrational way.

Ad-hoc organisation

All in all, seven years were necessary to take the project to completion (2004-2011). This long time span is due to the fact that the artist's project that was selected in 2005 had to be dropped in 2008 and a second commissioning process[13] had to be organised consequently. More

---

[12] See also how city fabric has been eroded by arterial roads in FAB's "grey doughnut" map, available at: http://www.forumbelfast.org/projects/Maps.php

[13] Both commissioning processes–led by the BCC–followed conventional rules in the sense that they sought to attract artists with an international profile and that they were led by a panel representing a variety of groups (BCC, Roads Services, Department of Social Development, local community representatives and local councillors). The 2005 and 2008 processes comprised two stages: an expression of interest across Europe followed by a presentation for the short listed artists. Details

precisely, in 2005, Californian artist Ed Carpenter's Trillian project was selected but shelved in 2008 as the economic climate led to increasing costs for raw materials. A second commission selected Buttress' RISE project in 2008 (Development Committee, 12th November 2008).

There is, however, another reason for the delay. Although the Roads Services and the BCC were committed to the project at the onset, there soon emerged questions as to who was leading the project and how the decision-making process ought to be run. One of the obstacles to effective work was the multitude of actors involved comprising funding bodies (Roads Services, Department of Social Development DSD, ACNI and the BCC) and bodies responsible for the management of the project (Roads Services for the "structural work", i.e. M1/Westlink improvement scheme, the BCC for the commissioning process). In an ad-hoc manner, the original 2004 joint venture became a disorganised group of bodies in the 2004-2007 period. The BCC's Development Committee stated in January 2007 that: "The delays in progress have resulted from a lack of clarity about roles and responsibilities and a funding shortfall. No organisation has yet agreed to perform a leadership or project management role which has resulted in confusion and frustration" (Development Committee, 14th February 2007). The problem lay in the fact that the body that would take on the leading role would have to provide management services, which would cost approximately £50,000 (Development Committee, 14th February 2007). The Roads Services seemed reluctant to provide extra funding, so the BCC eventually became the leading body in 2007 (Development Committee, 17th January 2007).

Such confusion in governance methods contributed to the fact that important issues were neglected. It is only following the 2007 decision by BCC to take on the leading role that some key aspects of the project began to be mentioned, such as the need to finalise a schedule, to agree on a contract with the artist or to engage with the local communities (Development Committee, 12th December 2007). One example illustrating ad-hoc decision-making is that the initial budget-estimated at £300,000 in 2004 (Development Committee, 3rd November 2004)–kept rising as the project drivers stumbled upon unanticipated requirements (such as staffing)[14].The 2004-2007 period highlights a lack of interest in the process of finding adequate modes of organisation to lead the project.

---

provided by Janice Smith, Tourism, Culture and Arts Development Officer at BCC in a series of messages exchanged in 2011/12.

[14] Initially estimated at £300,000, the project eventually cost £536,000. Some of the unforeseen expenses were related to a series of checks that the Roads Services

Eventually, in December 2007, the BCC proposed to set up two bodies (Development Committee, 12th December 2007):

- The Project Board was a decision-making body composed of representatives from the funding groups (such as the Department for Social Development and ACNI) and from the two original partners (Roads Services and BCC). The Board's function was to manage the project, and was to meet once every two months.
- The Steering Group was a consultative group composed of councillors from local areas as well as community representatives[15] and groups working on business and environment issues. They could "Advise the Project Board of key issues of stakeholders within the local, city and national contexts" (Development Committee, 12th December 2007) and were to meet quarterly.

As part of a consultation process with local populations, several meetings were organised[16] and schools were involved too. However, this notion of consultation must be qualified as local populations were "consulted" only once decisions had been made. They were included in the process at a late stage and were principally asked to endorse the project. This is confirmed by the BCC document specifying the role of the Steering Group, one of which is to "Develop consensus throughout constituencies with regard to the Broadway sculpture" (Development Committee, 12th December 2007). The form of participation proposed here is substandard and is reminiscent of past methods, when statutory bodies were criticized for proposing "sham"[17] participation exercises in the 1970s. When

---

had to complete in order to grant a Technical Approval/Certification. They were not included in the original budget (KPMG, 2010: 6-11).

[15] Community group representatives were not included in the BCC's first proposal, but an amendment was brought forward asking for local community workers to be included, namely representatives of the Saint James' Residents Groups and the Greater Village Regeneration Trust. See Development Committee, 12th December, 2007 and amendment voted in January 2008 (Development Committee, 16th January 2008).

[16] Public meetings took place in the Village in Spring 2009 and in the Falls in December 2010 and January 2011–interestingly, no one attended the second meeting. (BBC News Northern Ireland, January 20th 2011, "No show for meeting on Belfast roundabout sculpture")

[17] Ron Wiener contended in his 1975 book on a Shankill redevelopment project that participation was "restricted and controlled", and that it was "a sham exercise". See Ron Wiener's Chapter 7, "Participation or Negotiation?", *The Rape and Plunder of the Shankill*, 130-153

interviewed by BBC News Northern Ireland, Saint James' representative Breige Brownlee confirmed that local communities did not take part in the decision-making process and described the sculpture as a "fait accompli":

> Local Sinn Fein councillor Breige Brownlee said she hoped the sculpture would bring communities together. However, she claimed the public consultation had been inadequate and pointed out that the decision had been taken three years ago by others in a very different economic climate. 'There's still a lot of poverty around these areas and there's been a lot of objection to this piece of work and a lot of worries about the amount of money that was spent on it,' she said. 'A lot of local people would prefer to have seen the money better spent elsewhere. But now that it's a fait accompli, people are beginning to warm to it, which is good.' (BBC News, 2011)

Leaving aside the questions of cost and spending legitimacy[18], this reaction is interesting for two reasons. The first reason is that the project is considered as a "fait accompli", meaning that communities have been involved in the process at a late stage and, above all, once the main decisions to create a piece of public art there and to select Buttress' project were made. In fact, BCC meetings minutes show that local councillors have been asking for more community engagement regularly between the 2004-2008 period, but efforts were made on that level from 2008 only. Community representatives were included in the Steering group between 2008 and June 2011, when this was made redundant. Their participation was essential in addressing significant safety issues[19]. The second reason why Breige Brownlee's reaction is interesting lies in the fact that local residents slowly "warmed" to the project, showing that culture-led regeneration projects may become an interesting opportunity to build confidence or to improve relations provided that statutory groups are aware of its potential and that they know how to integrate local communities in the process. In that sense, the RISE project, and particularly the 2004-2008 period, may be seen as a missed opportunity[20].

---

[18] In general, local communities often criticise the legitimacy of public art and would prefer public bodies to address more pressing needs (such as unemployment or housing in poor urban contexts)

[19] The issue of safety was crucial during and after construction. During construction, there were concerns regarding the protection of the site, which was vulnerable to vandalism. After completion, the roundabout–being in an interface area–could become a contested space.

[20] The reactions from community representatives voiced during the meetings organised by the BCC testify to that. See for instance BCC, 2011.

Concluding remarks

Liam O'Dowd noted in 2010 that "contemporary Belfast remains nobody's project". He went on to explain that: "more accurately, it is the product of an extraordinarily fragmented governance system of government departments and agencies, a city council with limited powers, localized 'masterplans' and partnership boards, and publically subsidized development corporations" (O'Dowd, 2010: 36). This multi-layered system of urban governance has been described by academics such as Neill (Neill, 2010, 303). The study of the RISE project confirms O'Dowd's analysis about the "fragmented governance system" on two aspects particularly. Firstly, decision-making has happened in an impromptu manner in the first period from 2004 to 2008 and secondly, working in collaboration with professionals (architects/planners[21]) or with partners from the community has not been considered as a possibility, except on limited issues such as safety.

In addition, while the RISE project was being developed, one of its funding members-the Department for Social Development-launched a radical, contested renewal policy in the adjoining Village area, parts of which became an Urban Renewal Area in April 2008. This gave the Housing Executive (NIHE) essential powers to get demolition of some 600 houses[22] and regeneration processes underway. Several houses were earmarked for demolition and consequently boarded up. Eventually demolition began in June 2011. Both projects (RISE and the Urban Renewal Area project) promise nicer surroundings, but have locals had a chance of working out what that meant for them? Local community worker William Dickson claims that they have not[23]. The very notion of "nicer surroundings" remains unclear as the last phase of the URA project might leave some sites empty if no former resident asks to be re-housed in the area.

When assessing the current situation in Belfast, urban studies and peace specialist Scott Bollens concluded that:

---

[21] Partnerships could have been developed with members of FAB or with people involved in architecture following the *Architecture and Built Environment for NI* document mentioned earlier.

[22] In total, 538 homes will be demolished to be replaced by 273 new houses. In addition, 730 houses will be refurbished. See The Belfast Telegraph, 2011.

[23] As stated by William Dickson, Chairman of the Blackstaff Community Development Association, in a series of messages exchanged in 2012. See also their website: http://www.blackstaff-residents.org.uk/

> The fundamental challenge of how to intervene effectively and strategically in the human and built landscape of this splintered city remained as problematic in 2011 as when 'peace' first was announced in 1998. Meaningful, mutually beneficial urban interventions have a vital role in nurturing and sustaining Belfast's 'clenched teeth' peace. Handshakes are not enough (Bollens, 2012: 68).

The study of the RISE project has not provided evidence that "mutually beneficial urban interventions" were being devised. On the contrary, this paper gave us an insight into who is claiming the use of public space, in this case statutory bodies, and how they are gaining the right to place-making. In the case of the RISE sculpture, the process of place-making is essentially owned by statutory bodies. Community ownership is not sought or encouraged, or only at a late stage, despite the recommendations that such processes should now be collaborative (Gaffikin and Morrissey, 2011). We must note, however, that from 2008 a collaborative approach was adopted with regular meetings between the BCC, community representatives from both sides and other partners (such as the Police Service NI). The approach was highly appreciated by the different partners, who considered it to be "essential" and stressed that it "should continue" (BCC, 2011: 2). However, it was developed late in the place-making process. The conventional solutions that were brought forward–a consultative Steering Group, public meetings, and so on–were rather inadequate and did not follow a coherent strategy. This enhances the need for a premeditated approach on collaborative place-making in Belfast. Achieving this would undoubtedly mean that change is underway.[24]

[24] Recent developments tend to indicate that the BCC is seeking to adopt a more strategic approach based on partnership. In their 2012 Draft Investment Programme, the council party leaders are committed to finding working methods based on innovation and partnership. The following Consultation Feedback Report shows that they are considering regeneration ideas submitted by organisations or local communities, and, more importantly, that they are willing to develop collaborative methods. How they intend to do it, however, remains unclear.

Bibliography

Primary sources

Arts Council of Northern Ireland, *Public Art Handbook for Northern Ireland*, Belfast: ACNI, 2005

BBC News Northern Ireland, "No show for meeting on Belfast roundabout sculpture", http://www.bbc.co.uk/news/uk-northern-ireland-12236994, 2011

—. "Demolition of houses in the Village area gets under way", http://www.bbc.co.uk/news/uk-northern-ireland-13719213, 2011

Belfast City Council, *Draft Investment Programme 2012-2015*, Belfast: BCC, 2012

—. *Draft Investment Programme 2012-2015, Consultation Feedback Report,* Belfast: BCC, 2012

Development Committee (Arts Sub-Committee), *Meeting of Development (Arts) Sub-Committee, Wednesday 7th April, 2004*, Belfast: Belfast City Council, 2004

—. (Arts Sub-Committee), *Meeting of Development (Arts) Sub-Committee, Wednesday 3rd November, 2004*, Belfast: Belfast City Council, 2004

—. *Meeting of Development Committee, Wednesday 21st September, 2005*, Belfast: Belfast City Council, 2005

—. *Meeting of Development Committee, Wednesday 16th November, 2005*, Belfast: Belfast City Council, 2005

—. *Meeting of Development Committee, Wednesday 17th January, 2007*, Belfast: Belfast City Council, 2007

—. *Meeting of Development Committee, Wednesday 12th December, 2007*, Belfast: Belfast City Council, 2007

—. *Meeting of Development Committee, Wednesday 16th January, 2008*, Belfast: Belfast City Council, 2008

—. *Meeting of Development Committee, Wednesday 12th November, 2008*, Belfast:Belfast City Council, 2008

—. *Meeting of Development Committee, Wednesday 14th October, 2009*, Belfast: Belfast City Council, 2009

—. *Meeting of Development Committee, Wednesday 11th November, 2009*, Belfast: Belfast City Council, 2009

—. *Meeting of Development Committee, Wednesday 11th August, 2010*, Belfast: Belfast City Council, 2010

—. *Meeting of Development Committee, Wednesday 15th June, 2011*, Belfast: Belfast City Council, 2011

—. *Meeting of Development Committee, Wednesday 27th June, 2011*, Belfast: Belfast City Council, 2011
Belfast City Council, *Final Artists Pack*, Belfast: Belfast City Council, 2005
—. *Broadway Final Artists Pack*, Belfast: Belfast City Council, 2008
—. "Summary of RISE Community Monitoring Group, Summer Review and Evaluation, Tuesday 11 October 2011", Unpublished, 2011
Belfast City Council Tourism, Culture and Arts Unit, *RISE leaflet*, Belfast: Belfast City Council, 2012
(The) Belfast Telegraph, "Bulldozers move in as £100m regeneration scheme gets under way in Belfast", http://www.belfasttelegraph.co.uk/news/local-national/northern-ireland/bulldozers-move-in-as-100m-regeneration-scheme-gets-under-way-in-belfast-16010284.html#ixzz1wX5z38ul, 2011
Better Public Buildings Group, *Better Public Buildings. A Proud Legacy for the Future*, London: Department for Culture, Media and Sport, 2000
Department of Culture, Arts and Leisure Northern Ireland, *Architecture and the Built Environment for Northern Ireland*, Belfast: Department of Culture, Arts and Leisure, 2006
KPMG, *Green Book Economic Appraisal for a Public Art Sculpture at Broadway Roundabout on behalf of Belfast City Council*, Belfast: KPMG, 2010
Land and Property Services, Greater Belfast Electoral Wards, Belfast: Department of Finance and Personnel Northern Ireland, 1992
Northern Ireland Information Service, *Nine Point Package to Spell the Rebirth of Belfast*, Belfast: The Northern Ireland Information Service, 1978
Office of the First Minister and Deputy First Minister, *A Shared Future. Policy and Strategic Framework for Good Relations in Northern Ireland*, Belfast: OFMDFM, 2005
Roads Services, *M1/Westlink Improvements Public Information Leaflet*, Belfast: Roads Services, 2006
Stakeholder, "Titanic Quarter scoops top award for regeneration", http://www.stakeholdergroup.com/news/titanic-quarter-scoops-top-award-for-regeneration, 2011
Titanic Quarter, *Titanic Quarter, Regenerating Belfast,* London: 3Fox International, 2007
(The) Urban Task Force, *Towards a Strong Urban Renaissance*, London: Routledge, 1999
UTV News, "Rise sculpture unveiled in Belfast",

http://www.u.tv/news/Rise-sculpture-unveiled-in-Belfast/f1d95092-04ba-4f5c-960c-309d302af2ce, 2011

Secondary sources

Augé, Marc. *Non-places: Introduction to an Anthropology of Supermodernity*. London/New York: Verso, 1995

Bollens, Scott. *City and Soul in Divided Societies*. Oxford/New York: Routledge, 2012

Community Relations Council, *Towards Sustainable Security–Interfaces, Barriers and the Legacy of Segregation in Belfast*. Belfast: CRC, 2008

Dennett, Toby. "Foreword", *Public Art Handbook for Northern Ireland*. Belfast: Arts Council of Northern Ireland, 2005

Etchart, Joana. "The Titanic Quarter in Belfast: Building a New Place in a Divided City". *Nordic Irish Studies Journal* 7, (2008) 31-40.

Forum for Alternative Belfast (FAB), *Shared Space 2011*. Belfast: Forum for Alternative Belfast and Belfast Conflict Resolution Consortium, 2011

Gaffikin, Frank and Morrissey, Mike. *Planning in Divided Cities: Collaborative Shaping of Contested Space*. Oxford: Blackwell Publishing Ltd, 2011.

Goldie, Roz and Ruddy, Brid. *Crossing the Line, Key Features of Effective Practice in the Development of Shared Space in Areas close to an Interface*. Belfast: Belfast Interface Project, 2010.

Jarman, Neil. *Mapping Interface Barriers*. Belfast: Belfast Interface Project, 2005

Jones, Paul. *The Sociology of Architecture*. Liverpool: The University of Liverpool Press, 2011

Komarova, Milena. "Shared Space in Belfast and the Limits of A Shared Future". *Divided Cities/Contested States Working Paper No3,* 2008

Komarova, Milena and O'Dowd, Liam. "Regeneration in a Contested City: A Belfast Case Study". *Divided Cities/Contested States Working Paper No10,* 2009

Lederach, John Paul. "The Challenge of the 21st Century: Justpeace", *People Building Peace: 35 Inspiring Stories from around the World*. Utrecht: European Centre for Conflict Prevention, 1999

Miles, Malcolm. "Interruptions: Testing the Rhetoric of Culturally Led Urban Development". *Urban Studies* 42 (5/6) (2005), 889-911.

Murtagh, Brendan, "New Spaces and Old in 'Post-Conflict' Belfast", *Divided Cities/Contested States Working Papers n°5,* 2008

Neill, W.J.V. "Northern Ireland, an Introduction", in *Urban Design and the British Urban Renaissance* edited by John Punter, London: Routledge, 2010.

—. "Belfast. Rebranding the 'Renaissance City': from 'the Troubles' to Titanic Quarter in *Urban Design and the British Urban Renaissance* edited by John Punter, London: Routledge, 2010

O'Dowd, Liam. *Where are the People? Contemporary Photographs of Belfast 2002-2010*. Belfast: Belfast Exposed Photography, 22-37, 2010

Wiener, Ron. *The Rape and Plunder of the Shankill. Community Action: the Belfast Experience*, Belfast: Normaens, 1975

CHAPTER THREE

"I COULD NOT TELL": THE REPRESENTATION OF MEMORY AND TRAUMA IN CONTEMPORARY NORTHERN IRISH CULTURE

SHANE ALCOBIA-MURPHY

> The tragedies of the past have left a deep and profoundly regrettable legacy of suffering. We must never forget those who have died or been injured, and their families. But we can best honour them through a fresh start, in which we firmly dedicate ourselves to the achievement of reconciliation, tolerance and mutual trust, and to the protection and vindication of the human rights of all. (Anon. 1998: Paragraph 2)

When searching for ways to impose a meaningful order upon reality, we rely on memory for "the provision of symbolic representations and frames which can influence and organize both our actions and our conceptions of ourselves" (Misztal, 2003: 13). Yet following the Belfast Agreement, which was signed on 10 April 1998, a pronounced tension emerged in Northern Irish society between the urge to remember and the desire to forget the atrocities carried out during the period of the so-called "Troubles", with politicians time and again walking the fine line between amnesty and amnesia, whether willingly or not. In the effort to maintain existing ceasefires, and to seek a political solution, it had been deemed expedient for Justice to remain blind (or rather, to turn a blind eye) to certain past crimes: for example, due to the early release scheme negotiated under the auspices of the Agreement, Torrens Knight, convicted of eleven murders carried out at Greysteel and Castlerock, served only seven years out of eight life sentences, and Norman Coopey was allowed to align himself with the Loyalist Volunteer Force whilst in prison and thereby claim political status (and eligibility for early release) for what was a non-politically motivated sectarian murder (McKay, 2008). Thus, there appears to be a determined effort to overwrite the "legacy of suffering", a reflex symbolised most visibly in the Belfast City Council's new logo for the city with its heart-shaped "B", a design which, as Colin Graham has contended, effectively "pitches Belfast as a place of unspecified but all-encompassing 'warmth', its history bundled safely into a kind of distanced quaintness attuned to its function as a spectacle of and for tourism" (Graham, 2009: 105). Graham's recent research demonstrates how a recurrent trope has emerged within post-Ceasefire Northern Irish culture, namely "an ache which notices, knows, but can barely comment on the cauterisation of the dark complexity of the past, since to point to, or even test out, the fragile post-consociational consensus would be to remember a future that is now consigned to history" (Graham, 2005: 568). This chapter examines the poetic, novelistic and photographic responses to the Agreement, and explores the ways in which the writers and artists expose an uneasy relationship to Northern Ireland's violent past. If, as Andreas Huyssen argues, "[r]emembrance shapes our links to the past, and the ways we remember define us in the present" (Huyssen, 1995: 249), then what does the erasure of one's past say about one's self-conception in the present?

A perfect (and much commented upon) example of the "cauterisation" of the past is Michael Winterbottom's *With or Without You* (1999), a film which aestheticises the Belfast urban environment and which searches for "'a new imagery' that would rescue the city from its association with 'violence, fear and division'" (Hill, 2006: 230). Rather than featuring sectarian murals, peace-lines and graffiti, the film erases markers of conflict, "replacing the rundown streets, the Saracens, and the ever-hovering helicopters with a new vision of Belfast as a glass and chrome space of pleasurable consumption" (Barton, 2004: 174). Symbolising the forward-looking nature of the city is the film's focus on the Waterfront Hall, the "ultra-modern concert, conference and exhibition centre that came to symbolise the new, aspiring and increasingly affluent Belfast of the late 1990s" (McLoone, 2008: 59). That urge to forget is also encapsulated by the images used for the part played by Belfast in Coca Cola's *Open Happiness* (2009) global marketing campaign. Designed by the *eboy* collective[1] and commissioned by the McCann Erickson service communications agency, the pixel art and isometric projections used for the advertising posters depicting the "Coke Cities" which were displayed

[1] The *eboy* collective was founded in 1998 by Steffen Sauerteig, Svend Smital and Kai Vermehr to explore and expand the possibilities of pixel art.

throughout Belfast on billboards, bus-shelters, phone kiosks and other advertising spaces, portray the city as being over-run by tourists and culture vultures: in the post-Troubles context, the weather is always sunny, airport security is surprisingly lax, the Titanic is resurrected and filmed, and the only potential violence is from a wayward golf shot and a Ravenhill rugby fracas. In the words of one of Colin Bateman's characters, it is as if "the entire country had ducked into Mr Benn's changing room and emerged fresh and vibrant" (Bateman, 2005: 278).

However, a significant trend has emerged within Northern Irish cultural responses to the Belfast Agreement and the ensuing peace process, one which indicates a determined resistance to amnesia and which promotes an ethical-political approach towards the act of remembrance. For example, in Ciaran Carson's poem "Peace" (Carson, 2008: 55), the speaker does not foreground the progress resulting from the paramilitary decommissioning of arms and the prisoners' amnesty; rather, he underscores the inherent dangers of the strictly presentist concerns of Northern Irish *real-politik* by meditating on significant absences:

> And all the unanswered questions of those dark days come back
> To haunt us, the disabled guns that still managed to kill,
>
> The witnesses that became ghosts in the blink of an eye.
> Whom can we prosecute when no one is left fit to speak?

In these lines, as Neal Alexander observes, "the imperfect present is haunted by the past, by a silencing of memory that renders justice impossible and the duty to remember unfulfilled" (Alexander, 2010: 136). Here, Alexander refers to Ricoeur's contention that remembrance is an "action", one that is a prerequisite for bearing witness to atrocities and the subsequent achievement of justice. "The first reason why it is a duty to tell," Ricoeur states, "is surely as a means of fighting against the erosion of traces" (Ricoeur, 1999: 10); hence, the rush to forgive and forget may bring about "peace", but it utterly fails to salve the mind's wounds. Ricoeur does admit that, in order to get beyond fixating on anger and to become reconciled with the past's legacies, there is, alongside the duty to remember, a complementary "duty to forget" (Ricoeur, 1999: 11); nevertheless, he concedes that the two duties are not comparable and that progress cannot be achieved by the erosion of traces and archives.

Such an erasure is (understandably) writ large in Belfast Council's glossy window into the future, *Invest in Belfast: A City Guide for Investors*. The document highlights the significant investment in infrastructure, commercial ventures and urban regeneration, including the

£5 billion waterfront development, the Titanic Quarter, which aims to utterly transform 185 acres on the site of the former Harland & Wolff shipyards, and the projected development of the Lagan Corridor[2]. It has been noted that, in the recent past, factors such as the inner city developments, incorporating high-rise buildings out of scale and sympathy with already existing edifices, and traffic pressure have each contributed to the decline in Belfast's visual character (Brett, 2001: 90), but that the main contributor has been the legacy of the thirty years of violence (peace-lines, sectarian graffiti, destroyed buildings). Nevertheless, official responses to city planning have tended to strategically implement a policy of cultural amnesia. The graphics employed by the Belfast Urban Area Plan (1989), for example, projected "a suite of positive images of newly built or planned developments" which were "counterpointed by anaemic-toned panoramas of the city of the past"; indeed, as William J.V. Neill points out, all reference to "the sectarian divisions with which the city is riven was studiously avoided in both text and photographs" (Neill, 2001: 47). However, when artists and writers address the impact of Belfast's economic growth their approach is far more diachronic, rarely losing sight of the past. For instance, in Alan Gillis' "Progress" (Gillis, 2004: 55), the speaker wryly comments upon the effects of the city's newly found prosperity by positing, via a surreal filmic rewind, what it can never ultimately achieve, namely the resurrection of those killed during the Troubles and the healing of old wounds:

> They say that for years Belfast was backwards
> and it's great now to see some progress.
> So I guess we can look forward to taking boxes
> From the earth. I guess ambulances
> will leave the dying back amidst the rubble
> to be explosively healed.

Similarly, in John Duncan's photographic exhibition, *Trees from Germany* (2003), the modern Belfast cityscape resulting from recent economic investment is caught in an uneasy juxtaposition with evidence of continuing sectarianism. One image, *Days Hotel, Sandy Row*, features a worker in the process of laying turf in the front area of the largest hotel in Northern Ireland. As part of the Cordia Hotel Group, the location is an emblem of global capitalism, and the activity symptomatic of promised new growth; however, facing this area, but separated from it by the hotel's

---

[2] See
http://www.belfastcity.gov.uk/investinbelfastguide/docs/investinbelfast2010.pdf, 7.

railings, is an emblem that bespeaks a defensive local insularity, namely a large mural declaring "You are now entering Loyalist Sandy Row Heartland of South Belfast Ulster Freedom Fighters". The adjacent photograph is taken from behind the hotel and features a gigantic 11th July bonfire (once again separated from the hotel by railings). Thus, familiar and backward-looking markers of the Troubles lay siege to the indices of consumer-led progress. As Aaron Kelly has noted, with such photographs Duncan "achieves a collision between a fragmented past and a fractious future"; the images "do not simply document the ruins of the past but also form an inventory of the present and its future trajectory, which does not live up to its own apparent promise" (Kelly, 2010: 96). Divisions between communities are not erased here; rather, they are intensified.

What is remarkable is the consistency of approach by contemporary photographic projects focused on Belfast. Duncan's *Trees from Germany* echoes an earlier exhibition by John Davies, *Metropoli* (2000), which sought "to document the multi-layered character of metropolitan areas and to produce a coherent series of images which [would] reflect the positive achievements and realities within our continually changing urban space" (Davies, 2000: n.p.). His black and white photographs of Belfast depict a city in transition with modern and Victorian designs uneasily co-existing within the frame. The elevated vantage-point from which the images are taken enables the photographer to capture the icons of global capitalism in the same frame as the crowded terraced houses of the Donegall Pass. Davies here combines a synchronic gaze, that which "registers the varieties and patterns of present usage", with a diachronic gaze that "opens up the urban palimpsest" and "goes back through layers and accretions, perceiving history, influence, development, change"[3]. In one key image, that of an almost completed apartment block covered by scaffolding and tarpaulin, Davies, as Colin Graham astutely argues, "catches the moments in which a city's nostalgia is made, when the tarpaulin is pulled back like the curtain on an unveiled plaque, and in the midst of the achievement we feel that twinge of regret for its completion, because the future of a city space revealed is the beginning of a life-in-death for many pasts" (Graham, 2001: 10). That past is never fully erased in Davies' photographic texts, nor is it in Lai-Olaf Hesse's *Topography of the Titanic* (2007), a project which resonates with the work of both Davies and Duncan.

Hesse's interior and exterior shots of vacant and eerily depopulated spaces centre on the site of the projected Titanic Quarter development.

---

[3] For the distinction between the two types of gaze, see Barry 2000: 224-26.

Juxtaposed with contemporary images of memorial statues, abandoned docks, disused workshops and fenced-off areas are archival photographs from 1907-1912 documenting the building and first sailing of the Olympic-class passenger liner, R.M.S. Titanic. Past, present and projected-future are conjoined, yet sit uneasily together. One image, taken at a motorway underpass off Corporation Street, presents two differently coloured pieces of graffiti: U.D.A. (the acronym for the Ulster Defence Association) is sprayed in red, whilst over it we have in black a door, window and the phrases "What was here before? Who was here before?" (Hesse, 2007: 35). While the niggling, insistent questions bespeak a loss and erasure, they act as a call for remembrance of a past which is in danger of being by-passed. As Aaron Kelly has noted, the photograph suggests "that some people pay the price for the progress of others, that progress is not necessarily so progressive after all or a thing that is universally enjoyed" (Kelly, 2010: 100). The acronym "U.D.A.", although faded, still persists in the background: as a graffito, it functions as a marker "not only in the material, territorial sense but also of political possession and assertion" (McGonagle, 1987: n.p.). The past, then, has not been successfully archived here.

One of the crucial thematic foci of art centred on post-Agreement Belfast, particularly by those artists sponsored by Belfast Exposed Photography, is that of the archive itself. In *Archive_Belfast* (2004), Claudio Hils' photographs of "inaccessible video recordings, files and books stowed away on shelves, in locked and closed cabinets" (Eifert-Körnig, 2004: 104) self-reflexively engage with how memories are recorded and kept for posterity. In one image, taken at Schomberg House, the Grand Orange Lodge of Ireland, Hils presents the viewer with competing forms of data storage, each differently encoding the past: three framed images-a photograph and a colour portrait of people in Orange Order regalia, an illustration of King Billy-hang over two computer terminals and two colourfully decorated lambeg drums, replete with commemorative inscriptions. Juxtaposed to this photograph is a similarly composed image taken at the headquarters of the Irish Republican Socialist Party, Costello House: hanging over the computer terminals and ceremonial pikes are plaques commemorating the St Patrick's Day parades in San Francisco. In both images there is a tension between traditional and modern methods of recording and displaying historical memory; no indication is provided as to which takes precedence or which is more effective, and no interpretative framework is provided to guide the viewer as to what they are actually witnessing. The computers in both are turned off, thus suggesting that the archives of these institutions are closed off to outsiders. Similarly, while the viewer can see rows of video cassettes in a photograph taken at Knocknagoney Police station, only someone privy to the classification codes will know what each contains when glancing at their individual covers. In many of the photographs we see storerooms full of photographs, uniforms and iconic memorabilia, yet the organisational principle in each is uncertain: which items have evidential status and which constitute unimportant clutter is uncertain. The lack of a coherent archival structure could connote historiographical uncertainty whereby a society in transition has yet to determine the shape of public memory; however, while an archive is meant to be a repository in which important public documents and records are kept, Hils' photographs depict spaces in which items are disregarded, suffer wilful neglect and are shielded from the public gaze. Thus, rather than mere uncertainty about the historical record, what the exhibition presents is a form of archival amnesia, or the "erosion of traces" against which Ricoeur had warned. The consequence of such amnesia is psychic dislocation, or trauma.

The forceful return of an uncontainable, recalcitrant past, resulting from attempted repression or denial, is writ large in contemporary fiction focused on Northern Ireland. In her recently published monograph on Scottish and Irish fiction, Stefanie Lehner analyses Glenn Patterson's *That Which Was* (2004) and Eoin McNamee's *The Ultras* (2004) in a post-ceasefire context and argues persuasively that "both novels emphasise the importance of accounting for this burdensome past which the official *arkhe*-taintment attempts to lighten" (Lehner, 2011: 114). Such an approach could equally be applied to Seamus Deane's *Reading in the Dark* (1996), with its key motifs of enclosure and haunting. In that novel, the characters attempt to seal off and re-write the past. As such, it is, as Elmer Kennedy-Andrews contends, "a story of the suppressions, omissions, withholdings and evasions that are part of the narrative process" (Kennedy-Andrews, 2003: 217). Throughout, the reader witnesses the wilful erasure of uncomfortable familial and communal truths. Indeed, in the concluding chapter the narrator surmises that perhaps the only way "they […] could go on was by forgetting, forgetting" (Deane, 1996: 228). Yet Deane's text suggests that the consequence of such enforced amnesia is paralysis and not progress: suppressing her story, the narrator's mother suffers from aphonia. Archive fever is here both an activity and an ailment with disabling symptoms. She moves, we are told, "as though there were pounds of pressure bearing down on her; and when she sat, it was as though the pressure reversed itself and began to build up inside her and feint at her mouth or her hands" (Deane, 1996: 139). That "pressure" must find a release. That which is repressed returns in the form of a spectre: "I would come in to find her at the turn of the stairs, looking out the lobby window, still haunted, but now with a real ghost crouched in the air around her" (Deane, 1996: 139). In Deane's text, forgetting can only result in a hiatus: the ghost is neither of this world nor the next; the lobby window is located between the interior and exterior. Indeed, the mother's position is doubly liminal, caught as she is at "the turn of the stairs".

The return of the past in spectral form is also central to the plot of Stuart Neville's 2009 novel, *The Twelve*. Set during the Peace Process, it focuses on Gerry Fagan, an ex-prisoner and paramilitary haunted by the ghosts of those whom he has killed. When focalised through Fagan, the narrative reflects with some bitterness on the politicians' rewriting of the past: "The politicians on the outside had bartered for his freedom, along with hundreds more men and women. They called people like him political prisoners. Not murders or thieves, not extortionists or blackmailers. Not criminals of any kind, just victims of circumstance" (Neville, 2009: 7). In the new political climate, Fagan is viewed as a casualty of war and thus absolved of all responsibility for what were once deemed "crimes". Like Duncan's *Trees from Germany*, Neville's text suggests that capital investment, the development of the city's infrastructure and historical amnesia must go hand in hand for progress to occur: "The lights of the Odyssey complex shimmered across the water. The nightclubs inside it would be thronging with the young and the affluent; young enough to have no memory of men like Fagan, affluent enough not to care" (Neville, 2009: 14). For Fagan, however, memory persists and is seen as a "curse" (Neville, 2009: 16). To stave off psychic collapse he is conjoined by the ghosts to take vengeance on those who "engineered" their deaths. While the plot may be crude, nevertheless the central spectral motif works to suggest that the machinations of the new political regime are self-defeating if they simply erase the traces of the past: as the narrator states, "The old ways were dead and gone, but still their ghosts might come to haunt the political process" (Neville, 2009: 213).

Memory in both Deane and Neville's texts is of a particular kind, and is qualitatively different to that explored in Davies, Hesse, and Duncan. Rather than simply looking at historical memory as such, the novel's focus on trauma which, as Cathy Caruth states, "describes an overwhelming experience of sudden, or catastrophic events in which the response to the event occurs in the often delayed, and uncontrolled repetitive occurrence of hallucinations and other intrusive phenomena" (Caruth, 1996: 11). Trauma is characterised either by the compulsion to repeat the initial experience either in order to achieve a belated mastery or, as Otto Fenichel states, due to "the tendency of the repressed to find an outlet" (Fenichel,

1946: 542). The power of the traumatic experience lies not simply in the fact that it is "repeated after its forgetting" but, as Caruth argues, "that it is only in and through its inherent forgetting that it is first experienced at all" (Caruth, 1996: 17). A key text which demonstrates this in a Northern Irish context is Willie Doherty's 2007 exhibition *Ghost Story* which comprises a fifteen minute colour video installation and an accompanying soundtrack, both of which are continuously played on a loop. Structurally, the piece is unending and lacks closure. The voiceover by the actor Stephen Rea presents a narrative that is said to "evoke memories of the dead and a sense of loss and foreboding". More specifically, the speaker's first memory returns to the events of 30 January 1972 in Derry and to what he witnessed on Bloody Sunday:

> I found myself walking along a deserted path. Through the trees on one side I could faintly make out a river in the distance. On the other side I could faintly hear the rumble of far away traffic. The scene was unfamiliar to me. I looked over my shoulder and saw that the trees behind me were filled with shadow- like figures. Looks of terror and bewilderment filled their eyes, and they silently screamed, as if already aware of their fate. The scene reminded me of the faces in a running crowd that I had once seen on a bright but cold January afternoon. (Doherty 2009: n.p.)

Doherty's previous work on Bloody Sunday, in works such as *30 January 1972* and *How It Was*, focused primarily on the transmission and dissemination of memory and emphasised "how mediated images become the dominant images and replace or embellish other forms of forgetting" (Doherty, 2007: 40). Doherty's interest in *Ghost Story* lies elsewhere:

> The subtext of the work I'm showing here, *Ghost Story*, addresses the deeper-seated problems of how we deal with the memory and loss and tragedy of the past 30 years–or some people might say of the past 300 years–of the conflict in Ireland. That is what the political process is not dealing with, but there is an opportunity of being here in the context of representing Northern Ireland to flag up these issues. (Doherty in Jury 2007: n.p.)

The opening statements of *Ghost Story* are characterised by passive constructions, indicative of the subject's lack of both volition and agency. His inability to engage with his memories results in incomprehension. The lexis used places us in the realm of representational discourse: "scene", twice mentioned, marks the experience as unreal and this is symptomatic of his dissociative behaviour. He remains a witness rather than an active participant in the experience being related. Lacking corporeality the disembodied "shadow-like presences" which crowd the speaker's memory all suggest the spectral return of the repressed. The silent scream is an emblem of the subject's own current predicament since the initial event "is such that beyond it there remains only a speech in pieces, splinters and fragments of speech" (Nichanian, 2003: 112). With trauma, there is an inherent tension between the desire to recount and master one's experience and the need to repress the memory. As Gabriele Schwab notes, "[w]riting from within the core of trauma is a constant struggle between the colonizing power of words and the revolt of what is being rejected, silenced. […] Trauma as a mode of being halts the flow of time, fractures the self, and punctures memory and language" (Schwab, 2006: 95, 96). As spectators, we follow the subject as he retraces his footsteps along the paths and streets that, as he relates, he had thought he had forgotten. Yet all that remains are shadows, footprints, tracks and traces of the crowd. At one point the narrator finds that his "train of thought" is interrupted by what he calls "a further incursion of unreality":

> My eyes deceived me as I thought I saw a human figure. No matter how quickly or slowly I walked the figure did not seem to get any closer. When I took my eye off the figure he disappeared. When I stared at the point where the path vanished the figure emerged once again from the trees or from the path itself. I could not tell. (Doherty, 2009: n.p.)

This irruption of the uncanny once again marks the return of the repressed but the fact that he "cannot tell" also suggests that the trauma marks the limits of both perception and narration. That Doherty gives *Ghost Story* a circular, looped structure, one that is endlessly replayed in the exhibition space, is important as it conveys the subject's experience of trauma. What we have here is trauma in the sense of "a disease of time [which] permits the past to relive itself in the present, in the form of intrusive images and thoughts" (Young, 1997: 7). Because trauma is a "breach in the mind's experience of time" (Caruth, 1996: 4), the standard experience of time as a linear, chronological progression from past to present to future is disrupted. Traumatic events are timeless: for the victim, trauma appears to have "no beginning, no ending, no before, no during, and no after" (Laub, 1992: 69). Lacking closure, *Ghost Story* allows the viewer to get an understanding of what trauma may be like; as viewers we adopt the subject's point of view and are forced to bear witness to his pain. "Pain," as Veena Das argues, "is not that inexpressible something that destroys communication, or marks one's exit from one's existence in language. Instead, it makes a claim […] which may be given or denied. In either case, it is not a referential statement that is simply pointing to an inner object" (Das in Bennett, 2005: 49). If the viewer is receptive to the claim that *Ghost Story* makes on us, then we become more inclined to question the institutional imperatives to forget, move on or progress.

Yet one caveat must be made: while there is an ethical imperative to resist archival amnesia, there is also a danger that art might co-opt, sanitise and aestheticise suffering. In other words, art may take a past atrocity as a theme and treat it as mere "subject", thus doing it an injustice. A poem like Medbh McGuckian's "Butterfly Memory Object" (McGuckian, 2005: n.p.), which centres on trauma, is alive to this danger. Like Doherty's *Ghost Story*, it is a text concerned with the memories which inhere within a place:

> Still deadly places are folded
> Into an unburial ground, where resting
> Soldiers tell the munitionettes
> They're easy to sleep with,
> And for your button a kiss.

Citing heavily from Nicholas Saunders' *Trench Art: Materialities and Memories of War*, the poem highlights the persistence, rather than erasure, of the past. Once the corpses in these "still deadly places" are merged with the natural features, the landscape becomes a "multi-vocal palimpsest" (Saunders, 2003: 127). The ground is marked as an open wound. "Unburial ground" is Susan Sontag's coinage to describe the location of Felice Beatto's photograph taken inside the Secundra Bagh after two thousand rebels had been slaughtered by British forces in 1857. Yet the act of "folding" the soldiers into the ground, and the presentation of them as "resting", suggests pacification and silencing. Indeed, the narrative trajectory indicates a movement backwards, before death as if denying what has (or will) happen: the "resting" soldiers are not lying dead on the ground, but playfully flirting with the munitionettes prior to going out to battle. The "Butterfly Memory Object" of the poem's title suggests a further silencing: although such an artwork, made from shells and other destructive armaments, serve in the first instance to remember the dead, Saunders acknowledges that now the narratives which lie behind the artworks remain unknown (Saunders, 2003: 7). That McGuckian is mistrustful of art's propensity to transmute rather than to transmit pain can be seen in a final example, entitled "Life as a Literary Convict" (McGuckian, 2002: 18), a memory poem which borrows heavily from Graham Robb's biography of Balzac:

> Signs of the still recent war
> creep among the people like a plague,
> dressed as Phoebus.
> while I wander about in search of the dead,
> all I see are the living
> being pulled into existence [...]

While the speaker is preoccupied "in search of the dead", those around her are concerned with pulling the living "into existence". The "signs of the still recent war" have become transformed and have lost all their horror: they are "dressed as Phoebus", or Apollo, the god of art. The poem's speaker is separated off from such activity and plays no part in the covering over or transmutation of suffering. For her, the wounds must remain visible.

In conclusion, rather than foreground the imperatives to forgive and forget, or highlight the need to enter into the seductive embrace of cultural amnesia, or promote what Senator George Mitchell termed "the decommissioning of mindsets", much Northern Irish art focuses upon the dangers of forgetting the past. For the visual artists and writers alike, a wilful neglect of history may result in the return of the repressed and in psychic breakdown on both the communal and individual levels. Thus, contrary to those who indulged in the euphoric post-conflict jubilation, writers and artists like the poet Michael Longley weighed in with prudent counsel, arguing that "amnesty isn't amnesia" and that "[i]n order to make sure it doesn't happen again, you've got to remember it in great detail. Those who forget history are the ones who are doomed to repeat it" (Longley, 1997: 35-6).

Bibliography

Anon. *The Agreement*, 10 April 1998. http://cain.ulst.ac.uk/events/peace/docs/agreement.htm. Accessed 15 December 2011.

Alexander, Neal. *Ciaran Carson: Space, Place, Writing*. Liverpool: Liverpool University Press, 2010.

Barry, Peter. *Contemporary British Poetry and the City*. Manchester: Manchester University Press, 2000.

Barton, Ruth. *Irish National Cinema*. London: Routledge, 2004.

Bateman, Colin. *Belfast Confidential*. London: Headline, 2005.

Bennett, Jill. *Empathetic Vision: Affect, Trauma and Contemporary Art*. Stanford: Stanford University Press, 2005.

Bradley, Fiona. “Uncommon Ground”. *Buried.* Edinburgh: The Fruitmarket Gallery, 2009. 5-7.

Brett, C.E.B. “Victorian and Edwardian Belfast: Preserving the Architectural Legacy of the Inner City” in *Urban Planning and Cultural Inclusion: Lessons from Belfast and Berlin* edited by William J. V. Neill and Hanns-Uve Schwedler. Basingstoke: Palgrave, 2001. 85-99.

Carson, Ciaran. “Peace”. *For All We Know.* Oldcastle: Gallery Press, 2008. 55.

Caruth, Cathy, ed. *Trauma: Explorations in Memory.* Baltimore: The John Hopkins University Press, 1995.

—. *Unclaimed Experience: Trauma, Narrative, and History.* Baltimore: The John Hopkins University Press, 1996.

Davies, John. http://www.johndavies.uk.com/metropoli.htm. 2004. Accessed 30 July 2009.

Deane, Seamus. *Reading in the Dark.* London: Jonathan Cape, 1996.

Doherty, Willie. “Ylimaz Dzierwior in Conversation with Willie Doherty”. *Willie Doherty: Anthology of Time-Based Works.* Ostfildern, Hatje Cantz Verlag, 2007. 39-42.

—. “Ghost Story”. *Buried.* Edinburgh: The Fruitmarket Gallery, 2009. N.p.

—. “Some Notes on Problems and Possibilities”. *Buried.* Edinburgh: The Fruitmarket Gallery, 2009. 155-57.

Duncan, John. *Trees from Germany.* Belfast: Belfast Exposed Photography, 2003.

Eifert-Körnig, Anna M. “Of Memory Spaces: Photographic Thoughts on the Repressive Effect of Media”. *Archive_Belfast.* Belfast: Belfast Exposed Photography, 2004. 103-10.

Fenichel, Otto. *The Psychoanalytic Theory of Neurosis.* New York: W.W. Norton, 1945.

Gillis, Alan. “Progress”. *Somebody, Somewhere.* Oldcastle: Gallery Press, 2004. 55.

Graham, Colin. “Metropoli”. *Source Magazine.* 26 (2001): 7-16

—. “‘Every Passer-by a Culprit?’: Archive Fever, Photography and the Peace in Belfast”. *Third Text.* 19.5 (September, 2005): 567-80

—. “Gargarin’s Point of View: Memory and Space in Recent Northern Irish Art”. *Irish Review* (Winter 2009): 104-13.

Hesse, Kai-Olaf. *Topography of the Titanic.* Belfast: Belfast Exposed Photography, 2007.

Hill, John. *Cinema and Northern Ireland.* London: BFI, 2006.

Hils, Claudio. *Archive_Belfast.* Belfast: Belfast Exposed Photography, 2004.

Huyssen, Andreas. *Twilight Memories: Marking Time in a Culture of Amnesia*. New York: Routledge, 1995.

Jury, Louise. "Whose Art Is It Anyway?" *The Scotsman*. 11 June 2007. http://living.scotsman.com/index.cfm?id=907892007. Accessed 30 July 2009

Kelly, Aaron. "Spaces of Politics". *Where Are the People?: Contemporary Photographs of Belfast, 2002-2010* edited by Karen Downey. Belfast: Belfast Exposed Photography, 2010. 96-105.

Kennedy-Andrews, Elmer. *De-constructing the North: Fiction and the Northern Ireland Troubles since 1969*. Dublin: Four Courts Press, 2003.

Kirmayer, Laurence J. "Landscapes of Memory: Trauma, Narrative, and Dissociation". *Tense Past: Cultural Essays in Trauma and Memory* edited by Paul Antze and Michael Lambek. New York: Routledge, 1996. 173-98.

Laub, Dori. "Bearing Witness, or, the Vicissitudes of Listening". *Testimony: Crises of Witnessing in Literature* edited by Shoshana Felman and Dori Laub. New York: Routledge, 1992.

Lehner, Stefanie. *Subaltern Ethics in Contemporary Scottish and Irish Fiction: Tracing Counter-Histories*. Basingstoke: Palgrave, 2011.

Longley, Michael. "'Walking Forwards into the Past': An Interview with Michael Longley". Interview by Fran Brearton. *Irish Studies Review*. 18 (Spring, 1997): 35-9.

McGonagle, Declan. "Troubled Land". *Troubled Land: The Social Landscape of Northern Ireland*. London: Grey Editions, 1987. N.p.

McGuckian, Medbh. "Life as a Literary Convict". *The Soldiers of Year II*. Winston-Salem: Wake Forest University Press, 2002. 18.

—. "Butterfly Memory Object". *Qualm* (October, 2005). www.qualm.co.uk/mainpr.html#mmcgukian. Accessed 15 December 2011.

McKay, Susan. *Bear in Mind These Dead*. London: Faber, 2008

McLoone, Martin. *Film, Media and Popular Culture in Ireland: Cityscapes, Landscapes, Soundscapes*. Dublin: Irish Academic Press, 2008.

Misztal, Barbara, *Theories of Social Remembering*. Maidenhead: Open University, 2003.

Mitchell, George. "The Mitchell Report". http://www.dfa.ie/home/index.aspx?id=8741. Accessed 15 December 2011.

Neill, William J.V. "The Urban Planning Context in Belfast: A City between War and Peace". *Urban Planning and Cultural Inclusion:*

Lessons from Belfast and Berlin edited by William J.V. Neill and Hanns-Uve Schwedler. Basingstoke: Palgrave, 2001. 42-53.

Neville, Stuart. *The Twelve*. London: Harvill Secker, 2009.

Nichanian, Marc. "Catastrophic Mourning". *Loss: The Politics of Mourning* edited by David L. Eng and David Kazanjian. Berkeley: University of California Press, 2003. 99-124.

Ricoeur, Paul. "Memory and Forgetting". *Questioning Ethics: Contemporary Debates in Philosophy* edited by Richard Kearney and Mark Dooley. London: Routledge, 1999. 5-11.

Saunders, Nicholas J. *Trench Art: Materialities and Memories of War*. London: Berg Publishers, 2003.

Schwab, Gabriele. "Writing against Memory and Forgetting". *Literature and Medicine*. 25.1 (Spring, 2006): 95-121

Young, Allan. *The Harmony of Illusions*. Princeton: Princeton University Press, 1997.

PART II

LIFESTYLE AND ENTERTAINMENT

CHAPTER FOUR

GUINNESS GO LEOR: IRISH PUBS AND THE DIASPORA

KATHLEEN HEININGE

Any study of ethnicity, especially diasporic ethnicity, must somehow engage with the question of "authenticity," and Irish studies is no different. Irish cultural identity is performed on stage (with Irish plays, dance, and music), at St. Patrick's Day celebrations (witness the parade in New Orleans where Irish Spring soap, potatoes, cabbages, and ramen noodles are tossed from floats), in markets (where shamrock boxer shorts, Guinness hats, and Celtic cross snow-globes are sold), and in pubs. Such performances proliferate all over the world, often eliciting debate about the authentic representation of ethnicity. Is Martin McDonagh, touted as some by one of the most important Irish playwrights working today, really Irish, although he was not raised in Ireland? Does Riverdance really replicate traditional Irish dancing? Do the production values of Celtic Woman hearken back to the feis (Irish festival) or to pub music? At stake seems to be the need for members of the diaspora to align themselves with a romanticized and glorious past, one that has produced a considerable number of cultural artifacts, from James Joyce to Guinness. Because the story of Ireland has been largely one of emigration rather than immigration, the Irish diaspora can be found everywhere, not only in Boston and New York and San Francisco, but in Butte, Milwaukee, New Orleans, and Atlanta; not only in England and the United States, but in France, the Caribbean, Italy, South Africa, Hong Kong, Mexico, French Polynesia, and Croatia. Those who claim Irish connections, even when those connections are relatively tenuous or perhaps mendacious, can be found in a diversity of places far from Ireland. Consequently, how is Irishness marked? What happens to authenticity when it is exported, and how does that sense of the authentic contribute to (or detract from) participation in an imagined community, as defined by Benedict Anderson?

As is true for many ethnic groups, the markers of ethnicity often hew to stereotypes, and stereotypes about the Irish abound, although none so prevalently as the assumption that the Irish are prodigious drinkers. Some question the origin of such stereotypes, with theories proposed from a cultural preference to drink in public rather than at home, to the belief that drink was nutritious (see Porter 2002 and Barich 2009). Whatever the origins of the stereotype, its perpetuation has resulted in the association of the Irish with their drinking establishments, and the pub has spread as pervasively as the diaspora itself. Around the world, Irish pubs have become one of the ways the diaspora and others associate themselves with things Irish, and the familiar black Guinness sign proclaiming that comradery and affability can be found even when far from "home".

These pubs, found around the world, however, do not resemble the pub found in Ireland. Those in Ireland need not self-consciously identify as specifically Irish; they are already in Ireland, and need no further identification. Once, however, the pub leaves Ireland, it requires markers to set it apart from its "foreign" surroundings, and a particular kind of diasporic Irish pub is created: the imagined community of those with connections (both physical and wishful) to Ireland. Its self-consciousness, reflecting the self-consciousness of its connoisseurs, is oddly cliquish, choosing its own stereotypes to portray Irishness. The pub, then, becomes an interesting site for the contestation of Irish identity, and a determining factor in trying to assert a strange kind of authentic historical memory.

Cultural markers are not unusual in ethnic transplanting. When a Chinese restaurant opens in Dublin, the sign will include Chinese writing, though few patrons read Chinese, and the food served differs dramatically from that found in China, especially when it is served on chips rather than rice. When an American restaurant advertises Italian pizza, one assumes it will come loaded with cheese, meat, and vegetables, with little resemblance to a pizza ordered in Rome. The Irish pub is different, however, from other translated cultural artefacts in that its global commodification is beginning to change the nature of the Irish pubs found in Ireland, so that the latter "seem" more authentic to those from the imagined community of the diaspora. I wish to examine the markers at work here, both within and outside Ireland, as they stake a particular hierarchical claim for authenticity, and as that claim grows increasingly unclear.

Homi Bhabha, in *The Location of Culture* (1994), questions the very concept of authenticity, claiming the site of transculturation, where cultures rub together and influence each other, is where we find culture becoming "more transnational and translational" (Bhabha,1994: 5), and that concerns about authenticity are irrelevant in a global world. He would argue, then, that Irish pubs across the world are merely reflective of the cultures in which they find themselves, and have been "translated" in a sense. Agreeing with Benedict Anderson in the idea of an imagined community, one in which "the members ... will never know most of their fellow-members, meet them, or even hear of them, yet in the mind of each lives the image of their community" (Anderson, 1983: 5), Bhabha notes that culture must also be rooted in something, and that the "recognition that tradition bestows is a partial form of identification. In restaging the past it introduces other, incommensurable cultural temporalities into the invention of tradition" (Bhabha, 1994: 2). Believing we ought to celebrate the result of such hybridity as tradition is being invented, he argues, "The borderline work of culture demands an encounter with 'newness' that is not part of the continuum of past and present. It creates a sense of the new as an insurgent act of cultural translation" (Bhabha, 1994: 7).

While such a description helps us to understand Chinese restaurants in Dublin, it only goes so far, I would argue, to explain the particular nature of Irish pubs abroad. The pub, in its association with stereotypes of Irish identity, becomes the locus for the Bakhtinian carnivalesque, where riotous behaviour reigns for a time, but all is put right in the end (Bakhtin, 2009). The pub is a site where the stereotype of the Irish drunkard can be found, performed, interacted with, played upon, and then left behind. As Homi Bhabha notes in *The Location of Culture*:

> The stereotype is at once a substitute and a shadow. By acceding the wildest fantasies (in the popular sense) of the colonizer, the stereotyped Other reveals something of the 'fantasy' (as desire, defence) of that position of mastery. (Bhabha, 1994: 82)

The fantasy is to become Irish, to align oneself with a stereotype that, because of its spatial location in the pub, can be adopted temporarily.

To maintain the illusion, then, of authenticity, there appears to be considerable investment in perpetuating the traditional pub, and all that it means. Long a symbol of Irish hospitality, a pub requires a certain aesthetic, and comparisons of various houses are common. As an example of one especially provocative salvo in the exchange, architect Ben Davis, concerned with what he saw as the degradation of the true pub, wrote what he believes is the definitive text, *The Traditional Pub: A Way of Drinking* (1981), responding to an earlier architectural study of the Victorian pub by Mark Girouard (1978). His argument epitomizes the concerns with pub devotees. Despite the generally caustic and opinionated tone of the book, the instructions given therein to preserve the perfect pub are quite thorough. Davis, fearful about a movement in the 1970s to modernize older pubs, aware of what he considers to be the damage that such modernizations did in the 1930s and then in the 1950s, decided to publish some fundamental guidelines on what a pub ought to be. The level of his specificity is telling: he gives the necessary height for bar stools to attain maximum comfort (450 mm), the dimensions for the perfect footrail (50 mm), the material of which counter facings ought be made (wood is wasteful because in a good pub, the facing would be obscured by the crowd of people standing at the counter) (Davis, 1981: 24), the colour of the countertop (never green because of the "unfortunate" effect on the appearance of beer) (Davis, 1981: 30), the purpose of lighting, screens, alcoves, dadoes, anaglypta, and so on (Davis, 1981: 18-42). His opinions about the elements of a quality pub are very specific, including his blatantly stated prejudices against finding in pubs women (Davis, 1981: 98), children (Davis, 1981: 99), homosexuals (Davis, 1981: 100), televisions (Davis, 1981: 58) and Formica (Davis, 1981: 32).

Davis evaluates pubs first for their social impact and then for their architecture, although he assumes they are nearly inseparable, as the appropriate architecture should preserve the social experience. He insists that a man goes to a pub seeking a number of factors: He likes to feel welcome, as if he were at home. To that end, a pub should provide a sense of seclusion, of refuge from the world, with cozy alcoves and privacy; it should not have wide open unoccupied spaces, or large windows that would allow a customer's eyes to be drawn to the outside (Davis, 1981: 48). Ideally, the alcoves should be enclosed with screens of a sort, but those screens should never extend to the ceiling, as a customer does not want to feel he is in a cave; he wants to be secluded away; he wants to be a part of a whole, and likes to feel informal (Davis, 1981: 14). A pub with too much frippery will never succeed, as a man does not want an excess of curtains or carpets or flowers (Davis, 1981: 48). In fact, Davis points out that a move to feminize pubs would not be welcome by women any more than by men, since women like the masculinity of pubs. Indeed, according to Davis, the feminization of pubs would only draw homosexual males, and women would certainly not want that either (Davis, 1981: 100). (Women were only allowed in Irish pubs beginning in the 1960s, and even then, up until 2000, it was legal for a licensee to refuse to serve "on grounds of gender, marital status, family status, sexual orientation, religious belief, age, disability, race or membership of the Traveller community" (Molloy, 2002: 90).) In fact, argues Davis, the general pub-goer would not be comfortable around evidence of riches, and so the simpler the pub, the happier the customer. The simple decor will, in turn, foster friendliness and ease amongst the customers, and the more the customer feels at home, the longer he will stay (Davis, 1981: 8).

The pub-goer likes to feel a sense of goodheartedness in his watering-hole, and Davis defines this as the difference between gossip and spite (Davis, 1981: 24). He wants to be able to discuss with his friends all the news of the area, but to do so in a way that conveys news rather than nastiness. Consequently, the only appropriate seating in a pub is a backless stool, in order to encourage drinkers to sit forward and engage in conversation rather than lean back and distance themselves from their friends. Davis even argues that the only appropriate position for sitting in a pub with friends is to have one hand around a drink (preferably a pint, but a whiskey is acceptable), and the other elbow on the table to facilitate leaning in eagerly (Davis, 1981: 50).

Pervading all of Davis's recommendations is the suggestion that the pub-goer likes to feel a sense of tradition and continuity. He insists licensees and owners avoid following the fads of younger people, claiming the younger people will ultimately appreciate their time in pubs more if they are made to feel part of an on-going tradition, part of the continuity pubs represent. Davis acknowledges the benefits of occasional change, but urges pub owners to attempt such change in the Lounge section of the pub, where the clientele would be more amenable to updates (Davis, 1981: 79).

Although Davis fails to distinguish between English and Irish pubs, he does comment that the Irish are the only ones smart enough to leave intact the glorious pubs given them by the English, revealing a bias which points to the colonial history of the Irish pub, but which also suggests that the history of the pub reflects the same radical changes that other cultural artefacts experience as the political, social, and economical environment shifts. Writing in 1981, he addresses a pre-Celtic Tiger economy, one still tied to a nationalist rather than a global discourse. He would have been unable to imagine the effects of a booming high-tech industry or of an influx of immigrants as well as a return of many emigrants; he would have been still more startled by how abruptly that boom could turn around again. His unifying concern is in sustaining tradition and authenticity, but it is a battle that cannot be sustained.

Davis is of course also attempting to set the standard for the exportation of pubs around the world, an exportation which bewilders considerations of the authentic. The transported pub, while being a recreation of the original, must also define itself in terms of its environment; in doing so, it becomes something else, something that rings both true and false in comparison to pubs in Ireland, a hybrid in the sense that it is neither one thing nor the other. The specific markers of these pubs present a kind of nationalist narrative, identifying whether a pub is marketed for those with a rather indistinct attraction to Ireland, or for those native to Ireland who are either exilic or vacationing. Literary symbols, such as photographs of renowned authors like James Joyce, William Butler Yeats, Samuel Beckett, and sometimes even Lady Gregory, are common to both kinds of pub. The ubiquitous Guinness signs, both old and new, seem almost a requisite. A map, someone's coat of arms, street or county signs from Ireland, menus in Celtic script, old jugs or bicycles, battered furniture, and other such items suggest the country cottage feel, clearly attempting an association with the "auld sod." Gaelic Athletic Association (GAA) memorabilia strikes a different chord, often occurring in sports pubs, and the performance of "traditional" music is yet again different. A flag of Ireland, photos of the Easter Rising, Bloody Sunday, the Belfast murals, and other key icons announce political affiliation designed to strike a particular affinity in a particular customer, appealing to those more comfortable with Irish history than with Irish kitsch. Shamrocks and leprechauns attract those nebulously Irish members of the diaspora, those who have a loose affiliation, or those who simply like the idea of an Irish pub. As Kymberly Porter (2002) also notes, customers are rarely attracted to both the kitschy and the political or country kinds of Irish pub, each group harbouring completely different sets of expectations. Regardless of the nuances, the pub must proclaim itself as definitively Irish, unique in its foreign surroundings.

The reproduction of the pub as a site of identity construction, however, is fraught with difficulty. Walter Benjamin notes:

> The authenticity of a thing is the essence of all that is transmissible from its beginning, ranging from its substantive duration to its testimony to the history which it has experienced. Since the historical testimony rests on the authenticity, the former, too, is jeopardized by reproduction when substantive duration ceases to matter. And what is really jeopardized when the historical testimony is affected is the authority of the object. (Benjamin, 1968: 221)

Consequently, Irish pubs abound in places like Rome, Corfu, Paris, Taormina, Dubrovnik, Tahiti, Haifa, and Malta. The easiest way to find them is to look for the Guinness sign protruding from the building; the marker is so reliable that in Rome, the Guinness sign alone is posted on several major streets, with smaller signs indicating that the Trinity College pub is a mere three blocks away. The owner (as of 2004), a young man who also owns another Irish pub in Rome, is not of Irish descent and expressed some puzzlement over the pubs' popularity. He had bought the pub from someone else who sold despite its commercial success, and said the hardest part of running the pub, for him, was that he had to perfect his English since so many of his customers are English-speaking. The vast majority of English-speaking customers buy Guinness, as it is part of the continuity of experience for which they come; the few locals who frequent his pub only occasionally buy Guinness, but do buy other European beers and cocktails. The pub has a distinctly cosmopolitan feel, perhaps because the majority of people present on the off-season night I was there were not English-speaking, but there are, upstairs, the stock pictures of Yeats, Joyce and Padraic Pearse, as well as the requisite Irish tomes.

A number of Irish pubs in Paris, especially along the Rue St. Denis, offer something for both the kitschy pub-seekers and those seeking a more "traditional" experience: some are quite ostentatious in their symbolism, and some are less so. In every pub we explored, the clientele was definitely English speaking, and nearly everyone was drinking beer, most often stout. The James Joyce Pub, near the Arc de Triomphe, is owned by the man who began the chain of Kitty O'Shea pubs that are now found throughout the world, from Boston to Brussels. These pubs tend to define the type that attracts the diaspora, filled with symbols of Irishness: in the Paris pub, the owner's own Gaelic Athletic Association championship awards (from the late 1940s) are on display, as well as a remarkable collection of James Joyce editions. All of the furniture is built of wood, according to the style Davis extols, and the multiple levels help make the pub seem small, with discrete areas to either socialize or segregate in. Along with many of the other Irish pubs in the area, such as McBride's, this pub provides the illusion of home for those away from Ireland. But even so, these pubs have to identify themselves with outward, very distinct signs that mark them as Irish, very unlike pubs in Ireland which don't need such signs. Those familiar with the genre throughout the world outside of Ireland find themselves quite at ease in these pubs, despite the disparity between an "authentic" Irish pub in Ireland and those found in the rest of the world. There will be no chrome, no high beamed ceilings, no marble or granite or anything that appears modern.

The point here is that the "authentic" Irish pub is coming to be redefined because of the very mechanics of reproduction about which Benjamin speaks: when the historicity and context of the original are severed from the reproduction, the authority is affected. Bhabha notes:

> It is only when we understand that all cultural statements and systems are constructed in this contradictory and ambivalent space of enunciation that we begin to understand why hierarchical claims to the inherent originality or 'purity' of cultures are untenable. (Bhabha, 1994: 37)

The significance of this impulse to be "authentic" lies in its complications. Speaking with a number of Irish pub owners, I find that many Irish-Americans, for example, have learned what to expect from an Irish pub based on the models they have most often seen in the rest of the world, and they find themselves disappointed to find "real" Irish pubs are nothing like that. The pub owners, eager to provide the *failte* (welcome) sought by the diaspora and other tourists, are torn between the market forces and the commodification of Irishness, turning finally, in a strange twist, to produce pubs that look more like those in the United States, as can be seen in several pubs in Dublin's Temple Bar, or in cities such as Killarney. What, then, becomes of "authenticity"?

A prime example of this complication is the Irish Pub Company (funded by Guinness), who manufactures and markets Irish pubs, pre-built and decorated, and sells them all over the world (see Grantham 2009 as well as the Irish Pub Company website (www.irishpubcompany.com)). In order to maintain the "continuity" of tradition, to mimic the appearance of cozy and intimate pubs, heavy wooden furniture is built and then purposely distressed with chains and hammers so the furniture appears to be old and used. According to The Irish Pub Company brochures, you might choose between "Victorian Dublin Style" (in the style of the more lavish Dublin pubs with polished hardwood and etched glass), "Gaelic Style" (designed to demonstrate the "merry-making, music and craftsmanship" of the Gaelic people), "Traditional Style" (as in the old "corner of the grocery store" pub), "Country Cottage Style" (to reflect the days when a pub was simply someone's house which was open to the "public" for hospitality), or the "Brewery Pub" (designed with memorabilia from the brewing process, including wooden casks and drays). Other companies compete, such as The Celtic Dragon Pub Company, which can build a replica of an Irish pub in your own home, and which sells "pub mirrors, sepias, Guinness signs, historical posters, Guinness posters, Irish art work, bodhrans, Celtic prints, pub tabletops, flags and prints, personalized license plates," etc. Subscriptions to computerized "traditional" music are promoted as well, programmes devised to manipulate customers to desired behaviour; U2 plays during the bustling lunch crowd, and Enya plays during the mid-afternoon lingering crowd (Grantham, 1009: 259). Guinness also intermittently runs contests, primarily marketed in the U.S., in which the prize is a pub in Ireland, although the benefits of this are unclear, since the contest rules specify that there is no need for someone to actually live in Ireland to "run" the pub. Clearly Guinness itself is aware of the impulse within the diaspora to maintain this continuity of tradition. One of the questions, therefore, is how much the Irish pub represents a diasporic association with tradition and how much is Guinness's attempt to expand its own empire throughout the world by first ensuring the need for the world to drink its beer.

The influence of the tourist industry, guided by the push for the "authentic" experience, is changing the very face of pub culture in Ireland. These strange trends illustrate what Françoise Lionnet calls "transculturation," two cultures which rub off on each other, each wielding so much influence that it is impossible to separate the two into their origins. The concept is useful, she notes, because

> the prefix 'trans-' suggests the act of traversing, of going through existing cultural territories. . . [and] corresponds more accurately to the notion of 'appropriation,' a concept more promising than those of acculturation and assimilation, and one that implies active intervention rather than passive victimization. (Lionnet, 1996: 326)

Thus, the American version of the Irish pub cannot help but have an effect on the Irish version. With all their modernity, today's pubs can be said to subvert tradition in Ireland, not reinstate it. From decor to beverage choice, all is not as it once was, as pubs cater to an expanding demographic. People, concerned about their health, drink less; in 2004, nationwide smoking bans took effect; the laws against drinking and driving have become much stricter; people have less ready money. Many pubs have large televisions, often loudly airing sporting events, changing the very nature of the pub as social network. Brass and glass are as commonly seen as wood, and wide open spaces are replacing the snug. In city pubs, and in some country pubs, cocktails and wine may be found, choices virtually unheard of as little as ten years ago. Even in the country pubs, well-populated by the rural population, the drink of preference is more often Budweiser than it is Guinness, particularly among the younger generations. The change has been gradual: when I first visited my cousin's rural midlands pub in 1982, the men drank Guinness almost exclusively, and the women were expected to drink a glass of shandy, half lager and half lemon-lime soda. By 2000, Budweiser was the drink of choice for many because, according to a number of my own informal surveys of both pub owners and drinkers in Ireland, it was more expensive, and therefore more exotic. Budweiser, I was told, is American, and is therefore obviously a better beer, which of course is the reverse of what one finds in American bars, where any imported beer is more expensive and is thought to be, thus, better. (These conversations took place, for the most part, before the 2009 economic troubles began; the willingness to pay extra to appear more exotic may very well be different now.) The majority of U.S.

Americans and other foreigners, however, largely preferred Guinness or Harp. They didn't, as they explained, travel all this way to drink the very same thing they could get at home.

While these changing predilections may look like the simple attraction to all things foreign, they are related to the push of globalization and, for better or worse, the desire of the Irish to align themselves with the United States (and vice versa) as the two cultures continue to influence each other. The tradition of the Irish pub in Ireland continues, but it changes to accommodate the new influences of a globally aware clientele. As Bill Barich notes in his book, *A Pint of Plain* (2009), it becomes harder and harder to find the quaint pub portrayed in *The Quiet Man* (1952). Instead, cropping up in the cities are larger and brighter bars, such as those found in Rathfarnham or Dun Laoghaire, Galway and Cork. They have more floor space than those in a more distinctively tourist area such as Dublin's Temple Bar, and they have a more industrial look. Largely populated by a younger crowd, these pubs are indistinguishable as specifically Irish pubs, and look more like up-scale bars. The same crowd that goes to these, however, often finds itself, later in the night, in a more traditional pub, perhaps seeking the very things that Davis enumerated, despite the continued consumption of Budweiser.

There are other signs that Ireland's pub scene is migrating towards a more globalized version of bars. Anecdotally, in my cousin's small town in County Westmeath, "everyone" has always known that Mike pours a better pint than Murphy (I have changed the names), but that Murphy's is a tonier establishment (Murphy's regulars, of course, disagree.). For special occasions, people go to Murphy's for a pint (and always on Sunday after church), but for a more casual time, to bet on the horses or to watch the match, most people go to Mike's. Around 2000, Guinness decried this disparity in "pints", insisting a Guinness ought to be a Guinness no matter where it is ordered. The debates about who pours a better pint, what the temperature ought to be, how thick the head should be, have formulated part of pub ruminations for generations, and are inseparable from the debates about aesthetics. The true connoisseur could tell the difference between a fresh tank and an older one, or the benefit/tragedy of cleaning out the pipes often. Guinness embarked on a mission to regulate every pint of Guinness that was poured, not just in Ireland but in the world. Gone, they opined, would be the detectable differences between Mike's pint and Murphy's pint. A person could actually feel secure in getting that pint in any pub around the world that displays the Guinness sign.

According to many of the people to whom I spoke in Ireland, this uniformity of pints contributed greatly to their switch to Budweiser. After they cleaned the pipes, Mike's pints tasted different, and no one liked the new temperature at Murphy's, even on a Sunday morning. Apparently Budweiser (especially in a long-necked bottle) isn't so fickle a character as Guinness, and the younger drinkers especially are more concerned with getting a decent pint of anything than with continuity of tradition. Rumour has it, now, that Guinness isn't sending out quite so many representatives, having "successfully trained" everyone in the country, at least, as to how Guinness ought to be poured, and so many establishments have returned to the way they formerly poured it. Guinness, in fact, appears to be conflicted about its message. On the one hand, the desire to regulate a pint suggests a desire for a consistent and authentic Irish experience anywhere in the world where Guinness is poured. It is a product on which one can rely. On the other hand, the construction of a new and impressive tourist centre, the opening of a relatively new Guinness store (not to buy Guinness but to buy Guinness-related souvenirs, the "true" symbol of Ireland), encourages tourism to Ireland in order to experience the real culture. This other strategy is in keeping with the tradition of GIGFY ("Guinness Is Good For You"), insisting that its stout will keep one healthy, as well as with the claims that the stout is superior in Ireland because of the water (a story perpetuated at the Guinness brewery itself for many years). Visiting Ireland will always be more desirable as it allows one to taste the difference between stout brewed in Ireland and that brewed elsewhere and bottled under the Guinness name. Guinness's marketing seems to straddle the competing interests of ethnic identity and globalization.

The competing interests are, of course, the urge for people to identify with the continuity of tradition that legend tells us is Ireland, versus the hybridity and transculturation that must necessarily occur if such identification is acted out the world over; the desire to have an experience that has been anticipated through cultural representations such as film and literature, versus the desire to have an experience with which we are already familiar through example; the proliferation of the pub ambience and experience, accessible anywhere and anytime because of such dynamic expansion, versus the hope for that unique and intimate experience that a pub seems to proffer. If, as Bhabha notes, "in order to be effective, mimicry must continually produce its slippage, its excess, its difference" (Bhabha, 1994: 86), the Irish pub in the world is effective. The slippage lies in the notion of an originary authentic community of pub goers, reproduced at the very moment that it loses its authority in Ireland. But if Irish pub clientele, whether in Ireland or not, whether of Irish descent or not, whether savvy about issues of authenticity or not, is so conflicted about the desired product/experience, perhaps Guinness is less muddled than it appears in its marketing approach, as it targets everyone, transcending all the competing interests. As the ultimate marker for an Irish pub, the Guinness sign extols: Guinness Is Good For You.

Bibliography

Anderson, Benedict. *Imagined Communities: Reflections on the Origin and Spread of Nationalism*. London and New York: Verso, 1983.

Bakhtin, Mikhail. *Rabelais and His World.* Indiana: Indiana University Press, 2009.

Barich, Bill. *A Pint of Plain: Tradition, Change, and the Fate of the Irish Pub*. New York: Walker and Company, 2009.

Benjamin, Walter. *Illuminations.* New York: Harcourt Brace Jovanovich, 1968.

Bhabha, Homi. *The Location of Culture.* London and New York: Routledge, 1994.

Davis, Ben. *The Traditional English Pub: A Way of Drinking*. London: The Architectural Press, 1981.

Grantham, Bill. "Craic in a Box: Commodifying and Exporting the Irish Pub." *Continuum: Journal of Media and Cultural Studies* (23, no. 2). 2009: 257-267.

Kelley, Austin. "Ireland's 'Crack' Habit: Explaining the Faux Irish Pub Revolution." *Slate*. slate.com 1/3/2007.

Lionnet, Françoise. "'Logiques métisses': Cultural Appropriation and Postcolonial Representations." *Postcolonial Subjects: Francophone Women Writers* edited by Mary Jean Agreen, et.al. University of Minnesota Press, 1996: 321-343.

Mays, Michael. "Irish Identity in an Age of Globalisation." *Irish Studies Review* (13.1). 2005: 3-12.

Molloy, Cian. *The Story of the Irish Pub*. Dublin: The Liffey Press, 2002.

Porter, Kymberly Helbig. "Being 'Irish': The Market, Transnationalism and the Experience of Ethnicity". *Dissertation Abstracts International, Section A: The Humanities and Social Sciences*, (63.5) 2002.

http:www.irishpubcompany.com 1/3/2007

http:www.celticdragonpubcompany.com 1/3/2007

CHAPTER FIVE

SPORT, CULTURE AND IDENTITY

DAVID STOREY

Michelle Smyth's three swimming gold medals and one bronze at the 1996 Atlanta Olympics make her Ireland's most successful ever Olympian. However, allegations relating to the possible use of performance enhancing substances served to somewhat tarnish her achievement and image, and this Irish national sporting success became woven into a broader international narrative of "doping" in sport. At the 2002 football World Cup finals Republic of Ireland captain Roy Keane raged over what he saw as the unprofessional set-up and inadequate logistical arrangements for the Ireland team at the tournament in South Korea and Japan. His stance and subsequent withdrawal from the team provoked considerable debate and controversy in the country and could be interpreted as symbolic of a refusal to buy into an older Irish sporting and cultural narrative of happily tolerating a peripheral place in the world order. Keane's outburst appeared to project a new assertiveness centred on ambition and success rather than mere participation and noble failure. In 2006 an Irish business consortium led by former Republic of Ireland player Niall Quinn acquired a majority stake in the ownership of English football club Sunderland. Quinn and his associates' acquisition of the club reflected the broader phenomenon of significant overseas investment in property and other assets by Irish business people. These events occurred during a period of unparalleled economic growth in Ireland, and broader social, cultural and political change, and it might be argued that these sporting phenomena reflect some of those wider trends. Just as the Irish economy entered into an increasingly globalised era, it might also be argued that a more outward-looking dimension emerged in which Irish sport has been projected onto a more global stage, one on which sporting success was taken more seriously and in which commercial considerations became ever more central. This evolution, with all the positive and negative implications which surround it, raises many interesting issues about sporting traditions, social change and territorial identities in Ireland.

Despite what some appear to think and what others might wish, sport is not an autonomous arena and the varied intersections between sport, politics and society have been extensively examined in academic literature with the connections between sport and national identity a particular focus (Duke and Crolley, 1996; Giulanotti, 2000; Bairner, 2001; Jarvie, 2003; Smith and Porter, 2004). The nature of Irish history and the continuing issue of partition render it no real surprise that the island displays "a sporting culture … closely bound up with such potentially potent themes as the meaning of being Irish and the relationship of Irish people with each other and with the world beyond" (Bairner, 2005: 1). This chapter explores selected aspects of Irish sport and their intersections with wider dimensions of Irish society and identity in the 1990s and early 2000s. It is not the intention here to offer a comprehensive analysis of sport in Ireland during this period; instead the chapter offers some tentative insights that demonstrate the inter-connections between sport and wider developments in Ireland and beyond. The chapter is organised in three sections. The first of these focuses on examples of the modernising of traditional dimensions of sport in Ireland; the second focuses on the impact of shifting patterns of migration, while the third deals with sporting issues linked to the political conflict in the north of Ireland. Themes of place, culture and identity, set against the backdrop of an economy moving from bust to boom and back again, run through the various examples used.

Tradition and Modernity

Perhaps one of the most obvious (and least surprising) developments in sport in Ireland in the past two decades has been an increasing commercialisation. This has been very evident even within what might be regarded as the most traditional of Irish sporting arenas–Gaelic games. The Gaelic Athletic Association (GAA) is a sporting and cultural organisation whose activities permeate many aspects of Irish life both at home and amongst Irish emigrant communities abroad. The association's organisational structure has a strong geographical base using Ireland's provinces, counties and parishes as its key units. GAA matches and associated activities are major social events at the parish level and this has served to inculcate or reinforce a strong sense of place and an attachment to locality amongst its members where inter-parochial and inter-county rivalries are an important backdrop to fixtures (Cronin *et al*, 2009). While the playing of Gaelic games is largely confined to the island of Ireland and to Irish communities abroad, through various forms of sponsorship (and other processes) the GAA has formed an array of relationships with various multi-national companies and has engaged in broader processes of branding and image creation. Although Gaelic games remain primarily amateur sports, the rise of commercial sponsorship nationally and locally was a marked feature of the 1990s onwards as both club and county teams endeavoured to raise money to improve training and playing facilities. The branding of Gaelic sport was exemplified in a deal in 1995 when Guinness became official sponsors of the All-Ireland Hurling Championship, a deal portrayed as a coming together of two uniquely Irish brands. In recent years the GAA has actively engaged with marketing agencies in a conscious attempt at brand promotion mainly associated with the commercial sponsorship of selected events. The major insurance company Allianz (with its headquarters in Germany) is the current sponsor of the GAA's National Hurling and Football Leagues while Etihad Airlines are amongst the sponsors of the All-Ireland Hurling Championship. Alongside these sponsorship arrangements, merchandising has become a very obvious feature with sales of replica club and county shirts, together with flags, banners, hats and rosettes, a trend that mirrors developments in many other sports. One notable feature of the commercial sponsorship of sport was the involvement of the banking sector. Ulster Bank are sponsors of the GAA Senior Football Championship, while AIB, a central player in the financial collapse, are a sponsor of the GAA hurling and football club championships utilising advertisements making much of their "community" involvement.

In some ways this commercialising trend might appear paradoxical for an organisation often portrayed as holding onto what are seen by some as overly narrow perspectives on the nature of Irishness (Arrowsmith, 2004). However, for all that the GAA is seen as the custodian of traditional amateur games, it is worth remembering that its very origins and founding vision reflect an engagement in a process of modernisation through the codification and regulation of sport within Ireland, and the creation of administrative structures, phenomena paralleling sporting developments elsewhere in the late 19th century (Holt, 2009). Moreover, while the GAA has been cast in some circles as a conservative and backward-looking organisation, it has always shown itself very adept at accommodating changes for a variety of reasons. In recent decades a series of modifications and adaptations to playing regulations reflect a strongly pragmatic stance. Such things as the introduction of safety helmets in hurling and yellow and red cards for player misdemeanours reflect a willingness to adapt and to borrow from other "non-Irish" sporting codes

(Storey, 2012). The major refurbishment of the GAA's "home" at Croke Park might be seen as symbolising the association's marriage of tradition with modernity. The reconstruction, completed in 2005, has resulted in the creation of one of the largest sporting venues in Europe (though not one instantly recognised outside the country). Not surprisingly, such an investment reflected more than merely sporting interests and the stadium boasts a conference centre and hospitality suites while also housing the GAA museum opened in 1998 and revamped in 2010.

Despite the increasingly commercial (and more global) framework within which it now operates, the association has endeavoured to maintain a national orientation and to preserve and strengthen its local and community base. It continues to promote a policy of buying Irish products wherever possible and official footballs and sports clothing are produced by the Irish company O'Neills with whom the GAA have a long-standing business relationship. Many individual county teams endeavour to maintain local links through sponsorship. However, these place associations may be slightly less local that they first appear. While Leitrim's shirts bear the name of a local hotel, the Kerry Group (sponsors of the Kerry team) and Avonmore (whose logo adorns Kilkenny shirts) are companies that have long since outgrown their local and community origins. The GAA's "local" associations can also prove problematic. Until recently, businessman Seán Quinn headed a group of companies with interests in construction, packaging, insurance and a range of other sectors and with an extensive overseas property portfolio. Bankruptcy means the Quinn family no longer control the group and their financial difficulties are closely bound up with the property and banking collapse. The family have very close associations with the GAA and the Quinn Group were sponsors of a range of local GAA activities in the Fermanagh and Cavan region where Quinn lives and where many of the enterprises are based. Notwithstanding the problems which may arise linked to commercial sponsorship, it might be argued that the GAA and its affiliated clubs and county associations have endeavoured to steer a course that attempts to ally the pragmatic need to earn revenue with its traditional role as keepers of the island's sporting heritage, while remaining firmly embedded in local communities.

While Gaelic games remain primarily an amateur set of sports, rugby has in recent decades shifted at senior level to a more professional footing in which a strongly commercial and international orientation has been clearly discernible. While success for the all-Ireland national team has been sporadic, the four Irish provincial teams have been placed on a professional footing and compete in European competitions providing an international dimension for what are now effectively club teams rather more than provincial representative ones. This has had a number of outcomes. Firstly, Irish players who might otherwise have plied their trade with professional outfits in Britain or France are more likely to remain within Ireland. Secondly, the provincial teams have also attracted some overseas talent so that players from New Zealand, South Africa, Argentina and elsewhere can now be found wearing the colours of the Irish provinces. An integral element in this professionalisation of the sport has been sponsorship and enhanced television coverage. Many matches involving the provincial teams are shown live by the UK-based satellite broadcaster Sky Sports and this has served to widen the potential audience. Although long seen as a middle class sport, recent years have witnessed a broadening out from its original core. The professionalisation of the teams and the parallel growth of a provincial identification (set within a broader national frame) as Irish teams regularly play against others from England, Wales, Scotland, France, Italy and elsewhere in league and cup competitions links the game more consistently into a wider European context. These have also afforded a measure of success, particularly for Leinster and Munster. This internationalising of the sport, combined with the importation of overseas players, has simultaneously enhanced the quality of the game while actually serving to promote (to some extent at least) a heightened sense of territorial identity, though we need to be mindful that such identities, and the ways in which sport and place are linked, are of course constructed and subject to contestation (O'Callaghan 2011). The sale of replica shirts, scarves and related merchandising, as well as commercial sponsorship of both teams and competitions, has been another integral feature of the transformation. Ulster Bank (as part of the RBS group) is sponsor of the rugby Six Nations tournament and makes much of its community-focused initiatives, styling itself as the "16th man" (http://gaa.ulsterbank.com/force). These changes in Irish rugby, as in the case of the GAA and other sporting contexts, reflect a broader professionalisation and commercialisation of sport while simultaneously serving to (re)produce territorial identities. However, while the national team selects players from the provincial sides and they feed off each other in terms of player profile and recognition, it might also be argued that the strengthening of the provincial teams has somewhat overshadowed more local club teams.

Although the 1990s and early 2000s might be seen as bringing economic benefits to Gaelic games and rugby the same is not true of all sports. The experience of domestic soccer on the island has been less successful, despite the sport's obvious popularity. Clubs within the League of Ireland in the Republic moved towards employing players on a full-time professional basis in recent years but this has been accompanied by financial difficulties for many with a number of clubs going into liquidation. Clubs in Ireland have traditionally suffered from living in the shadow of the game in England with many supporters choosing to travel there to attend matches, while the traditional "brawn drain" of young playing talent heading to Britain remains a persistent phenomenon (McGovern, 2000). While there has been increased television coverage of domestic club games, this remains somewhat peripheral to media coverage of the game in England. The game in the north of Ireland has suffered similarly and a re-organisation of structures there has not had any huge transformative effect. Clubs from both sides of the border have enjoyed very limited success in European club competition. The emergence of the Irish satellite broadcaster Setanta in the early 1990s could be seen as mirroring the rapid rise and subsequent demise of the Celtic Tiger. Initially created to broadcast Irish sports to emigrant audiences in the UK and elsewhere it grew rapidly to televise live English and Scottish soccer matches in an attempt to rival Sky. However, it ran into financial difficulties and its British operations collapsed in 2009.

In considering the economic and political significance of sport in Ireland, it is worth briefly alluding to horse racing. This is a sport with a long history in Ireland and is one arena in which the country has long excelled. The breeding and sale of horses as well as the revenue generated from race meetings and through betting have made it a significant part of Ireland's sporting economy. It is also one deeply bound up with wider dimensions of Irish politics. The Tiger years witnessed an increase in the numbers of race meetings and an expansion of the stud farm industry. However, favourable tax conditions on the equine sector have proved controversial and raise broader questions about the incentives offered to sports and the economic benefits which might accrue from them (*The Economist* 2004, Ó Ríordáin, 2012). The annual Galway race festival is a centrepiece of the Irish horse racing calendar and has long been a place in which political and business figures are wont to be seen but the demise of the tiger has been reflected in the diminishing numbers of business people attending the Galway festival and a decline in what might be regarded as more ostentatious displays of wealth (Hayes, 2010). In turn, this appears symptomatic of a broader decline in the number of entries at race meetings and attendance figures at equine events.

Migrant Players and Plastic Paddies

The Celtic tiger years witnessed a novel demographic phenomenon as Ireland became a magnet for immigrants rather than an exporter of people and this reversal had very clear impacts on sport. In the past, substantial emigration left some GAA clubs in rural areas finding it difficult to field teams due to the loss of young talent, a phenomenon that now appears to be re-emerging following the economic collapse. Conversely, persistent out-migration had resulted in the formation of GAA clubs in places such as London, New York, San Francisco and other cities with sizeable Irish emigrant communities (Brady, 2005; Darby, 2010). In recent years many Irish emigrants departed for what might be seen as non-traditional destinations and this led to the establishment of GAA clubs in various parts of Europe and further afield. An Asian County Board was established in 2006 with auspices over clubs such as the Arabian Celts, Dalian Wolfhounds and Singapore Gaelic Lions. Consequently, an organisation that, superficially, may appear insular and nationally defined and concerned with the preservation of a distinctive sporting and cultural heritage, seems to have benefited enormously from Ireland's global interconnections and shifting demographic trends.

Immigration into Ireland from the mid-1990s through to about 2008, a reversal of previous established trends, resulted in immigrants and the children of immigrants becoming involved in Gaelic games. Where Irish emigrants have found a sense of "home" through GAA clubs in London, New York and elsewhere, the children of immigrants to Ireland are becoming involved in the association and its sporting activities. This has resulted in a broadening of the cultural milieu in which Gaelic games operates. While this may have contributed to a more multi-cultural ethos, problems have emerged with issues of racist abuse becoming a cause for concern (see, for example, O'Connor, 2012). In response, the GAA now has guidelines prohibiting discrimination and has enshrined anti-racism principles within its regulations. In a further example of progressive social change the broadly supportive response to a leading GAA player publicly declaring himself gay would seem to reflect wider shifts in social attitudes in Ireland (Horan, 2012).

As suggested earlier, the economic changes of the Celtic tiger years did little to improve the quality of domestic soccer within Ireland (either north or south of the border). Nevertheless, the League of Ireland in the Republic has not been immune from the global phenomenon of migrating sports people (and the more specific phenomenon of in-migration to Ireland) and it now has a sprinkling of foreign-born players from places such as Cameroon, Benin, Sweden, Germany and Italy. It has already been noted that Irish provincial rugby teams now include players from places such as New Zealand, South Africa, Argentina and elsewhere. However, Ireland's long-standing out-migration came to play a perhaps unanticipated role in Irish soccer, particularly in the Republic. Two notable features of the game since the late 1980s have been the relative success of the Republic of Ireland national team and the fact that this enhanced profile was achieved through a heavy reliance on non-Irish born players of Irish descent. A deliberate policy of selecting players of Irish ethnic origin was pursued following the appointment of Englishman Jack Charlton as national team manager in 1986. In a context of sustained and endemic out-migration this reclaiming of the Irish diaspora, while pursued for pragmatic purposes of widening the player pool, had a certain symbolism. It also dovetailed with President Mary Robinson's emphasis on the importance of Ireland's emigrant communities upon taking office in 1990. The team reached its first ever major tournament finals with the European Championships in 1988 followed by the World Cups of 1990 and 1994. Subsequently the team appeared at the World Cup finals of 2002 and European Championships of 2012. This relative success has been portrayed in many ways as a reflection of these broader shifts in Irish economy, society and culture (Holmes, 1994; Free, 2005). Throughout this period of moderate success the selection of non-Irish born players has remained an enduring phenomenon. The policy has provoked some negative reactions over what some see as the diluted sense of Irishness contained within the team and lingering suspicions that for some players a careerist rather than cultural motivation is at work. Conversely, for many others the phenomenon has been seen as a justifiable reclaiming of the diaspora, reflecting a more global sense of Irishness and a recognition of the multi-layered nature of national identity (Holmes and Storey, 2011). The fact that the Irish soccer team continues to be composed of players drawn from both within and outside the country and with differing levels of connection to it allows a much more multifaceted image of the "embodied nation" to emerge. Dermot Bolger's 1990 play about Irish soccer supporters, *In High Germany*, highlighted how the composition of the team allowed Ireland's diaspora communities to engage with an Irish identity in a way they knew and understood, reflected in second-generation support for the team from people born in Britain, sometimes disparagingly referred to as "Plastic Paddies" (Free, 1998; Arrowsmith, 2004). The Bolger play captures the way in which the team, with its amalgam of Irish and non-Irish accents were seen to be "playing for all those generations written out of history" (Bolger, 2002: 97).

As already noted, the Celtic tiger era witnessed large-scale migration into Ireland leading to heightened debate over immigration, citizenship and belonging (Fanning and Munck, 2011). Within a sporting context, this has opened up some interesting possibilities. As one Irish sports columnist has pointed out (with regard to soccer), "we are coming fast towards a time when there will be kids born and raised in Marino [a suburb of Dublin] who will be declaring to play soccer for Latvia or Lithuania or Nigeria. Good luck to them" (Humphreys, 2005). While this has yet to occur it co-exists as a possibility alongside the prospect of O'Briens, Murphys and Kellys opting to represent Poland, Lithuania or Nigeria (Holmes and Storey, 2011). Although this may not yet have happened in soccer, the Irish cricket team's modest successes in recent years have, in part, been due to the selection of non-Irish-born players from countries such as South Africa and Australia who have become resident in Ireland. Conversely, however, two of Ireland's best home grown cricketers, Ed Joyce and Eoin Morgan, have both been included in England cricket teams. Their selection is a consequence of their residency within the UK and of their own desire to play international cricket at the most senior level. As with soccer, Irish-born cricketers are more likely to enhance their careers through playing in England while international representation at the highest level is not possible with the Irish national team who have not been accorded "Test" status.

North and South

At the 1992 Olympic Games in Barcelona boxers Michael Carruth and Wayne McCullough won gold and silver medals respectively for Ireland. McCullough's achievement had a broader significance in that he was a northern Protestant and hailed from the staunchly loyalist Shankill Road area in Belfast. Not surprisingly, his decision to represent Ireland was not universally popular in unionist circles in the north. In July 2012 the two boxers were present at the border between the north and the Republic as the Olympic torch was passed onwards on its journey to Dublin. The presence of the torch on the soil of a non-hosting country was presented as a symbolic acknowledgement of peace, and the torch was subsequently paraded at Croke Park. These events, which bookend the period under consideration in this chapter, serve as useful reminders that the northern conflict has impacted on sport in many ways.

It is hardly surprising that the GAA has found itself at the heart of many dimensions of the conflict (Sugden and Bairner, 1993; Cronin, 2001; Bairner, 2003; Hassan, 2005). For many northern nationalists involvement with the GAA has provided an obvious platform for assertions of an Irish identity within British-controlled territory. At the same time, the association's promotion of Irish sports and its championing of the Irish language and other aspects of Irish culture has led many unionists to view it as a hostile organisation with loyalist paramilitaries characterising it as part of the broader Irish republican threat. A long-standing rule prohibiting members of British security forces and police in the north from membership was a major bone of contention. While many people within the organisation (and outside it) felt the rule was anachronistic, it was largely supported by those in northern counties who tended to view themselves as living in an occupied territory. The shifting context emerging out of the peace process in the late 1990s ultimately led to the rule being abolished in 2001 despite intense opposition from many GAA members in the north. As well as the abolition of that rule, the association's long-standing ban on Gaelic sports grounds being used for "foreign" games was temporarily suspended in 2007 to allow rugby and soccer to be played at Croke Park during the refurbishment of their regular venue at Lansdowne Road. Although this sparked some debate both within and outside the organisation, opposition appears to have been limited and relatively muted. The opening of the revamped stadium at Lansdowne Road (now known as the Aviva Stadium) as home to rugby and soccer means the ban has once again been implemented and the rule continues to be a source of controversy. In 2010 the Cork GAA club Nemo Rangers were censured for allowing the Irish rugby team to briefly use their training facilities (Keys, 2010). However, signs of the shifting political context in the north were amply demonstrated in January 2012 when Northern Ireland First Minster Peter Robinson (leader of the Democratic Unionist Party) attended an inter-county GAA match in January 2012, a move indicative of a more accommodating attitude towards the association in unionist circles.

Soccer within Northern Ireland has experienced a number of difficulties related to the political situation. One of the more notable was the demise of the Derry City club, based in the nationalist Brandywell area of the city and their controversial exit from the north's Irish League in the 1970s. The club re-emerged in the 1980s but as members of the Republic's League of Ireland. Alongside episodes of sectarian chanting and occasional violence at certain games soccer has been far from immune from the wider political issues of the contested territory. In a wider sense, the contested nature of the territory has made it difficult for many nationalists to identify with sports teams representing Northern Ireland while even liberal unionists have experienced a degree of ambiguity in their sporting allegiances (Hassan, 2005; Jamieson, 2011). A more specific controversy has recently emerged at international level. If the selection of the sons and grandsons of Irish emigrants for the Republic's soccer team could be seen as a manifestation of a more complex interpretation of Irishness (see above), one specific facet of the selection policy has begun to prove particularly contentious. Tensions have emerged over the decision by some northern-born players from Irish nationalist backgrounds to elect to play for the Republic, an option available to them by virtue of their entitlement to Irish citizenship. Controversy erupted in 2006 when Derry-born Darron Gibson switched his allegiance from Northern Ireland (Hassan *et al*, 2009). Subsequently Marc Wilson, Shane Duffy and James McClean have been notable defectors from north to south. While not discounting the possibility of careerist motivations, this phenomenon seems a logical extension of a tendency amongst those from a nationalist background in the north to regard themselves as Irish, to opt to carry an Irish (rather than British) passport and, amongst those who follow the game, to support the Republic's team rather than Northern Ireland (Fulton, 2005). Suggestions that players from Catholic backgrounds have felt somewhat marginalised within the Northern set-up appear to have provided a further justification (McGee and Bairner, 2011). This recent trend has, not surprisingly, generated a considerable negative reaction amongst both supporters and officials of the game in Northern Ireland. A match in Dublin in 2011 between the Republic and the North was boycotted by many northern supporters protesting what they perceived as poaching of their players by the Republic. Following a 5-0 victory for the Republic, the crux of the issue was made clear when Northern Ireland player Niall McGinn (somewhat unusually and perhaps not very wisely) declared himself a Republic of Ireland fan, an utterance that led to a very hostile reaction from Northern supporters. In 2012, the decision of Derry-born James McClean to play for the Republic provoked an extremely virulent reaction from some northern supporters. Michael O'Neill, appointed as Northern Ireland team manager in 2012 (and himself from a Catholic background), has made clear an intention to ensure an inclusive environment in which those from nationalist backgrounds would feel comfortable playing for Northern Ireland. Meanwhile, the complexities of this identity issue were apparent at the 2012 Olympic Games and Paralympics where competitors from Northern Ireland were to be found amongst the ranks of both the Great Britain and Ireland teams. Significantly perhaps, this phenomenon did not provoke the same level of debate as McCullough's decision twenty years earlier.

If soccer appears to have reflected the political and sectarian divisions of the northern conflict, there has been a tendency in some quarters to project rugby as sitting above and beyond the messy realities of Irish politics, in particular the northern issue. The all-island nature of the national team (which has regularly included players from a unionist background) has been presented as a case of sport transcending politics but such a view seems somewhat naïve. Debates over identity and the accompanying paraphernalia of flags and anthems has not been absent from the sport. As Bairner (2003) and others have noted the unionist orientation of some members of the team is far from diminished by their participation, perhaps functioning as a public acknowledgment of an Irish dimension to their Ulster Britishness. In a similar vein, Tuck (2003) suggests a distinction between an official constructed and consumed identity and the embodied one felt by the players. Hassan (2003) has also argued that participation in rugby has increased amongst northern Catholics which he attributes to the growth of a middle-class taking on the interests and mores of their Protestant counterparts and eschewing what they might perceive as the divisive politics of nationalism. However, despite claims to the bridging potential of the sport, controversies still occur. The Irish team uses a specially written anthem, "Ireland's Call" in order to accommodate unionist sensitivities and to reflect their all-Ireland composition though the anthem of the Republic of Ireland, "*Amhrán na bhFiann*" is still played in addition to "Ireland's Call" at matches in Dublin. Controversy surrounded a friendly encounter between Ireland and Italy played at Ravenhill in Belfast in 2007 with calls in some unionist quarters for "God save the Queen" to be played. In the event "Ireland's Call" was the only anthem permitted for the team.

Elsewhere, the political ambiguities of rugby in Ireland were highlighted by the presence of Sinn Féin's Gerry Adams and Martin McGuinness at Lansdowne Road for Ulster's victory in the final of the 1999 European Cup. This could be said to have a certain symbolism as the leaders of northern nationalism displayed support for a team composed of players from a predominantly unionist tradition representing ostensibly the nine counties of Ulster but in reality a Northern Irish team (Hassan, 2003). More recently, McGuinness's lauding of the Ulster team on reaching the 2012 Heineken cup final (in his capacity as Deputy First Minister in the northern assembly) points to the political paradoxes thrown up by sporting events.

Conclusions

As Ireland has undergone profound economic, social, cultural and political changes in recent decades many of these shifts have been reflected within the realm of sport. Irish sports have displayed an increasing professionalisation and commercialisation and these tendencies mean that some sports are now more firmly linked into broader international networks. These shifts have been accompanied by inevitable tensions. Gaelic games in particular have endeavoured to retain a local sensitivity, attempting to modernise while maintaining specific traditions, balancing commercial ambitions with community obligations while simultaneously encouraging both participation and competition. While continuing to emphasise Irish sporting heritage and the importance of community and place the GAA has shown a high degree of adaptability and pragmatism through which the local and parochial intertwine with the global and modern (Doak, 1998; Cronin, 1999; Ó Tuathaigh, 2009). The selection of non-Irish born players (of Irish ethnic origin) for the Republic's international soccer team has contributed to debates over the relationship between the Irish "homeland" and the Irish diaspora. The recent trend of Northern Irish-born players from nationalist backgrounds opting to play for the Republic has fuelled north-south footballing tensions while casting further light on territorial identities and raising questions of citizenship and belonging. While the game of rugby has sometimes been lauded as a symbol of harmonious north-south relations, debates over the playing of anthems and flying of flags at Irish international matches periodically re-emerge. Although sport in Ireland has undergone transformations, the territorial nature of support remains at its core. Indeed at the level of the individual multi-sport supporter, a spatial hierarchy may well be employed ranging from Dublin soccer club Shamrock Rovers, through the Dublin county GAA team, Leinster rugby team and up to Republic of Ireland soccer team and the all-Ireland rugby team at international level.

While acknowledging Free's (2005) stricture about reading too much into sporting events or incidents, and recognising that the complexities of recent Irish history, politics and culture are not reducible to such "collective fantasies", it is still the case that an examination of sporting phenomena can provide us with insights into wider society, culture and politics. Sport also becomes a reference point for wider issues. In 2012 the Irish Tánaiste (Deputy Prime Minister), Eamon Gilmore, controversially urged opposition politicians to "put on the green jersey" and support the government in negotiations over Ireland's economic bailout programme. But political figures are not the only ones deploying sporting metaphors. Playwright Dermot Bolger (author of *In High Germany* referred to earlier) has recently returned to a sporting theme. He uses the handball incident by France's Thierry Henry that led to a goal in a match against Ireland, and which is deemed to have cost the team a place in the 2010 football World

Cup finals, as a metaphor for contemporary Ireland. In the author's words people have been "robbed of jobs, robbed of hope, robbed of our children's future by a self-regulated elite of bankers, developers and politicians" (Bolger, 2011). Against the backdrop of economic collapse and the resultant imposition of massive cuts in government spending, sporting disappointment comes to symbolise broader loss, anger and injustice.

Acknowledgements

This chapter has benefitted from the insights and suggestions of Michael Holmes, Anne Sinnott and Andy Storey.

Bibliography

Arrowsmith, Aidan. "Plastic Paddies vs Master Racers: Soccer and Irish identity". *International Journal of Cultural Studies* 7 (4), (2004) 460-479.

Bairner, Alan. *Sport, Nationalism, and Globalization: European and North American Perspectives*. Albany: State University of New York Press. 2001

—."Political Unionism and sporting nationalism: an examination of the relationship between sport and national identity within the Ulster Unionist tradition". *Identities: Global Studies in Culture and Power* 10 (4): (2003) 517-535.

—. "Sport and the Irish", in *Sport and the Irish. Histories, Identities, Issues* edited by Alan Bairner. Dublin: University College Dublin Press 1-4. 2005

Bolger, Dermot. *In High Germany*, in *Plays 1*, London: Methuen: 69-99. 2000

—. *The Parting Glass*, Dublin: New Island Books. 2011

Brady, Sara. "Performances of Irishness at New York's Gaelic Park", *New York Irish History* 19: (2005) 17-34.

Cronin, Mike. "Global, parochial, still anti-imperialist and Irish". *Peace Review* 11 (4): (1999) 517-522.

—. "Catholics and sport in Northern Ireland: exclusiveness or inclusiveness?" *International Sports Studies* 21 (1) (2001): 25-41.

Cronin, Mike, Duncan, Mark and Rouse, Paul. *The GAA. A People's History*, Cork: The Collins Press. 2009

Darby, Paul. "The Gaelic Athletic Association, transnational identities and Irish America", *Sociology of Sport Journal*, 27 (4) (2010): 351-370.

Doak, Richard. "(De)constructing Irishness in the 1990s-The Gaelic Athletic Association and cultural nationalist discourse reconsidered", *Irish Journal of Sociology* 8 (1) (1998) 25-48.

Duke, Vic and Crolley, Liz. *Football, Nationality and the State*. London: Addison Wesley Longman, 1996

Fanning, Bryan and Munck, Ronaldo (eds) *Globalization, Migration and Social Transformation. Ireland in Europe and the World*, Farnham: Ashgate, 2011.

Free, Marcus. "'Angels with drunken faces?' Travelling Republic of Ireland supporters and the construction of Irish migrant identity in England" in *Fanatics! Power, Identity and Fandom in Football* edited by Adam Brown, London: Routledge: 219-232. 1998

—. "Keeping them under pressure: masculinity, narratives of national regeneration and the Republic of Ireland soccer team", *Sport in History*, 25 (2) (2005): 265-288.

Fulton, Gareth. "Northern Catholic fans of the Republic of Ireland soccer team", in *Sport and the Irish. Histories, Identities, Issues* edited by Alan Bairner, Dublin: University College Dublin Press: 140-156. 2005.

Giulianotti, Richard. *Football. A Scoiology of the Global Game*, Cambridge: Polity Press, 2000.

Hassan, David. "Rugby union, Irish nationalism and national identity in Northern Ireland", *Football Studies*, 6 (1): (2003) 5-18.

Hassan, David. "Sport, identity and Irish nationalism in Northern Ireland", in *Sport and the Irish. Histories, Identities, Issues* edited Alan Bairner, Dublin: University College Dublin Press: 123-139. 2005.

Hassan, David, McCullough, Shane and Moreland, Elizabeth. "North or South? Darron Gibson and the issue of player eligibility within Irish soccer", *Soccer and Society*, 10 (6) (2009): 740-753.

Hayes, Cathy. "Debt-ridden developers shun Galway Races. Celtic Tiger a distant roar as reality bites", *Irish Central*, August 2nd, http://www.irishcentral.com/news/-Debt-ridden--developers-shun-Galway-Races-99749874.html (Accessed September 14th 2012). 2010.

Holmes, Michael. "Symbols of national identity and sport: the case of the Irish football team", *Irish Political Studies* 9: (1994) 81-98.

Holmes, Michael and Storey, David. "Transferring national allegiance. Cultural affinity or flag of convenience?" *Sport in Society* 14 (2): (2011) 253-271.

Holt, Richard. "Ireland and the birth of modern sport", in *The Gaelic Athletic Association 1884-2009* edited by Mike Cronin, William Murphy and Paul Rouse, Dublin: Irish Academic Press: 33-46. 2009

Horan, Niamh. "Donal Og Cusack fights back against the bigots", *Irish independent* September 7th 2012

Humphries, Tom. "Identity is a sense of place not birthplace", *The Irish Times*, January 10th 2005.

Jamieson, Teddy. *Whose Side Are You On? Sport, the Troubles and Me*, Yellow Jersey Press. 2011.

Jarvie, Grant. "Internationalism and sport in the making of nations", *Identities: Studies in Global Culture and Power* 10 (4) (2003): 537-551.

Keys, Colm. "Croker issue warning to Nemo". *Irish Independent* May 5th 2010.

McGee, Darragh and Bairner, Alan. "Transcending the borders of Irish identity? Narratives of northern nationalist footballers in Northern Ireland", *International Review for the Sociology of Sport*, 46 (4): (2011) 436-455.

McGovern, Patrick. "The Irish brawn drain: English league clubs and Irish footballers, 1946–1995", *British Journal of Sociology* 51 (3): (2000) 401–18..

O'Callaghan, Liam. *Rugby in Munster. A Social and Cultural History*, Cork: Cork University Press. 2011.

O' Connor, Ruaidhri. "Players' group backs ban for pair over racist abuse of GAA star", *Irish Independent* June 20th 2012.

Ó Ríordáin, Aodhán. "Funding of sports needs to be played by fairer rules", July 30th 2012

Ó Tuathaigh, Gearóid. "The GAA as a force in Irish society: an overview", in *The Gaelic Athletic Association 1884-2009* edited by Mike Cronin, William Murphy and Paul Rouse, Dublin: Irish Academic Press: 237-256. 2009.

Smith, Adrian and Porter, Dilwyn (eds) *Sport and National Identity in the Post-War World*, London: Routledge. 2004

Storey, David. "Heritage, culture and identity: the case of Gaelic games", in *Sport, History and Heritage: Studies in Public Representation* edited by Jeffrey Hill, Kevin Moore and Jason Wood, Woodbridge: Boydell Press. 2012

Sugden, John and Bairner, Alan. *Sport, Sectarianism and Society in a Divided Ireland*, London: Leicester University Press, 1993.

The Economist. "'Horses for courses'. The beauty of an equine heritage", October 14th 2004.

Tuck, Jason. "Making sense of emerald commotion: rugby union, national identity and Ireland", *Identities: Global Studies in Culture and Power* 10 (4): (2003) 495 – 515.

CHAPTER SIX

FOLLOWING IN THE FOOTSTEPS OF JOHN HEWITT: ASSOCIATION FOOTBALL IN NORTHERN IRELAND AND THE SEARCH FOR AN INCLUSIVE IDENTITY

ALAN BAIRNER

Introduction

Unlike their American counterparts, Irish writers have paid relatively little attention to sport, at least in their published work. In the case of Northern Ireland/Ulster, although Samuel Beckett, educated in County Fermanagh, has a place in cricket's almanac, Wisden, the most notable exception is Sam Hanna Bell. Born in Scotland in 1909 to Ulster-born parents, Bell was taken "home" to Ireland at the age of seven. He spent most of his life in the Strangford area of County Down, worked for the BBC as a producer and wrote a number of novels, the best known of which is *The December Bride* (1951). In 1961, he published *The Hollow Bell*, a story set in 1930s Belfast and centred on the life of a young footballer. Football is used in this work as a window through which to examine heightened sectarian tensions of the time. Bell had little interest in the sport per se[1]. Nevertheless, he has shown a willingness to discuss, albeit superficially, an important aspect of working-class life in Northern Ireland, one which had and continues to have a close relationship with

[1] The author is grateful to Mr Fergus Bell, Sam Hanna Bell's son, for sharing his recollections of his father's sporting interests which involved playing rather than spectating and rugby union as opposed to football. He had taught himself the latter by reading players' autobiographies and by having the good fortune to know Danny Blanchflower, the cerebral captain of Tottenham Hotspur and Northern Ireland in the late 1950s and early 1960s.

identity formation (Bairner, 2000). This cannot be said of many other Northern Irish writers, including those who have professed a commitment to the interests and aspirations of the working classes.

The politics of identity have, of course, been central to social life in Northern Ireland since partition. As John Wilson Foster (1975: 17) argues, "the urgent task facing anyone with a benevolent interest in Ulster is to explore as honestly as possible those cultural differences between Protestant and Catholic that seemingly irrational sectarian conflict". Even in an era in which that conflict has abated, if not completely disappeared, such differences remain worthy of comment. As Foster goes on, "it is less than helpful, even with the best will in the world, merely to assert that beneath the orange and green camouflage Protestants and Catholics are all Irishmen and only political scoundrels prevent their mutual recognition of the fact". More contentious, however, is Foster's use of the term "Ulster" with reference, one assumes, to Northern Ireland.

Arguably, not since the formation in 1921 of the Northern Ireland state, comprising for the most part, six of the provinces of Ulster's historic counties, has there been such a good opportunity to assess the meaning of Northern Ireland in relation to the identity formation of those who live there–to consider what Northern Ireland has been and what it can become, particularly in light of the evolving constitutional context of the United Kingdom in general. Ulster unionists can explore to a greater extent than ever before their precise feelings about Northern Ireland *vis à vis* the rest of the United Kingdom. Is the continued constitutional relationship with Britain an end in itself or merely a means to an end–namely, a bulwark against incorporation within the Republic of Ireland, itself no longer a possibility without their consent? As Todd *et al* (2009: 87) point out, the signing of the Good Friday Agreement in 1998 posed "new questions for ordinary Protestants in Northern Ireland, casting into doubt older assumptions, requiring of them new modes of practice and interaction". More significant perhaps is the question of where the Peace Process and the re-introduction of institutions of devolved government for Northern Ireland have left Irish nationalism and, perhaps even more controversially, republicanism. Is former republican prisoner Anthony McIntyre correct to claim that the majority of republicans in the north of Ireland, especially in Belfast, were never fully committed to the idea of a united Ireland, motivated as they were primarily by the desire for social justice which could be, and arguably has been, accommodated through reform within

Northern Ireland[2]? As McIntyre (2008: 228) has commented, "before the Provisional IRA was founded the Unionist prime minister of Northern Ireland, Terence O'Neill, pompously stated that if the Unionist community would only treat Catholics well and allow them some prosperity, they would stop having seventeen children and come to live like Protestants". According to McIntyre (2008: 228), "his day has come".

The signing of the Good Friday Agreement and the subsequent difficult, but at present relatively successful, quest for an acceptable basis upon which to establish devolved government, have led to the two more extreme nationalist and unionist political parties entering the mainstream of political life and agreeing to share power. Yet, concerns continue to be expressed about the extent to which the public at large have moved forwards in the same spirit. In particular, to what extent do the new political arrangements either reflect or encourage the emergence of a widely shared sense of being Northern Irish. Have traditional rivalries simply been masked by political change or is there a possibility, now as never before, of a shared Northern Irish identity?

This chapter examines the on-going search for an inclusive Northern Irish consciousness. In so doing, it looks back to the poetry and politics of John Hewitt as well as at the current role of the Northern Ireland football team in relation to the formation and reproduction of identity. Two questions dominate the discussion–first, is it inevitable that the terms "Northern Ireland" and "Ulster" (in the sense of the six counties) are so closely associated with unionism and Protestantism that they are unlikely ever to form the basis for an inclusive civic consciousness and, second, have shifts in nationalist thinking made a Northern Irish identity more acceptable than at any time since partition?

As Bryonie Reid (2004: 109) argues, "Northern Ireland may be described as a hybrid, borderline area, but this context has resulted more often in fossilisation of identity and difference than any kind of acceptance and celebration of ambiguity". That said, basic ethnographic evidence tells us that Northern Irish people, whether nationalist or unionist, have for many years regarded themselves as different–unionists, of course, different from "the Irish" but also, it can be argued, from the British, and especially the English, and nationalists from the British but also, in a more nuanced way, from their compatriots in the Irish Republic. Conversely, a history and a landscape shared by unionists and northern nationalists, even though interpreted differently, is undeniable. But to what extent, if at all, does this

[2] This view was expressed by McIntyre to the author whilst the former was studying for a PhD at the Queen's University of Belfast.

provide a basis upon which to build a shared consciousness? One man who, for a time at least, believed in such a possibility was John Hewitt, whose poetry and politics have been a source of considerable interest to a wide range of scholars (Dawe and Foster, 1991). Unlike Bell, however, Hewitt showed no interest in sport and, most significantly football, which, through the existence of a separate governing body and national teams, provides highly visible evidence of Northern Ireland as a place apart.

John Hewitt's quest for a regional identity

Born in Belfast on 28 October 1907, John Hewitt was a socialist and a lover of art who is now best remembered for his poetry. In 1950, he became deputy director and keeper of art at the Belfast Museum and Art Gallery but he was subsequently denied the vacant post of director, believing that he had been branded as a pro-Catholic communist. In 1957, he left Belfast to take up a post as director of the Herbert Art Gallery in Coventry. He retired in 1972, returned to Northern Ireland and died there in June 1987.

Hewitt's Ulster regionalist project began during and after the Second World War and, with the outbreak of the Troubles in 1969, "took on an urgent contemporary dimension" (Longley and Ormsby, 2007: xiv). Working with Sam Hanna Bell, John Boyd and others, Hewitt believed that "if we could establish a regional consciousness for the North of Ireland it would give us something to cling to, a kind of key to our identity…" (cited in Mooney, 1998: 68). According to Martin Mooney (1998: 69), Hewitt "twinned his Regionalism and his socialism to give an account of the role of the writer in society, in opposition to the complacencies of the Unionist establishment and the kailyard provincials". But what exactly was the region to which Hewitt's regionalism alluded?

As Reid (2004: 103) points out, "constructions of place are often burdened with bitterness, and the ways in which Unionism and Nationalism traditionally construct their claims to the territory of Northern Ireland are centred on absolute ownership and mutual exclusion". The implications of this have been at the very heart of political contestation at least since the formation of the state.

> Northern Ireland was brought into existence in self-conscious refusal of the cultural and political identity of the Free State. However, the power of the Nationalist sense of place, and the statelet's existence on the island of Ireland, made difficult any separate and distinctive place-based imagining of Northern Ireland (Reid, 2004: 106).

Thus, although Hewitt wished to see the nine counties of Ulster or, perhaps more specifically, the six counties of Northern Ireland, as a region, his sense of place was markedly at odds with that of other poets, for example John Montague, and by extension of other Ulster men and women.

> John Hewitt's poetic locales lie east of Montague's hilly and Catholic Tyrone, in the green Glens of Antrim and the fertile corridor of the Lagan Valley. They are largely Protestant locales, lying on a clear day in view of the mainland that peopled them, though providing, in the Antrim moors and glens, opportunities for the planter poet to ascend into the older native culture (Foster, 1975: 23).

Indeed, as Hewitt was later to admit, "the trouble was that I didn't realize that there were several regions in the North of Ireland, and that the one region I thought it was, was heavily conditioned by Protestant planter background" (cited in Mooney, 1988: 73). By his own admission, Hewitt's regionalism was trying to bring together "incompatible pieces" as his poetry implicitly reveals.

Writing for Ulster

As Michael Longley and Frank Ormsby (2007: xx) note, "Hewitt always remains pretty clear about who he is (or who he is not)"–hence his "hierarchy of values".

> I am an Ulsterman, of planter stock. I was born in the island of Ireland, so secondarily I'm an Irishman. I was born in the British archipelago and English is my native tongue, so I'm British. The British archipelago consists of offshore islands to the continent of Europe, so I'm European (Hewitt, 2007: xx-xxi).

In "Rite, Lubitavish, Glenaan", he writes,

> …I am of Irishry
> by nature and by birth (Hewitt, 2007: 44).

However, he at times questions one level of that hierarchy, namely his sense of belonging to Ireland. For example in "Conacre", he writes,

> This is my home and country. Later on
> perhaps I'll find this nation is my own;
> but here and now it is enough to love

> this faulted ledge, this map of cloud above,
> and the great sea that beats against the west
> to swamp the sun (Hewitt, 2007: 4).

There is even a mildly embarrassing poem, "The Irish Dimension", in which he recalls childhood neighbours, in a slightly mawkish tone reminiscent of the sentimental parodies of Northern Irish life created by comedian, James Young:

> We shortly found that they were Catholics,
> the very first I ever came to know.
> To other friends they might be Teagues or Micks;
> the lad I quickly found no sort of foe (Hewitt, 2007: 114).

In England, he is able to describe himself as "an Irishman in Coventry" albeit before commenting on "the sick, guilt-clotted legend of my creed-haunted, godforsaken race" (Hewitt, 2007: 53). No matter the nods in the direction of his Irishness, however, Hewitt remains committed to the idea of Ulster as a place apart as he explains in "An Ulsterman",

> This is my country. If my people came
> from England here four centuries ago,
> the only trace that's left is my name (Hewitt, 2007: 68).

Or in "Freehold" where he writes,

> Mine is historic Ulster, battlefield
> of Gael and Planter, certified and sealed
> by blood, and what is stronger than the blood,
> by images and folkways understood
> but dimly by the wits, yet valid still… (Hewitt, 2007: 133).

All of this, of course, is central to his political dilemma,

> Born is this island, maimed by history,
> and creed-infected, by my father taught
> the stubborn habit of unfettered thought,
> I dreamed, like him, all people should be free (Hewitt, 2007: 69).

So how unfettered was his thought, particularly during the period when he sought to unite socialism with a particular brand of Ulster regionalism?

His here and now was undoubtedly Ulster. In "Once Alien Here", Hewitt (2007: 8) invokes memories "of all the buried men in Ulster clay". More than that, however, rather than the six counties, far less the nine, his here and now is east Antrim where “The moon will rise on a defeated world” (Hewitt, 2007: 10). It was this that spelled the end of his regionalist project even though his later poetry at times revisited what Peter McDonald (1992: 72) has described as “the grave of Regionalism”. However, there may now be signs that a six-county Ulster identity is finally in reach as, after the signing of the Agreement, political and academic debate began to resound with phrases such as “conflict transformation” and “the politics of transcendence” (Arthur, 2000). If so, where can it be found other than in the institutions of devolved governance? Not yet perhaps in the churches, the schools or in most other agencies of civil society but conceivably in sport where the Northern Irish association football team represents Northern Ireland formally at least on the international stage.

Playing for Northern Ireland

In fact, the challenge that Hewitt set himself and ultimately failed to surmount has proved to be equally daunting in the world of sport. The history of sport in Ireland is in many ways a microcosm of the island’s political and cultural history in its entirety (Bairner, 2005a). As Mike Cronin (1999: 190) has noted, “until there is only one idea of Irish nationalism, and a singular and commonly shared expression of identity, then sport will continue to reflect the multifaceted and ever-changing nature of Irishness”. In this respect, the historic province of Ulster has played a pivotal role standing as it now does with one foot in the Republic of Ireland and the other in the United Kingdom of Great Britain and Northern Ireland, with all of the political and sporting implications which that divide involves. The story of sport in Ireland is a significant element in the history of three different Irelands–pre-Partition Ireland, the Irish Free State (subsequently the Republic of Ireland), and Northern Ireland. It also embraces the distinct but dialectically interwoven narratives of Catholic and Protestant Ireland, urban and rural Ireland, post-imperial and post-colonial Ireland, and traditional, modern and even postmodern Ireland.

A superficial understanding of the topic tells us that sport has certainly played an important role in modern Ulster, latterly Northern Ireland, both as means by which to escape from political and social hardship and as a major influence on the construction and reproduction of competing identities (Sugden and Bairner, 1993). Not only has sport, particularly association football, been influenced by and implicated in the political struggles that have taken place within urban areas, it has also been a key feature of the rural landscape not least as a major signifier of cultural affiliation and a crucial conduit for community cohesion.

In relation to sport, one visible signifier of the existence of Northern Ireland as a separate place is participation as a "national" team in the Commonwealth Games. The fact that this puts Northern Ireland on a par with the Isle of Man, Jersey and Guernsey as well as England, Scotland and Wales serves to lessen its significance. More interesting is the manner in which the Gaelic Athletic Association (GAA), that most explicitly nationalist of Irish sporting organisations, has acquired two rather different roles since the partition of Ireland. It has even been suggested that the GAA in Northern Ireland has attained a *de facto* semi-autonomous status (Hassan, 2005). Certainly within the nine counties of Northern Ireland, most Gaelic football rivalries tend to follow the contours established by partition–Tyrone versus Derry and Down versus Armagh in the north and Cavan versus Monaghan on the other side of the border.

On 11 November 2009, an Ulster Sports Exhibition opened in Belfast's City Hall. Its aim was to celebrate the achievements of, amongst others, sporting luminaries such as footballer George Best, Olympic gold medal winning athlete Mary Peters, boxer Barry McGuigan and cyclist Wendy Houvenghel. The exhibition was organised by the Ulster Sports Museum Association, the ultimate objective of which is the establishment, in 2012, of a permanent museum dedicated to Ulster sport. In the interim period, a temporary exhibition has travelled to different locations and sporting events (http://www.nisf.net/proposals-to-create-an-ulster-sports-museum-485.asp). The association's honorary secretary, Brian Morrison, announced at the opening of the Belfast exhibition, "It is about celebrating the past and inspiring the future" (http://www.belfastforum.co.uk/index .php?topic=26506.0). The questions that this statement immediately raise, of course, are similar to those prompted by Hewitt's regionalist project– "whose past?" and "whose future?"-and those are precisely the questions that any account of the development of sport in modern Ulster must address.

Sports museums are relatively common features of the cultural landscape of North America and of many parts of Europe. This is hardly surprising. Museums are places in which memories are given meaning and few human activities are more enticing than sport in terms of imbuing specific memories with collective meaning. For example, The Alabama Sports Hall of Fame (ASHOF) in Birmingham, Alabama, reminds state residents and visitors alike of the significant role that sport has played and the contribution that has been made in the process by athletes and teams from Alabama. According to its website, "the ASHOF is a magnificent state treasure, dedicated to the celebration and preservation of Alabama's exceptional sports heritage" (http://www.ashof.org/). What makes things relatively easy for the museum staff, however, is the fact that the boundaries of Alabama are clearly delineated. The people and teams which the museum celebrates represent Alabama as a spatially identifiable entity. The word "Ulster", on the other hand, means very different things to different people, not least in the context of sport. Representing Ulster poses problems that representing Alabama does not (Bairner, 2010).

Representation is an important concept in the world of sport. Athletes represent their school, their club, their county, their province, their country and so on. However, in the context of Northern Ireland, representation has wider connotations which are bound up with the equally problematic process constituted by acts of naming. Acts of naming are of immense political and social importance because they are central to what Chang and Holt (2009: 303) describe as "the intricate intertwining of language, ideology, and identity construction". Whatever athletes represent has a specific name. This may be relatively uncontroversial–the name of a club, for example, or the name of a school–although even here the very act of naming can be fraught with difficulties. Even more contested, however, are names given to political and quasi-political entities and it is with these that sports people, arguably more than most, particularly in times of relative peace, are most prominently associated. It is these that they represent and in so doing they help to confirm the identity and perhaps the status of a specific geopolitical entity despite the fact that the association of the place with a specific name may be contested by many. Ulster is a case in point and sport is a particularly good lens through which to begin to glimpse the complexities involved in discussions of place, identity, ethnicity and nationality.

The term "Ulster" is used widely in the sporting world not only by unionists with reference to rugby union, for example, but also by nationalists in relation to Gaelic games. But the current political dispensation does not encompass the whole of Ulster, regardless of how that term is understood, but only the six counties of Northern Ireland which is precisely why football with its own Northern Irish league structure, cup competitions and national team is so significant. As a basis for shared identity, however, the sport may well be fatally flawed not unlike, and for comparable reasons, Hewitt's regional project.

In the past few years, a number of young Catholic association footballers, born in Northern Ireland, have chosen to represent the Republic of Ireland in international competition. At first glance, it might seem odd that this phenomenon has emerged at a time when the constitutional status of Northern Ireland has never been more secure. However, we can perhaps more easily understand this phenomenon by first considering briefly the experiences of those association footballers from a Catholic background who have represented Northern Ireland in international competition in the past, not least by examining their published life stories as representations of Northern Ireland as a particular place (see Bairner, 2010). Following this discussion is an examination of the more recent trend involving the "defection" of young nationalist players.

Two relatively minor terminological issues are worthy of consideration at the outset. The word "Catholic" is used here not as a consequence of any insight into the religious beliefs of the players under discussion. In other circumstances, the word "nationalist" would be preferable not least insofar as it attests to the fact that the conflict in and about Northern Ireland has been quintessentially political rather than religious. Given the subject matter of the chapter, however, it is important not to attach political labels to the players whose life stories are central to the discussion. The words "football" and "footballers" are also used here despite a recognition that in many parts of Ireland, "football" refers to Gaelic football and the word "soccer" applies to association football. Indeed, some of the players mentioned in this chapter frequently tend to favour the word "soccer" rather than "football", although in Belfast, the largest city in Northern Ireland, the usual distinction that is made, even in nationalist areas, is between "Gaelic" and "football".

Football and the Idea of Northern Ireland–then

Catholic players have always played for Northern Ireland regardless of the political circumstances of the time and their own political beliefs. However, events surrounding the end of Neil Lennon's international career have become hugely influential in terms of Catholic attitudes towards the Northern Ireland team (Lennon, 2006). It is no exaggeration to say that the player was forced to retire from international football because of taunts from his own supporters and threats to his life, provoked primarily because of his association with Celtic Football Club. It should be noted, however, that only towards the end of his career, and for those very specific reasons, did Lennon sever his links with the Northern Ireland team. Like numerous others Catholic players, he had previously performed conscientiously for the side. However, in addition to his Celtic connection, like former goalkeeper Pat Jennings (1984), Lennon (2006) had also expressed his preference for a united Ireland team. By contrast, Martin O'Neill's biographer hints at little controversy and, indeed, points to his subject's passion for the "national" i.e. Northern Ireland team (Montgomery, 2007). The autobiographies of two footballers from an earlier era, Charlie Tully (1958) and Peter McParland (1960), are uncontroversial overall and particularly with regard to international football. But they played their professional football in the pre-Troubles era and at a time when the team that represented the Irish Republic was still regarded as a football minnow. That said, it is apparent from all of the available relevant biographies and autobiographies that each of the players had a particularly close affinity with their Catholic and nationalist roots.

In the early stages of their life stories, their Irishness is most clearly demonstrated in their negotiation of the rival attractions of Gaelic games and football. The point is further established by references to adult relationships which are recognised as important–relationships with other Irish people or, in several cases, with Celtic FC. Examples of the influence of a Catholic/nationalist habitus highlight the extent to which Northern Ireland has been and remains (as shown in the treatment of Neil Lennon) a divided society (not only in terms of residence and education but also sporting representation).

These footballers' stories suggest that there is more evidence of division than of convergence–signs of a Northern Irish football consciousness, perhaps, but not of an emergent Northern Irish political consciousness, far less a "national" identity. The Good Friday Agreement has done much to strengthen the constitutional status of Northern Ireland. Ironically, however, it has also simultaneously allowed for greater freedom and more opportunities than in the past to choose one's own national allegiance. Thus, in an era when the political leaders of Irish nationalism and republicanism are helping to govern Northern Ireland as a constituent part of the United Kingdom, young players such as Darron Gibson have chosen the Republic of Ireland over Northern Ireland for whatever reasons. It is precisely those reasons that form the content of the final section of this discussion.

Football and the idea of Northern Ireland–now

Darron Gibson who made his decision to defect whilst playing for Manchester United is by no means alone in opting to represent the Irish Republic rather than Northern Ireland as recent research has demonstrated (see McGee and Bairner, 2011). One such player is Shane McEleney who recalls,

> Without a doubt, my main influence for going down south was the way that I was treated by them [the Irish Football Association-IFA], as at that age you need to feel welcomed but they never did that... I definitely would not consider ever going back to Northern Ireland because of their treatment of me and that basically, Protestants will always be selected over Catholics if at all possible (cited in McGee and Bairner, 2011: 445).

Seen in isolation, these feelings could be viewed as those of a dejected and resentful footballer who had failed to make the grade with the Northern Ireland team. But, in light of remarkably similar accounts from other players, it appears that major question marks remain over the commitment of the IFA to creating a shared future in Northern Irish football.

This is not to suggest that Catholic footballers see their involvement with the Irish Republic side as a counter-hegemonic gesture. As Shane McEleney's comments show, the decision to "go south" is not at all straightforward:

> I mean if you gave me two grand right now, I don't think that I would play for Northern Ireland again, that's the way I now feel about them (the IFA). I had that bad of an experience with the country through football that, whilst I have no idea how I will get on with the Republic, I certainly can't stay here after that (cited in McGee and Bairner, 2011: 445).

McEleney believes that he now has no choice in the matter, insofar as his experience with the IFA has meant that the Northern Ireland side option is no longer viable. Whilst some apprehension is discernible in his reference to the Irish Republic, the absence of equitable circumstances within Northern Ireland makes the alternative a risk he is prepared to take. At one level, we may question the extent to which McEleney, or the other Catholic players in the same situation, ever truly identified with Northern Ireland, especially given their childhood support for the Republic of Ireland team. However, this does not disguise the fact that many of them, as in the past, have exhibited a genuine willingness to represent the country's football team, only to be discouraged by what they perceive to be the exclusive governance of the IFA.

Those who choose to remain with the Northern Ireland team experience equally complex emotions. For example, commenting on his "choice" of sporting allegiance, Eugene Ferry observed:

> It would always have been the Republic as I supported them as a boy. But then when I got called up to the Northern Ireland team, I didn't care so much about that. I would say 'I don't care that my pride is with the

> Republic, I'm only playing football for them' (cited in McGee and Bairner, 2011: 449).

Such remarks offer fascinating insights into the ways in which the Catholic footballer in Northern Ireland understands and negotiates his sense of sporting allegiance. At one level, Ferry regards the Irish Republic as "his nation", with an admission of childhood support and, perhaps more significantly, of a sense of personal pride in the south. However, his latter reference to "only playing football for them" i.e. for Northern Ireland is equally revealing. Here, Ferry plays down the significance of his decision to represent Northern Ireland, appearing to indicate that a sense of sporting identity is relatively superficial. Indeed, considering the way he describes the Northern Ireland side as "them", one could be forgiven for questioning why he has made such a decision at all.

Hassan (2002: 73) suggests that the answer may well cohere around a "peculiar mix of sporting expediency and opportunism". To a certain extent, Hassan is correct to identify the pragmatic dimension, but such an explanation fails to acknowledge the complex ways in which athletes negotiate different layers of their identity. Niall McGinn's comments make this explicit:

> When it comes to football matters, you don't really think about whether it has to be the Republic of Ireland as 'my country'. That is kind of different to your football stuff. You don't really take that into consideration when it's about football (cited in McGee and Bairner, 2011: 450).

Here, McGinn clearly distinguishes football matters as separate from his sense of national identification with the Irish Republic. Indeed, as in the case of Ferry, McGinn's comments appear to suggest that his football identity is less embedded than his national identity. Therefore, the conception of a form of Northern Ireland football identity emerges through which Catholic members of the team are both happy and, in many cases, proud to represent what essentially becomes their "football nation".

However, adopting what initially appears to be an opposing position, Paddy McCourt who, like McGinn, has opted to play for Northern Ireland, suggested that "it's a great thing to be with the Northern Irish team as obviously you are very proud to be playing for your country as that is an opportunity that anyone would jump at". If we accept this declaration at face value, we could conceivably view McCourt's sentiments as evidence of a more general sense of an emergent Northern Irish identity within the nationalist community. However, when considered alongside his subsequent comments, such a reading becomes difficult. Explaining his reasons for choosing Northern Ireland, McCourt stated:

> When I got called up to play for Northern Ireland, I decided then that they would be my team. I wasn't going to go here and then there as I wouldn't want to be seen as someone who did a u-turn. I mean you pick a country to play football for and mine just happened to be Northern Ireland (cited in McGee and Bairner, 2011: 450).

Whilst exhibiting a commendable degree of personal integrity in his loyalty to Northern Ireland, McCourt nevertheless also trivialises his decision as being merely about playing football. It appears that he too is almost certainly expressing only a football identification with Northern Ireland or, what Bairner (2010) refers to as, a "Northern Irish football consciousness". As highlighted by McGinn, this football consciousness is constructed in conjunction with, rather than in opposition to, national identification with the Irish Republic.

It seems unlikely that it is an emergent sense of national consciousness that prompts Catholic footballers to represent Northern Ireland. Rather, their narratives reveal evidence only of a Northern Irish football identity, a relatively superficial and temporary dimension of their sporting habitus. Catholic footballers can benefit from the advantages of playing international football with Northern Ireland without necessarily recognising the legitimacy of the political entity which the "national" team represents–a condition which bears some comparison with that of Northern Irish unionist rugby union players and their relationship with an all-Ireland national team (Bairner, 2005b).

Conclusion

Writing in 1978, David W. Miller (2007) referred to Ulster loyalists, and perhaps by implication many unionists, as "Queen's Rebels" whose loyalty to the Crown was largely conditional. From John Hewitt to the present, it might also be argued that both for unionists and for nationalists loyalty to Northern Ireland is conditional–culturally and spatially restricted in the case of the former as it was for Hewitt himself and pragmatically so in the case of the latter. In the wake of the signing of the Good Friday Agreement, Paul Arthur (2000: 249) wrote that "a sense of civic consciousness is being developed". To what extent that can be transformed into a regional or even a national consciousness remains to be seen. However, Arthur (2000: 247-8) also claimed that "the genius of the agreement can be traced to a few innocuous words" i.e. "the birthright of all of the people of Northern Ireland to identify themselves and be accepted as Irish or British *or both*". It would be ironic, indeed, if an agreement which has consolidated Northern Ireland's political existence as never before has also made it easier for people to disavow the descriptor "Northern Irish". If even those young footballers who represent Northern Ireland find it difficult to identify with the place itself and what it stands for, then it is unlikely that the body of Hewitt's regionalism can be resurrected at least in the foreseeable future. Arguably had Hewitt taken the time, as Sam Hanna Bell had done, to consider understanding the divisions that have long existed within the most popular sport in working-class urban communities in Northern Ireland, he might have realised far sooner than he did just how elusive a shared Ulster identity might prove to be.

Bibliography

Arthur, P. *Special Relationships. Britain, Ireland and the Northern Ireland Problem*, Belfast: Blackstaff Press, 2000.

Bairner, A. "Football, Society and the Literary Imagination: Sam Hanna Bell's *The Hollow Ball* and Robin Jenkins' *A Would-Be Saint*", *Kunnskap om Idrett*, 4: (2000) 30-43.

—. "Irish Sport", in *Cambridge Companion to Modern Irish Culture* edited by J. Cleary and C. Connolly Cambridge: Cambridge University Press, 190-205. 2000a

—. "Sport, Irishness and Ulster unionism", in *Sport and the Irish. Histories, Identities, Issues*, edited by A. Bairner, Dublin: University College Dublin Press: 157-171. 2005b

—. "Representing the North: reflections on the life stories of Northern Ireland's Catholic footballers", in *Sport, Representation and Evolving Identities* edited by P. Dine and S. Crosson, Oxford: Peter Lang, 217-238. 2010.

Bell, S. H. *The Hollow Ball,* Belfast: Blackstaff Press. First published in 1961. 1990.

Chang, H. C. and Holt, R. "*Taiwan* and *ROC*: A critical analysis of President Chen Shui-bien's construction of Taiwan identity in national speeches", *National Identities*, 11 (3) (2009), 301-330.

Cronin, M. *Sport and Nationalism in Ireland. Gaelic Games, Soccer and Irish Identity since 1884*, Dublin: Four Courts Press, 1999.

Dawe, G. and Foster, J. W. (eds.) *The Poet's Place. Ulster Literature and Society. Essays in Honour of John Hewitt, 1907-1987*, Belfast: Institute of Irish Studies. 1991.

Foster, J. W. "The Landscape of Planter and Gael in the Poetry of John Hewitt and John Montague", *Canadian Journal of Irish Studies*, 1 (2), (1975), 17-33.

Hassan, D. "Sport, Identity and Irish Nationalism in Northern Ireland", in *Sport and the Irish. Histories, Identities, Issues* edited by A. Bairner, Dublin: UCD Press: 123-139. 2005.

Hewitt, J. *Selected Poems*, edited by Michael Longley and Frank Ormsby, Belfast: Blackstaff Press, 2007.

Jennings, P. *Pat Jennings. An Autobiography*, London: Panther Books, 1984

Lennon, N. *Man and Bhoy*, London: HarperSport, 2006.

Longley., M and Ormsby F. "Introduction", in J. Hewitt, *Selected Poems*, edited by Michael Longley and Frank Ormsby., Belfast : Blackstaff Press, xi-xxv. 2007.

Macintyre, A. *Good Friday. The Death of Irish Republicanism*, New York: Ausubo Press, 2008.

McDonald, P. "The Fate of 'Identity': John Hewitt, W. R. Rodgers and Louis MacNeice", *Irish Review*, 12, (1992), 72-86.

McGee, D. and Bairner, A. "Transcending the borders of Irish identity? Narratives of northern nationalist footballers in Northern Ireland", *International Review for the Sociology of Sport*, 46 (4) (2011): 436-455.

McParland, P. *Going For Goal*, London: The Soccer Book Club, 1960.

Miller, D. W. *Queen's Rebels: Ulster Loyalism in Historical Perspective, Dublin: University College Dublin Press*. 1978.

Montgomery, A. *Martin O'Neill. The Biography*, London: Virgin Books. 2007.

Mooney, M. "'A Native Mode': Language and Regionalism in the Poetry of John Hewitt", *Irish Review*, 3, (1988) 67-74.

Reid, B. "Labouring towards the space to belong: Place and identity in Northern Ireland", *Irish Geography*, 37 (1), (2004) 103-113.

Shirlow, P. and Murtagh, B. *Belfast. Segregation, Violence and the City*, London: Pluto Press, 2006.

Sugden, J. and Bairner, A. *Sport, Sectarianism and Society in a Divided Ireland*, Leicester: Leicester University Press, 1993.

Todd, J. "Nationalism,, Republicanism and the Good Friday Agreement", in *After the Good Friday Agreement* edited by J. Ruane and J. Todd, Dublin: University College Dublin Press: 49-70. 1999.

Tully, C. *Passed to You*, London: The Soccer Book Club, 1958.

PART III

MEDIA AND FILM

CHAPTER SEVEN

"IT'S IN BELGIUM": LOCATING IRELAND *IN BRUGES*

SARAH MARTINDALE AND CATHERINE REES

In writer-director Martin McDonagh's first feature length film *In Bruges* (2008) two hitmen are sent by their boss to hide out in the titular city, a picturesque and historic tourist destination in Belgium, in the wake of a botched killing in London. This much we learn from the opening voiceover. As the narrative progresses they explore the unfamiliar location and encounter both native residents and other international visitors, before the violent chain of events set in motion prior to their arrival in that place overtake them there, when the ruthless gangster who they work for arrives to enforce his warped principles. The two central characters around which the film revolves are Irish. Is this an incidental detail (perhaps a by-product of casting Irish actors in those roles) or a potentially significant component of the meaning of this film? This chapter will argue the latter, exploring Irish cultural identity as a factor of the text, its context and intertexts. In particular, we will look at the ways in which Martin McDonagh uses and engages with stereotypical images of Irish identity, especially religion and Catholicism, to expose and challenge assumptions about nationalism and to provide an ironic narrative on Irish stereotyping and the fluidity of national distinctiveness.

In many ways this must appear to be a perverse choice, given the rich variety of films made in recent years that are more obviously oriented towards Irish heritage, politics and society; just a few examples of which are *The Wind that Shakes the Barley* (Loach, 2006), *Garage* (Abrahamson, 2007), *Kisses* (Daly, 2008) and *The Secret of Kells* (Moore, 2009). What *In Bruges* offers as a case study, however, is the opportunity precisely to explore the tensions and contradictions inherent in the concept of national cinema. Writing about "The Instability of the National" Andrew Higson points out that "[i]n recent debates about identity, culture and nation, concepts such as instability and transnationality have come very much to the fore, with key metaphors now travel and mobility, liminality and the diasporic, marginality and the hybrid" (2000a: 38). These themes are obvious in this film in which criminals with Irish backgrounds arrive in Bruges from London and exist in a state of uncertainty in a world that is Belgian in setting but populated by English-speaking characters.

As is indicated by its title, this film is absolutely rooted in a specific location,[1] the architectural and cultural splendour of the town providing an incongruous backdrop for the amoral activities of the characters (verbal aggression, physical violence, drug abuse, racism, prostitution, illegal trade in firearms, theft and murder). In order to achieve this effect the film was shot on location, although it was produced by Focus Features, the speciality division of Hollywood studio Universal, and a number of British companies including Film4. The unstable and transnational identity of the text and context are consistent with the work of writer-director Martin McDonagh, a Londoner with Irish parents (who have now returned to live in County Galway), whose considerable reputation as a dramatist was established by five Irish-set plays that have garnered critical acclaim in America, Britain and Ireland. Although these are conventionally structured and utilise customary and highly recognisable Irish theatrical locations and characters, he does create situations which splinter and explode traditional theatrical form.

For example, the grimy and desolate torture scene in *Lieutenant of Inishmore* (2001) is arguably more influenced by Quentin Tarantino and the American gangster film genre than Irish theatrical tradition. Whilst his plays are peppered with intertextual references to Irish theatre, they also recall American drama such as that by David Mamet (another playwright-screenwriter-film director) and the work of absurdist British dramatist Harold Pinter[2]. This melange of influences confuses the somewhat

---

[1] It is interesting to note that all of Martin McDonagh's play titles (with the exception of *The Pillowman*) include references to locations–*The Beauty Queen of Leenane*, *A Skull in Connemara*, *The Lonesome West*, *The Cripple of Inishmaan*, *The Lieutenant of Inishmore* and *A Behanding in Spokane*–and this tendency is clearly also evident in *In Bruges*. This highlighting of geographical space draws audiences' attention to the question of place and landscape, and invites critics to view his work within a spatial framework although, of course, he also fractures and disrupts singular or simplistic images of nation or place with his preoccupation with global images and destabilising of stereotypes.

[2] The similarities between *In Bruges* and Pinter's *The Dumb Waiter* (1960) are clear. In both narratives, two male hitmen wait for instructions for their next target and while they kill time they discuss seemingly trivial matters. After instructions from their employer it seems as if the older colleague is instructed to murder his younger partner. Both film and play end without narrative closure, and so it is

restrictive categorisation of the plays as either "Irish" or not, and Martin McDonagh's own biography feeds into this unstable relationship between nation and drama. Thematic ambivalence around cultural identity therefore forms a point of continuity between *In Bruges* and the previous theatrical work of its writer-director. Although this chapter will comment on the film in connection to the plays, the aim here is also to consider how it relates to and reflects upon cinema as a national and international medium[3]. A fascinating point of comparison for the purposes of this analysis is provided by *The Guard* (2011), a film written and directed by Martin McDonagh's brother, John Michael.

Set in County Galway in the west of Ireland, *The Guard* stars Brendan Gleeson (who also plays Ken, one of *In Bruges*' hitmen) as an unruly Garda, Sergeant Gerry Boyle, whose highly individual and ethically dubious approach to policing the rural community, not to mention conducting his personal affairs, causes friction with FBI agent Wendell Everett, when the investigation of international drug smuggling necessitates international collaboration. The film explores Irish culture through interactions between locals and outsider characters,[4] given that "difference is constitutive of identity" (Morley & Robins, 2006: 294), and deliberately draws on and plays with the landscape, language, politics, customs and stereotypes of the country for comic effect. With this emphasis in terms of location, characters and subject matter it is not surprising that *The Guard*, like the other Irish films mentioned above, was supported by the national film development agency, Bord Scannán nah Éireann / the Irish Film Board (IFB). At the level of state media policy the concept of national cinema has clear definitional value as a means to differentiate film products, promote cultural difference and lay claim to critical/commercial success (Higson, 2000b: 69-70).

---

unclear if they actually are killed at the end. These similarities are explored at length by Lance Norman in his 2009 essay "Dumb Waiters, Dead Children and Martinizing the Pinteresque" in *Pinter Et Cetera*, Ed. Craig N. Owens. Newcastle: Cambridge Scholars Publishing.

[3] In the context of this chapter we will be concentrating on the system of English-language film production and distribution dominated by Hollywood. This is not intended to elide the fact that other film industries and cultures are in operation around the world.

[4] Higson's point that "the contingent communities that cinema imagines are much more likely to be either local or transnational than national" (2000b: 73) applies to *The Guard*, as there are Irish as well as foreign incomers to the local community depicted.

Simon Perry CBE was chief executive of the IFB during the period when both *In Bruges* and *The Guard* were made (outside and within the organisation's aegis respectively) and he generously agreed to share his professional insights with the authors for the benefit of this chapter. Perry's own career provides a useful illustration in this context of the complexity of the international film industry. He is a British producer whose work includes the adaptation of Orwell's *Nineteen Eighty-Four* (Radford, 1984). Prior to his involvement with the IFB, Perry headed British Screen, which financed films such as *Orlando* (Potter, 1992) and *Hilary and Jackie* (Tucker, 1998). His current role is president of Ateliers du Cinéma Européen (ACE), a Paris-based organisation that trains and supports independent European film producers, and he is also a member of the British Screen Advisory Council. As someone committed to sustaining alternatives to Hollywood, Perry defines the job of a national film agency as "a cultural aim, a set of objectives, on behalf of the country's artists and the visibility of the country's own culture around the world".

Martin McDonagh benefitted from the support of the IFB in making the transition from one medium to another. The agency financed his first foray into cinema, the short film *Six Shooter* (2004), a tragic-comic story of a bereaved man (also played by Brendan Gleeson) on a traumatic train journey in Ireland, which won the debut director an Academy Award. The critical acclaim received by *Six Shooter* established Martin McDonagh "as not just a playwright of high repute but a very interesting new filmmaker" (Perry, 2012). It also illustrates why national film bodies invest in the short cinematic form, which has a very limited commercial market of film festivals, DVD collections and television. As Perry explains, "short filmmaking is based very much on the principle that you hope you're identifying and giving a first start to interesting people. In the case of Martin there was no question that that happened". Although the director went on to build his profile within the international film industry by making *In Bruges* without the involvement of the IFB, Irish culture is made visible in this film by its stars, Brendan Gleeson and Colin Farrell.

Perry points out that these two actors are very popular in Ireland as bearers of national identity. Although internationally associated with roles in high budget global film products,[5] their national profiles are, in Perry's view, rooted in performances in Irish films like *The General* (Boorman, 1998) and *Intermission* (Crowley, 2003). Equally important to fuelling the

---

[5] Gleeson is probably best known for playing Mad-Eye Moody in three parts of the *Harry Potter* franchise, and Farrell for *Minority Report* (Spielberg, 2002), *Alexander* (Stone, 2004), *Miami Vice* (Mann, 2008) and most recently *Total Recall* (Wiseman, 2012).

impression of Irish cultural ownership of these international film stars, according to Perry, is a feeling of proximity. Gleeson is a familiar figure within public and artistic life and "there's no-one else in Ireland who has the adored star power"; and Farrell, despite his relocation to Hollywood, is still identified as a Dubliner, "their boy". This sense of presence, of being part of the community, is not something strongly associated with the McDonagh brothers as cultural figures hailing from and based in London. Bearing this in mind it is interesting to note that both writer-directors present gangster villains with cockney accents, who act as critical reflections on English identity.[6]

Both *In Bruges* and *The Guard* revolve around a central working relationship between two male characters, criminals in the former and lawmen in the latter, one of whom is played in each case by Brendan Gleeson. Indeed, there are similarities between the roles of Ken and Boyle in terms of narrative trajectories and character traits. Both are shown to be morally reprehensible in the sense that they deliberately engage in illegal activities, but both also display clear personal principles, including loyalty and care. A particularly poignant gesture is Ken's scattering of small change to ensure that his suicidal plunge from the tower does not harm innocent bystanders. This act, like Boyle's one-man assault on the drug traffickers supported only by covering fire from Wendell, is ultimately a self-sacrificial gesture motivated by a particular code of conduct and sense of integrity. Despite the parallels, however, it would be simplistic to argue that Boyle is a straightforward emulation of Ken, although the casting of Gleeson obviously establishes an intertextual connection. A Garda character called Gerry also appears in John Michael's short film *The Second Death* (2000; also supported by the IFB), included as an extra on

[6] Harry, the violent gang boss in *In Bruges*, adheres doggedly to a code of honour that requires that Ray must die because he accidentally killed a child. His view is "if I'd killed a little kid, accidentally or otherwise, I wouldn't've thought twice, I'd've killed myself on the fucking spot!". As a version of English "good form" this uncompromising position is the cause of Harry's downfall, when he takes his own life believing that he has shot a schoolboy in the course of trying to kill Ray. Of course, the hollowness of this self-destructive gesture on the part of a homicidal maniac is underlined by the fact that he has actually killed the adult dwarf actor Jimmy, who was dressed as a schoolboy. The character of Clive Cornell in *The Guard* is similarly high-handed, and his superior attitude is attributed by those around him to his national identity. Sheehy-Skelfington is incensed when Cornell nominates Bertrand Russell as his favourite philosopher because "low and behold, he's fucking English". When Cornell silences this criticism by pointing out that "Bertrand Russell was Welsh", his self-satisfied smirk suggests that he is indeed condescending.

the DVD of *The Guard*, the packaging of which states that he is "an earlier incarnation" of Inspector Gerry Stanton (both are played by Gary Lydon), but also "a prototype for" Sergeant Boyle.

The Production Notes that promote *The Guard* present it as a film that had a lengthy genesis dating back to *The Second Death*, inspired by the character Gerry who had "percolated" in the writer-director's mind ever since (6). John Michael's directorial debut, which screened at the Galway Film Festival in 2000, does not appear to have functioned as a professional springboard in the same way that *Six Shooter* did for Martin. In the eleven years between the release of the short film and the release of the feature film John Michael wrote the screenplay for *Ned Kelly* (Jordan, 2003), but did not gain further experience as a director. Without the status accorded to Martin as a successful playwright and Academy Award winning director, Perry explains that John Michael faced a greater challenge securing the financing necessary to make his first feature[7]. Thus it seems that *The Second Death* did not serve to establish a track record for John Michael as a marketable commodity. As an Irish story though *The Guard* had a natural ally in the IFB and the national agency was involved in the production process "right from the start, very involved in fact, and supported it very strongly" (Perry). Of course, the concept of an "Irish story" is not one which can be understood simply or singularly, as we will discuss later.

Other sources of funding were necessary in order for *The Guard* to be produced and key film industry figures played a part in attracting this financial backing. The Hollywood star Don Cheadle not only took the role of Wendell, he also acted as an executive producer, getting involved with the project before it had "a home" in order to "help get it made" (Production Notes, 6). Martin McDonagh was another of the film's executive producers, a move that Perry thinks "was designed to help the project and to give people confidence in John" on the basis that "Martin as a filmmaker carries commercially a lot of weight". In this sense the relationship between the brothers served pragmatic purposes, but it is also possible to discern thematic and stylistic links between their bodies of work, most notably in the way in which both writers engage with Irish stereotypes or sensitive topics in Irish politics or history. Interestingly, John Michael's film seems closer to Martin's theatrical oeuvre than *In*

---

[7] It is worth noticing the difference in the estimated budgets of *In Bruges* and *The Guard*: $15million and $6million respectively (http://www.imdb.com/title/tt0780536/ and http://www.imdb.com/title/tt1540133/ accessed on 8/11/12), indicative of different levels of commercial support for the projects.

Bruges itself is. The use of irreverent humour and distinctive syntax is a shared feature, and both also make use of rural Irish settings in which insider knowledge of the insular local community is crucial. There are also some more specific resonances.

Eugene Moloney, the boy who discovers the guns in *The Guard*, is always seen riding a pink girl's bicycle, an image which appears to mirror one from *The Lieutenant of Inishmore*, in which we see an adolescent boy with a bike described as "pink, with small wheels and a basket" (McDonagh, 2001: 5). The drug traffickers of *The Guard* also seem to have been inspired by the same play, as the scene in which they debate philosophy in the film has much in common with the INLA terrorists in *The Lieutenant of Inishmore*, and their discussion about Marx (McDonagh, 2001: 27). Other notable similarities include the discussion about ugly babies, in which Boyle responds to Wendell's comment that his joke was rude with the remark, "maybe it is and maybe it isn't", suggesting a lack of clarity in moral reflection. In *The Beauty Queen of Leenane*, Mag tells Maureen that her dream of her mother's funeral is mean to which she replies, "I don't know if it is or it isn't" (McDonagh, 1999: 16), which would seem to offer a similar vagueness in ethical clarity.

When Wendell goes house to house alone to make enquiries he is met with a Gaelic speaking couple (one of whom is called Bartley, which is also a character name from *The Cripple of Inishmaan*), and they berate him (though he is, of course, uncomprehending of this) for asking if they speak English when they are in Ireland. This discussion parallels one from *The Beauty Queen of Leenane*, in which Maureen criticises her mother for complaining about Gaelic on the radio, asking her what country she lives in and telling her "it's Irish you should be speaking in Ireland" (McDonagh, 1999: 4). Another direct reference from this play occurs when the young boy in *The Guard* complains to Boyle, suggesting his supposed mistreatment at the hands of the police is like the Birmingham Six. This is mirrored in Ray's complaint in the play that the police broke his toes. When no-one believes him he exclaims, "Isn't that how the Birmingham Six went down?" (McDonagh, 1999: 53). This subversive humour is potentially offensive and is used by both writers to expose Irish national "sacred cows" as potential sites for misunderstanding and misquoting (and thus rendered politically impotent). A final specific similarity is the debate in *The Guard* about homosexuals in the IRA and a similar discussion in *The Lieutenant of Inishmore* (McDonagh, 2001: 33).

Arguing more widely, both writers also have a rather ambiguous attitude to women and certainly focus most closely on masculine experience. In *The Guard*, the images of women as prostitutes resonate strongly, and the familiar Catholic virgin/whore dichotomy is rehearsed here as Gabriela McBride and Eileen Boyle (roles of wife and mother respectively) offer a counterpoint for Boyle's encounters with the only other two women in the film[8]. Interestingly, in our interview, Perry reveals that the character of Boyle's mother was nearly cut from the film. To do so would have been, in his view and ours, "absolutely fatal" because the interactions between mother and son form "part of the reason that you love him [Boyle]" as a character. To have taken these slower paced, but lovingly written and filmed, scenes out would eradicate a very touching aspect of the film, and yet further diminish the role of women in the narrative, which is, already "absolutely a man's world view" (Perry)[9].

A final point of comparison between the two writers comes not from Martin's Irish work, but his most recent play, *A Behanding in Spokane* (2010), which is set in the US. The play bristles with the sort of racial tension we see highlighted in *The Guard*, as a central character makes explicitly racist remarks, along the lines of Boyle's impression that only black men could be drug dealers. Although this is obviously a knowingly crass joke in *The Guard*, with Boyle being deliberately provoking in order to attract Wendell's attention, it is clear in the play that these comments are meant more seriously[10]. Another parallel between Martin's play and John's film is suggested by the endings of the two plots. Both leave the protagonists in an open ended narrative, either engulfed in flames or about to be so, and it is far from clear whether or not they survive. This refusal to provide closure leaves the narratives with poignant and suggestive endings, and this is exploited to full effect in *The Guard* as Wendell remembers Boyle fondly and we are left to wonder if it might have been possible for him to survive, and whether his actions were "really motherfucking dumb, or really motherfucking smart".

A Behanding in Spokane, like *In Bruges* before it, sees Martin McDonagh moving away from the Irish narrative context that so strongly characterises his earlier stage writing and his brother's feature film. This is

---

[8] There is a similar binary representation of women in *In Bruges*, with the pregnant and respectable Maria contrasting with Chloe, who seduces tourists so that her "boyfriend" can rob them, and the prostitutes hired by Jimmy.

[9] This masculine environment is also a feature of *In Bruges*, and in both films women are portrayed as vulnerable to male violence. There is dialogue in each case about the unacceptability of men hitting women, but this is motivated by the fact that female characters are shown to fall victim to attack, in "self defence" (*In Bruges*) and as a result of criminal intimidation (*The Guard*).

[10] Of course, racial tensions are also explored in *In Bruges* as well, most memorably in the scene involving "two manky hookers and a racist dwarf".

not to say, however, that Martin McDonagh's work is no longer concerned with Irish identity. *In Bruges* explores the relationship between signifiers and stereotypes of Irish identity. However, as the film is not actually located in Ireland, Martin McDonagh uses tropes associated with Irish identity to discuss the ways in which national identity can be created or evoked through images and symbols. This is played out with an engagement with Catholicism. At the outset of the film, Ray makes it clear that the botched assassination in which he killed "them", by which he means a priest and a young boy,[11] takes place in London. This event is depicted in flashback, later in the film, and the location is described in the screenplay as a "Catholic Church". This setting is supposedly London but feels Irish in every respect, causing the viewer to feel a disjuncture between the voiceover connecting this event to London and the images they are now faced with. Father McHenry, who is shot by Ray, is also played by the Irish actor Ciarán Hinds. Whilst there is a large Catholic community in London, the choice of the overtly Irish milieu in this scene seems intriguing. Indeed, it is only the beginning of a series of meditations about Catholicism that run through the film.

Ray and Ken visit the Basilica of the Holy Blood, ornately decorated with religious iconography and gothic crucifixes, and discuss the relic of the blood. They also visit an art gallery, and are particularly transfixed by various medieval paintings depicting a series of saintly deaths. They focus on Bosch's *Last Judgment*, which is surreally recreated in the final moments of the film as Ray contemplates death. They discuss various aspects of Catholic doctrine such as "who gets into Heaven and who gets into Hell and all that" and Ray fixates on questions of "the afterlife and guilt and sins and Hell". Realising he is referring to the murder of the little boy, Ken discusses religion with him, and Ray says that he was brought up Catholic and argues that "the things you're taught as a child never really leave do they?". The most striking Catholic image is the hotel owner's

[11] This particular combination of victims seems also to link the incident to the child abuse scandal that surrounds the Catholic Church in Ireland (and other parts of the world). There is a scene cut from the final edit of the film, but included on the DVD as an extra feature, in which Ray and Ken lie in their beds in the hotel room (a sleeping arrangement reminiscent of *Father Ted*, the Channel 4 comedy series about Irish priests) and discuss the circumstances of the shooting. Ray comments that he assumed the hit on Father McHenry "was some paedophile thing" and Ken explains that it was actually because the priest was "on the action committee" opposing their boss' housing development. The removal of this narrative information from the film means that there is ambiguity around the relationship between religion and morality.

wife Marie, (clearly a synonym for the Madonna) who is heavily pregnant. In a brief but touching scene, Ken looks over into her living quarters and watches her decorating a Christmas tree whilst softly speaking to her unborn child. The Catholic imagery and association is clear; Our Lady's Church in Bruges holds the only Michelangelo statue to have left Italy–a depiction of the Madonna and Child. Such religious iconography peppers the film, and creates a concrete link between the Catholic Belgium and Ray's religious upbringing in Dublin. This connection would not be possible if filmed in London; the somber and gothic imagery of Bruges communicates to the ornate Catholic Church in the flashback scene and the exposition of Ray's mortal crime. The film's meditation on sin, death and hell creates a connection between Ireland and Belgium which must bypass Protestant London.

Images of Ireland thus seem to haunt the film, despite, or perhaps because of, its European setting. A hybrid space is created; a place negotiated between Ireland and Belgium. To use Homi Bhabha's words, "the production of meaning requires that these two places be mobilized in the passage through Third space" (1994: 36) and "[i]t is that Third Space, though unrepresentable in itself, which constitutes the discursive conditions of enunciation that ensure that the meaning and symbols of culture have no primordial unity of fixity; that even the same signs can be appropriated, translated, rehistoricized and read anew" (1994: 37). Furthermore, *In Bruges* presents us with images of religion both medieval and modern. Twentieth-century images of Christianity are recycled through popular culture and present themselves to characters in mediated form. Harry calls Ken "Robert fucking Powell out of *Jesus of* fucking *Nazareth*" when confronted with Ken's self-sacrificing behaviour. His allusion to mass media representations of religion suggests that "[t]his scene does not allude to Jesus as an authentic figure, but refers to a popular media portrayal, and the values for which he stands are communicated by actors" (Rouse, 2011: 178). A mediated third space is thus required by these characters to make their engagement with religion and identity meaningful[12].

Despite the Belgian setting, Martin McDonagh is certainly engaging with images of stereotypical Irish identity. He has explicitly identified *In Bruges* as "not caring about the American market–saying, you know, in an Irish anarchistic way, 'I don't care about government or nationalism,' splurging with a kind of Pogues-like anger, using then subverting the

[12] American cultural identity exists in a mediated third space in *The Guard*; characters repeatedly assume that Wendell must be engaged in criminal profiling, in keeping with popular television depictions of FBI activity.

form" (quoted in Lonergan, 2012: 136-7). Encapsulated in this description is the paradoxical nature of the film, the desire to undermine concepts of national identity by directly calling upon them. This characterisation of the film as Irish in essence is at odds with its international production context in terms of funding, filming location and performers[13]. In this respect *In Bruges* is in complete contrast to *Six Shooter*, which was made and set in Ireland, with IFB backing and an Irish cast. Three of the actors from Martin's short film–Lydon, David Wilmot and David Pearce–appear in *The Guard* as well, and there is also crossover between the casts of John Michael's two films (Lydon, Wilmot, Liam Cunningham and Owen Sharpe). In this sense it is possible to identify a company of Irish actors that both the McDonagh brothers have drawn on in the course of their filmmaking[14].

Perry points out that "Irish audiences do respond to Irish actors in the right thing" and in the case of *The Guard* it seems that there was a successful conjunction of performers and material. For the IFB as an agency investing Irish public money in films it is important that those films "build and sustain an image of the country" (Perry), but this does not necessarily translate into popularity within Ireland. Ruth Barton writes that "few Irish films have made any significant impression at the Irish box office" (2004: 107) and argues that this is because they "tend to be tagged with the 'arthouse' label" (2004: 108). Perry echoes this view, commenting that Irish audiences often think Irish films are "going to be small and dark and not so interesting". This is not to say, however, that the film market in Ireland is limited; Perry stresses that "the number of visits per head of population is very impressive" but that this interest "is overwhelmingly for mainstream Hollywood films". Consequently what was particularly attractive about *The Guard* for him was his confidence

---

[13] *In Bruges* seems in some ways to play with and offer a warped reflection of the global film culture from which it emerges by means of reference to the blockbuster *Harry Potter* films. Ken, Harry and Chloe can be seen as extreme versions of the character types–mentor, villain and siren–played by the same actors in the Warner Brothers family franchise. In one of *In Bruges*'s deleted scenes the young Harry is shown swiftly dispatching a character named Potter (by decapitation), something that his counterpart Voldemort famously never manages.

[14] Indeed the relationships extend into Martin McDonagh's theatre work too. Lydon and Sharpe were in Nicholas Hytner's National Theatre production of *The Cripple of Inishmaan*, which opened in December 1996. Wilmot and Sharpe were in the cast of the first production of *The Lieutenant of Inishmore* at the RSC, The Other Place, in 2001. When that play was on Broadway in 2006 the role of Davey, previously played by Sharpe, was performed by Domhnall Gleeson, who appears alongside his father Brendan in *Six Shooter*.

that the film "would do something that Irish films were having great difficulty doing, which is appealing to Irish audiences". As suggested earlier, *The Guard* appeals to Irish audiences largely because it tells an "Irish story" and explicitly engages with Irish history, tradition, locations and stereotypes (albeit within the framework of a more traditional Hollywood crime thriller). These factors are exaggerated in the film for comic effect, and much of the film problematises the way in which shorthanded approaches to nationalism lead to prejudice and misunderstanding. It is hardly surprising that critiques of Irish stereotyping are popular with Irish film-goers, and Martin McDonagh's plays also found an enthusiastic audience in Ireland.

The logo of the IFB features people silhouetted against a screen, so appeal to an audience is implicit in their activities. This was particularly pronounced in regards to their involvement in *The Guard*, Perry explains, because they provided a large amount of additional funding over and above their normal maximum investment on the basis of the Irish market, which they carved out as niche revenue. Perry says "if I'm pleased, relieved, proud of one thing leaving the Irish Film Board just over a year ago it's that I did leave them this very nice legacy because the film worked so well in Ireland that all that money came back plus an enormous profit". Indeed, although *In Bruges* grossed nearly twice as much globally,[15] Irish Box office figures indicate that *The Guard* made about €1million more there, €4million in total[16]. In this sense it is clear that John Michael's film represents "indigenous cultural tradition" by depicting the locality in which it is performed (Higson, 2000a: 36).

Bruges offers Martin McDonagh a very different opportunity to explore place in relation to cultural identity. It is a blank canvas, a location devoid of previous cinematic depiction and manufacture. Indeed, this fact is made explicit through the self-referential feature of a film being shot within the film; Chloe actually remarks "[t]here's never been a classic movie made in Bruges, until now". In the DVD extras documentary, Martin McDonagh says there is an interesting conflict in the film between the whimsical location and the bloody gangster story. He argues that it is a location new to such narratives, and is free from associations of settings such as New York or London, where cinematic backdrops to gangster

---

[15] http://www.boxofficemojo.com/movies/?id=inbruges.htm and http://www.boxofficemojo.com/movies/?page=main&id=guard.htm accessed on 19/11/12.

[16] http://www.iftn.ie/distribution/boxoffice/irishboxoffice2008/?hl=in+bruges and http://www.iftn.ie/distribution/boxoffice/Irishweeklyboxoffice2011/irishboxoffice16-18september2011/ accessed on 19/11/12.

plots are more commonplace. This blank canvas can be populated with both national and international images, and these allusions ask the audience to consider the meaning of national distinctiveness. In his plays, Martin McDonagh makes frequent references to global products, international soap operas and American films; in this film too he uses global companies to fracture and disassociate the location with any place in particular. Ray mentions going to Burger King in London, they visit an Irish bar in Belgium, and Ray decides learning any specific European language is pointless as everyone speaks English. Furthermore, Ray tells Harry he had dinner at Pizza Hut, and that it was the same as in England because "that's globalisation". In a global world where Pizza Hut is the same the world over, national distinctiveness is undermined and simplistic generalisations about national culture are ridiculed.

International imagery destabilizes the singularity of national experience. It suggests that you need not travel to distinct locations; rather you are able to enjoy all global products in any global location. As geographer David Harvey pointed out, globalisation can be thought of as a "time-space compression" (1990) in which experiences can be simultaneously encountered in ways that belie the real geographical distances involved. However, it's worth reflecting on what might be lost in translation; whereas there certainly are pubs in Ireland, they frequently bear little resemblance to the numerous "Irish" bars found across the world (as Kathleen Heininge points out in this volume). What are often recycled are the stereotypical and simplistic images of national identity. So if Irish pubs are found the world-over perhaps that helps nourish a mythology about the Irish and their fondness for drinking. In *The Guard* there are widely recognisable images of Ireland perpetuated, like a confessional and a pub in which a ceilidh band plays, but these are complicated by some subtleties of representation. There are tensions throughout between the "big city boys" and Boyle as a provincial Garda (and the gentle mocking of characters from Dublin). Whereas the convention "in a number of Irish films" is that "country accents" mark out the Gardaí "as figures of fun" (Barton, 2004: 185), this film inverts that by demonstrating Boyle's (sometimes) superior intellect, integrity and professional aptitude.

In *In Bruges* Ray and Ken indulge in some stereotyping of American tourists; Ray advises some overweight Americans not to climb the bell tower and Ray tells Jimmy he will overlook his nationality so long as he does not say anything "too loud or crass". This is also found in *The Guard*, as the Irish are represented as laid back and instinctive (Boyle seems to have an innate knowledge and understanding of policing and the community) whereas the American Wendell is portrayed as uptight and rule-bound, struggling to connect with the environment and people around him. Of course, in *In Bruges* the superficiality of Ray's assumptions about nationality are made laughably obvious when it is revealed that the "Yankee fucking cunt" who he attacks in the course of an argument about intercultural arrogance, justifying his action with the comment "that's for John Lennon", is in fact a Canadian, a misapprehension that led to the escalation of their animosity in the first place.

Both McDonaghs create worlds in which national images, stereotypes and prejudices are either destabilised or mocked. The fact that their films depict characters out of their natural environment (Irish men in Belgium and an American in Ireland) helps accentuate the contrast (or celebrate the similarities) between national identity and popular prejudices. Travel allows for a global tourism and for anyone to pick and "sample" another culture. In *The Guard* Wendell is aghast to hear that Boyle's only experience of America was a trip to Disneyworld by himself; a commodified fantasy, the highlight of which was a "picture taken with Goofy". Through travel Ray and Ken are able to visit Belgium and experience its culture, but what they actually encounter is as subject to partiality as images celebrating the mythologised Irish are. Interestingly, throughout the film, the location feels resolutely Belgium, and no globalised images are depicted. In fact, Bruges is showcased and its major landmarks form the central location for the action. Yet, at the same time, that action represents a literal and symbolic assault on the customary locations and routines of the tourist experience, as criminal violence erupts in public leisure spaces of restaurant, hotel and visitor attraction.

The seeming conflict in the film between global images and a distinct national location can be seen as temporal as well as spatial. Margitta Rouse argues that *In Bruges* "destabilizes the binary opposition between the medieval past and the postmodern future" (2011: 172). In fact, we could argue that the characters enjoy a partial and stereotypical view of Bruges and that this experience is clearly old-fashioned, consisting of mainly medieval iconography. The global images Martin McDonagh peppers the film with (through dialogue rather than visual imagery) are part of the postmodern frame; they complicate the simplistic tourist experience Ray and Ken encounter. They also offer an example of mediation–global tourism demands images that can be understood easily and quickly, so the hitmen try to explain their experience of Bruges through contemporary products. Both are doomed to failure; the mediated version is simplistic and so is the "old-fashioned" tourist experience. Both package a geographical location for quick global consumption, and in this film there is therefore little distinction made between Pizza Hut and Bosch's *Last Judgement*.

Theatre director Garry Hynes describes Martin McDonagh's filmic and theatrical career as "perched on the cusp of two cultures… He's Irish, but also from South London. He feels no need to kneel at his heritage's shrine" (quoted in Nightingale, 1998). The use of religious imagery here too is interesting; Hynes is suggesting that Martin McDonagh's work does not pay homage to Irish imagery, either cultural or religious. Whilst he may not be reverent in his approach to Irish traditions, he certainly does not reject them outright; even *In Bruges* constantly reflects and muses upon Irish imagery. Indeed, Martin McDonagh's work, as is often claimed, uses Irish tradition in subversive, playful and parodic ways, and his international success as a playwright and film director is thus a confusing and complicated question. His image of Ireland is neither comforting nor sentimental yet he never abandons interrogation of Irish culture and heritage, even when setting a film in Bruges.

To return to Homi Bhabha, perhaps his description of mimicry is pertinent. Mimicry describes a negotiation in power between colonial forces whereby the colonized might start to mimic their oppressors in "an exaggerated copying of language, culture, manners, and ideas" (Huddart, 2006: 57). This constitutes a form of comic mockery and a resistance to the colonial power. Through mimicry, the image of the coloniser's stable identity is undermined and compromised because parodic representations of their behaviour are adopted and challenged. The effect of this is that identities are seen to be unstable and changeable: "The colonizer has no absolute pre-existent identity which can be mimicked, and the colonized likewise has no real identity which he or she is betraying through mimicry" (Huddart, 2006: 71) and "[m]imicry suggests that our construction of identity is necessarily fluid and imaginary" (Huddart, 2006:70). Indeed, the "discourse of mimicry is constructed around an ambivalence" and is an "ironic compromise" because it represents that which is "almost the same, *but not quite*… Mimicry marginalises the monumentality of history, mocks its power to be a model... It repeats rather than represents" (Bhabba, 1994: 86). Martin McDonagh's repetition of Irish imagery, through theatre and film, ensures it is an ironic commentary on colonial history. In exploring the extent of Irish commodification, Martin McDonagh may be contributing to it, but this double bind enforces his position as a hybrid and diasporic figure creating mimetic images of a recycled Ireland.

Bhabha's description of colonial power exchanges reminds us that national distinctiveness is a myth and that fixed national borders do not exist. Hybridity rejects the concept that nations are singular and when we apply this approach to national cinema it becomes increasingly difficult to pin down characteristics we might expect to see in "Irish" films. Lance Pettitt characterises Irish cinema as "a cinema that no longer aspires to attain a unitary form of national culture and which questions the validity of this definition of national project" (2000, 44); *In Bruges* and *The Guard* certainly appear to be more interested in probing the complexities and limits of Irish identity than in promoting a particular national myth. While John Michael does this within an Irish narrative and production context (maintained in his current project *Calvary*),[17] Martin's work is increasingly distanced from Ireland[18]. His new film *Seven Psychopaths*, which is (at the time of writing) about to be released in the UK, is a British production set in Los Angeles about a struggling screenwriter and featuring a number of recognisable Hollywood actors; and yet there remains an Irish presence in the form of Colin Farrell and the character he plays.

Despite the fact that their work is differently situated, both McDonaghs very consciously employ Irish imagery, tropes and stereotypes in their work. We may use Bhabha's concept of hybridity to explore their approach to Irish culture in their filmmaking; the McDonagh brothers are both Irish and British, and therefore their own identities transcend a singular definition. Although their fascination with Irish identity can perhaps be explained in commercial terms, as Perry acknowledges "the Irish love […] historical stuff, they love their culture on screen" and "Irish work can sometimes just appeal particularly to an American taste and sensibility", it is also fair to say that what makes a distinctly "Irish" film is impossible to pin down, and the concept defers final definition. In this chapter, our analysis of *In Bruges* and *The Guard* has applied "a flexible interpretive approach that focuses on immediate circumstances without feeling the need to apply an overarching theory of unified causes" (Gillespie, 2008: xiv). Both films can be identified as engaging with Irish cultural identity, in different ways and for different reasons, but they are also international and global products, and as such represent a postmodern engagement with the "imagined community" of contemporary Ireland.

---

[17] This film, written and directed by John Michael, is currently in post-production for release in 2013. It is about a priest, played by Brendan Gleeson, and is being made with the support of the IFB.

[18] This migration in Martin's film career away from Ireland to "British, American and mainland European filmmaking where, it appears, the opportunities are greater" mirrors that of many others; including "the foremost auteurs of Irish film culture", Neil Jordan and Jim Sheridan (Barton, 179).

Acknowledgements

The authors wish to thank Simon Perry for his time in conducting an interview with us and for sharing his invaluable insights.

Bibliography

Barton, Ruth. *Irish National Cinema*. London; New York: Routledge, 2004.

Bhabha, Homi K. *The Location of Culture*. London and New York: Routledge, 1994.

Gillespie, Michael Patrick. *The Myth of an Irish Cinema: Approaching Irish-Themed Films*. Syracuse: Syracuse University Press, 2008.

Harvey, David. *The Condition of Postmodernity*. Cambridge: Blackwell. 1990.

Higson, Andrew. "The Instability of the National" in Ashby and Higson (eds) *British Cinema, Past and Present* London: Routledge, 2000a, pp. 35-47.

—. "The Limiting Imagination of National Cinema" in Hjort, Mette and Scott Mackenzie, (eds), *Cinema and Nation*. London: Routledge, 2000b, pp. 63-74.

Huddart, David. *Homi K. Bhabha*, London and New York, Routledge, 2006.

Lonergan, Patrick. *The Theatre and Films of Martin McDonagh*. London: Methuen, 2012.

McDonagh, Martin. *The Beauty Queen of Leenane* in *Plays One*. London: Methuen. 1999.

—. *The Lieutenant of Inishmore*. London: Methuen. 2001.

Morley, David and Kevin Robins, "Spaces of Identity: Communication Technologies and the Reconfiguration of Europe" in Valentina Vitali and Paul Willemen (eds), *Theorising National Cinema* (London: BFI, 2006), pp. 293-303.

Nightingale, Benedict. "The Sort of Renown that would make any Troupe Weep". *The New York Times*. 22/2/1998.

Perry, Simon, Personal Interview with the authors of this chapter, 2012.

Pettitt, Lance. *Screening Ireland: Film and Television Representation*. Manchester and New York: Manchester University Press, 2000.

Production Notes, *The Guard*, Optimum Releasing. DDA Public Relations, 2011.

Rouse, Margitta. "Hit Men on Holiday Get All Medieval". *European Journal of English Studies*. 15: 2, pp 171-182. 2011.

CHAPTER EIGHT

COMMUNICATING DIFFERENCE AND DEVIANCE: ETHNIC MINORITIES ON IRISH CURRENT AFFAIRS TELEVISION

SHARON LEAHY

Introduction

Ireland exhibits its national identity on the international stage in the form of its unique culture and heritage, reflecting an outward image of a mature society, secure in its own identity. However, some suggest another reality; that of a nation state struggling to adapt socially and culturally to the rapid globalising influences of the Celtic Tiger era (Hurwitz, 2001; Share et al., 2007). This represented a period of accelerated change, economic growth and increased spending power, along with a socially mobile and an increasingly individualistic society (Mac An Ghaill, 2002; Penet, 2008). The relatively new experience of sustained in-migration exposed the ambiguous nature of the nation's boast of "céad mile fáilte" (hundred thousand welcomes) and revealed an ethnic insularity amongst its people (Aniagolu, 1997, Lentin, 1999). White has dubbed this altered Irish society "retro-global", seeing "Ireland presented as a global nation, while fostering state-level and social conditions that construct isolated spaces for immigrants, regardless of level of education, class and occupation" (2002: 258). Ireland was perceived to be experiencing a crisis of identity, or what White has called a "collective multiple personality disorder" (2002: 252).

The National Action Plan against Racism (NAPR) was the manifestation of an assurance given by the Irish Government at the UN World Conference against Racism, in Durban in 2001, to examine and establish improved procedures and policies, which would better serve an increasingly multicultural society. The NAPR noted that the media played an invaluable role in making the public more conscious of the diversity of cultures, and raised awareness of ethnic discrimination on a national platform. Nevertheless, it also expressed concern of irresponsible media reporting and noted that

> a key challenge is to ensure the media continues its valuable public interest reporting and awareness role while at the same time developing appropriate and agreed mechanisms to complain and to provide redress for irresponsible reporting (Dept. of Justice et al., 2004).

Consequently, the role of the national broadcaster, RTÉ, to influence interpretation in the Irish context requires greater attention and analysis. This discussion is part of a broader study, which involved a multi-method approach incorporating content and critical discourse analysis of a two year corpus of current affairs programming (Jan 2005-Dec 2006), broadcast at the apex of the Celtic Tiger period, an online questionnaire to members of the public, an online questionnaire to NGOs who work with ethnic minorities in the Republic of Ireland, and an analysis of online discussion groups that were launched after programmes had been aired. Current affairs programmes provide an arena for the expression of public debate and have been seen to be amongst the most dominant forces influencing societal relations (Van Dijk, 1988; Leudar and Nekvapil, 2000; Mastro and Robinson, 2000; Patrona, 2006). Patrona (2006) claims that these shows are "ultimately, the mediated construction of the public sphere in contemporary western societies" (2006: 5). For this research three shows, *Prime Time*, *The Late Late Show* and *Questions & Answers*, were chosen. This study aimed to uncover ways in which discourses concerning ethnic minority groups in Ireland are portrayed in current affairs television texts, and to establish the ways in which programmes construct and impart knowledge. It is contended that images of diverse ethnic groups displayed on the screen are portrayed in support of specific politically motivated narratives, consequently creating ideologies that can influence people's belief systems. How the media depict ethnic groups may thus contribute to the ideological racist discourse.

Cultural geographers see texts as more than just the written word; they incorporate any socially constructed medium (textual, visual or aural) with the potential to be deconstructed. When television programmes are viewed as texts to be analysed in this way, they provide a vast representative record. Hartley has argued that "television is one of the prime sites upon which a given nation is constructed for its members" (1978: 124). These programmes are active discursive performances from which cultural traditions and identity traits develop and solidify. How issues are transmitted and presented determines how they are received. Knowledge that is prioritised in the media narrative identifies the issues of significance in a given society, and contributes to the development, and reiteration, of the dominant ideological discourse. Discourses of "race" and "ethnicity" portrayed through media texts have been shown to play a significant role in the development of intolerant and prejudicial ideology (Gillespie, 1995; Stupples, 2003; Dittmer, 2005; Spencer, 2006). It has been illustrated that the constant reiteration of televisual discourse triggers perceptual markers that endorse and normalise society's stereotypes.

RTÉ's public institutional narrative explicitly outlines its impartial remit, highlighting issues of equality and inclusion at all levels, suggesting an all-encompassing, impartial and unprejudiced media service. The provision of these broadcasting principles of open-mindedness and liberalism will be called into question by the data presented in this study. Each transcribed broadcast was critically evaluated, using methods of content and discourse analysis, to unveil their discursive structure and reveal the negotiation of certain identity markers with respect to ethnic minority groups. There were several major news events that occurred during the time period under study (2005-2006), which impacted on the content of the programmes; these included, i) the investigation of a number of Irish companies with respect to the discrimination of foreign workers, ii) the killing of a member of the Traveller Community, John Ward, by an Irish farmer, Padraig Nally[1], iii) issues centring around the Danish cartoons insulting Islam, and iv) calls for the banning of Muslim dress. As a result of this, at various times there was a surge in programmes centred on a common topic. Individual broadcasts were initially classified, through content analysis, into seven thematic groupings. These were then further analysed to determine the extent to which they framed ethnic minority debate. For this study, three of these frames are discussed.

[1] In October 2004 a County Mayo farmer, Padraig Nally, shot dead a member of the Traveller Community, John Ward, who had entered the yard of his home. Nally shot him twice, the second time, the fatal shot, in the back as Ward ran away. Nally was convicted of manslaughter through "excessive force" but was freed upon appeal. The verdict was celebrated by many in Irish society, who felt that Nally had reason to be fearful of members of the Travelling Community, but it was also gravely criticised by those who believed it was a criminal act embedded in prejudice and inequality.

Framing ethnic minorities on RTÉ Current Affairs Television

Frames fundamentally encase an issue and contribute to their overarching discourses; through the use of particular narratives topics are moulded within demarcated imaginative boundaries. This flow chart visualises the programme corpus on the left, the themes covered in the 31 relevant broadcasts in the centre column, while the frames are identified in the right hand column. The interconnector lines emphasise the intertwined and repetitious nature of the central frameworks.

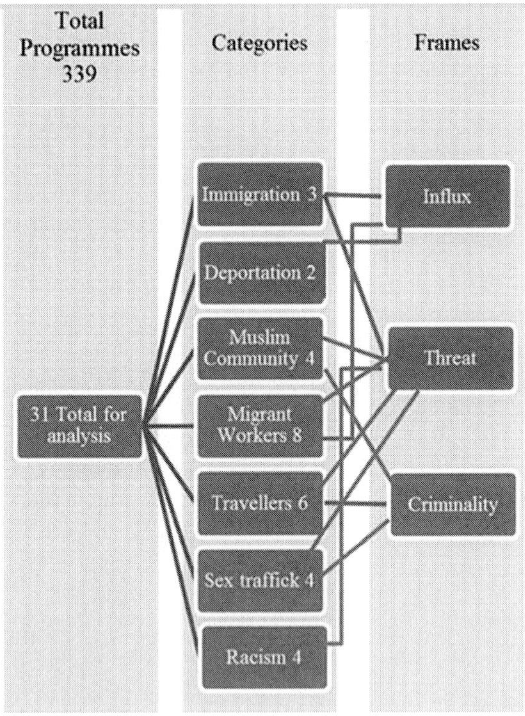

Table 8.1, Content of RTÉ programmes flowchart

The RTÉ Authority stated in 2008 that "central to RTÉ's vision of maintaining the trust of the people of Ireland is to provide news and current affairs that is impartial and fair" (RTÉ; 6). This critique provides a detailed analysis of the ways in which such information relating to minorities is presented. Language has long been seen to play a fundamental role in the dispersal of discourse, acting as a cultural tool, reflecting the world we live in using descriptive practices (Barthes, 1977). Spenser who refers to the work of Foucault, Fairclough and van Dijk, maintains that "our language itself mirrors and reproduces social divisions, at times it may serve to fix definitions or bound the debate, at others to challenge them" (2006: 9). An examination of lexical choice is central to an investigation of the representational treatment of ethnic minorities. Throughout the programmes, various discussions classified ethnic minority members in groups rather than as individuals; this strategy facilitated the formulation of "other" identities. The "majority Irish" in-group were classified as "free" (17)[2] and "Catholic" (10), while the out-group were constructed as "a danger" (26), "a threat" (25), "terrorist" (30), "criminal" (43) and "violent" (25). This strategy is reminiscent of colonial attitudes, evoking thoughts of demonization, "civilising missions" and the need for the enlightenment of the minority group. Ireland, once a nation at the thorny end of this classificatory method, was now the perpetrator. These approaches may not be immediately explicit, but they are consistent, subtle narrative mechanisms employed to tell a specific story. It is, in a sense, an obscured transgression; a "gradual slide in what is socially acceptable to say and suggest" (Haldrup et al., 2006: 176). This depicts a form of discrimination that is veiled within Irish public and everyday discourses, as issues around uniformity and sameness often prove to be more imaginative than real.

Analysis of the level of misrepresentation and under-representation in media texts pertaining to ethnic minorities is seen as a transparent marker of the levels of discrimination in mediated representations (Mahtani, 2001). Livingstone quotes Taylor (1992), stating "that misrecognition or misrepresentation can inflict harm, can be a form of oppression, imprisoning someone [or group] in a false, distorted, and reduced mode of being" (Taylor (1992) in Livingstone, 1998: 17). The voices which are heard and the voices which go unheard are a central aspect in the performance and articulation of discourse. Investigation for this study therefore, incorporated an analysis of the panel discussants on each broadcast to provide information about the representative nature of RTÉ's current affairs discussions. The interview panels on such broadcasts are usually made up of leading political and academic elites, who are perceived to hold the social power in a society, with their opinions influencing how the viewer appreciates an issue. They have been

[2] The number of occurrences of that word/phrase with the programme corpus

described as the "primary definers", dominating discursive diffusion in society (Maneri and ter Wal, 2005). Panellists are often repeated across the three programmes; a recognisable face and commonly heard name give a topic a more personable element and allows for greater identification with the narrative.

The marginalised position of ethnic minority groups in Irish society was reproduced through their lack of presence and influence in the televised debates. The guiding principles of RTÉ's government appointed charter assert that the national broadcaster should not discriminate against any group. The table below indicates that only one programme, *Prime Time Investigates*, afforded minorities with a majority voice on issues pertaining to them. While *Questions & Answers* merely placed two members of ethnic minorities groups on their debating panel, this figure contrasts significantly with the 55 majority voices that offered their opinions on topics pertaining to minorities.

Programme	Majority Panel Participation		Minority Panel Participation	
Prime Time Studio Debate	15	71%	6	29%
Prime Time Investigates	57	45%	71	55%
Questions & Answers	55	96%	2	4%
The Late Late Show	10	67%	5	33%

Table 8.2 Programme Panel Participation: numbers of participants from both majority & minority populations 2005-2006

The high number of ethnic minorities featuring in *Prime Time Investigates* broadcasts can be accounted for by the show's interviewing of various minorities throughout their filmed reports. These minority speakers frequently had their identity concealed, distancing them further from the viewer and prioritising the opinions of those who appeared fully on the screen. Regarding Traveller issues specifically, only three spokespeople have appeared on the panel discussions in the two year period; Martin Collins (Assistant Director of the Traveller Group, Pavee Point), Derek Hanaway (Director of An Munia Tober, the Traveller support organisation for Belfast) and Anne Costello (a community worker with Galway Traveller Movement). Only one of these commentators was a member of the Travelling Community. RTÉ's lack of input from ethnic minority groups was highlighted as a key issue by all 28 ethnic minority support organisations who responded to the survey for this study. It was argued that "by getting the correct and accurate information from minority groups themselves, instead of basing all their programmes on hearsay and assumptions" better and more impartial reports could be provided. It was continually reiterated that "more positive stories" need to be highlighted "in a meaningful way" (Organisation 8).

The discussions presented on Irish current affairs programmes throughout this period illustrate the utilisation of various lexical techniques. The first frame is that of influx, a common framework seen in studies of this kind. This type of debate is not a reasoned one, but rather a dialogue of fear and trepidation towards migrants and asylum applicants. Metaphors provide key cognitive frames from which reality can be imagined, offering an additional persuasive tool to facilitate symbolic representation. Their use has been shown "to simplify and make issues intelligible, to resonate with underlying symbolic representations, to stir emotions and to bridge the gap between the logical and the emotional" (Charteris-Black, 2006: 565). Metaphors of natural disaster and impending war were articulated through the use of words such as "influx" (8), "invasion" (6), and "spread" (15). These act as semantic scaffolds for the constitution of discourses of fear. Such metaphors have a significant impact on the understanding of needs for regulation and security, while also providing the under-pinning of notions of belonging and exclusion.

As Charteris-Black claims, these metaphors often serve to "discourage empathy" (2006: 569). They were generally applied in discussions about migrant workers. For example, the presenter of *Prime Time*, Miriam O'Callaghan, introduced the programme on the 18th of April 2006 stating that:

> When the European Union enlarged two years ago, Ireland was one of only three EU countries to open its borders to Eastern European workers straight away, anyone who said that decision wouldn't lead to an influx of tens of thousands of people seeking higher wages and a better life has been proved wrong.

This type of declaration covertly produces sentiments of fear, linked to the idea of border as barrier, while the reference to "influx" alludes to issues of a "floodgate being opened". It functions as a precursor to enliven and stir a debate. Such sentiment later manifested itself through the use of the word "invasion", insinuating an attack, which appeared in six instances throughout the broadcasts. Similar tactics were seen later on the same show when the Chairman of the Cork Builders Group argued that

> if you have a situation here that you have 70 million out there, and they can earn more in one week here on the minimum rate then what they can get back home in a month, well then they're going to keep heading this way, and going to keep heading this way for a long time (PT 18/04/06).

The use of such a number acts as a resounding threat of being "over-run", making it seem that a population of 70 million has the potential to come to Ireland to seek employment from one country alone. Additionally, it makes the situation of "flooding" seem like a constant, long-term threat, drawing attention to an immediate need for action. These metaphors foster images that may be linked to the establishment of doomsday scenarios, which in turn lead to widespread concerns about the burden migrants may be seen to be placing on the Irish state.

The second frame that became apparent was that of multiple threats posed by ethnic minority groups to the majority "Irish" population. This threat was often concealed within other discussions. For instance, migrant workers were viewed as "fuel" and "key supplier"(s) with a renowned "work ethic" required to "run" the Celtic Tiger economy. The reporter Donagh Diamond in his opening sequence of a *Prime Time* programme focusing on the Polish Community in Ireland, argued that "any economic boom has an almost insatiable demand for one fuel, people, and as the largest of the ten new EU member states it is Poland that is now our key supplier" (PT 08/06/06). He immediately marked the Polish community as products to "fuel" the economy, going further to stress that Polish migrants are now Ireland's "key commodity". Such a message was relayed throughout this programme, and can again be illustrated in a quote from an executive board member of the employers' union IBEC, Danny McCoy, when he claimed that the Polish Community "have a kind of characteristic that has a good work ethic" (PT 08/06/06). This serves to dehumanise the migrant and returns the debate to the idea of migrant employee as a "fuel" to run and serve Ireland. A sentiment such as this not only dis-engages the migrant from association as an equal member of Irish society, but furthermore, adds to the greater discourse that such migrants are posing a threat within Irish society to those native Irish people who may require this employment position. Overall, in this study issues centring on migrants as "fuel", "suppliers" of the economy and "cheap labourers" were discussed 21 times over six programmes. Such a sentiment broadcast in 2006 now feeds into wider demonisation of migrant workers within the post Celtic Tiger context.

Additionally, discussions were seen to regularly draw on viewers sensitivities' towards the Irish nation state, mobilising feelings of nostalgia, using, not only the challenging nature of accommodating ethnic minorities, but also problematising migrants with respect to national security. This harks back to Ireland's colonial past, striking a chord with Lentin's (1999) and Luibhéid's (2004) discussions of a renewed Irish racial state in colonialism's wake. One example of this becomes apparent from a *Question & Answers* broadcast about in-migration, when Joan Burton, a former Labour Party spokesperson on Finance, declared that "this is a very delicate issue, in which there is issues (sic) of Irish national state protection, as well as issues of being fair and just to people who come to the country" (Q & A 25/09/06). The state was positioned as a space in need of safeguarding, a rhetoric that was built upon throughout the programme corpus.

Further threatening frameworks were employed in dialogue relating to the Muslim Community, which highlighted the utilisation of hysterical and alarmist language. These lexical choices have various implications for the demonstration of Muslims as deviant and dangerous. Over five programmes the following nouns were used.

Noun	Occurrence
Terrorist (and variants)	30
Radical (and variants)	22
Extremist (and variants)	21
Violent (and variants)	6
Fanatic	2
Zealot	2

Table 8.3, Uses of extremist language on RTÉ

The extent of this rhetoric is clearly articulated by the high number of occurrences of each of these nouns in relation to one group of people. Discussions regularly promoted a connection between Islam and violent behaviour. An example of this is shown in a quote from the then Minister for Defence, Willie O'Dea, who argued that "you daren't say a word about Islam or there could be a suicide bomber sent to blow you up, or maybe a fatwa put on you, compulsory assassination now you know" (Q & A 18/09/06). Additionally, the author Richard Whelan argued that "they are fundamentally opposed to Western culture, those ideas are not being challenged by the West at any level, this is a war of ideas" (PT 18/12/06). Here we see the re-stressing of notions of barriers of difference in an altered way, highlighting ideas and beliefs that contravene "ours". This is exemplified by the word "war", which conjures notions of a need to fight against and resist these ideas. An example of this type of dialogue can be illustrated by a quote from Ian O'Doherty who stated that "there's a sickness at the heart of Islam, there's a sickness at the heart of the Middle East" (LLS 10/02/06). Not only has physical violence been insinuated, but so too have medical threats, imposing notions of apprehension in a subtler fashion. Such disease type metaphors are shown to "have a visceral appeal in that they help to convey a dangerous and darkly insidious threat" (Stares and Yacoubian, 2007: 5-6). This delivers an impression of anxiety that was often more blatantly apparent in other cases. For example, when discussing Muslim dress, Mark Dooley argued that "there was a threat within the Muslim Community to all of us" (LLS 16/09/05). Irish society is constructed as liberal and democratic, with Muslims projected as a physical threat, not only to the general public, but to Ireland's sense of nationhood and independence.

Sex trafficking was also seen as an outside threat, rather than an example of internal problems. Discussions fed into notions of national security and border control. Non-Irish nationals were predominately blamed, and perpetrators of sex trafficking were essentialised as male Eastern Europeans. Grave prejudice was aimed at such countries, and generalisations were made which maligned their collective family values. The narrative saw commentators having doubts about the morality of Eastern Europeans, the MEP Mairead McGuiness stated that "we're concerned about Romania and Bulgaria joining the European Union in January, and we have concerns sometimes about how they look after their children and abandon young adults" (PT 08/05/06). This classification of two separate nations as one draws attention to the people of these countries collectively, the speaker is insisting upon a derogatory rhetoric in relation to communities of people. At no time were Irish nationals implicated in any of the trafficking or abuse. The overall criticism was not placed on the Irish people who pay for sex, but on the lack of government action and policy in this area to keep traffickers out.

All these topics have in many ways been blamed on a lack of integration with the local Irish community, with minorities seen as unworthy and unappreciative because they have not adopted an Irish way of life. This is apparent in a comment made by Olivia Mitchell, a former Fine Gael spokesperson on transport, where she stated that "I think this is what we have to be wary of, is that (sic) the cultures never merged in any real way, they never became parts of society, they never integrated into society" (Q & A 07/11/05). This "othering" strategy is a further attempt to stress the disparity between groups. Similar sentiments were noted in a discussion on deportation a year later, when Eoin Wilson, the chief economist of KBC Asset Management argued that "the issue is how we manage and deal with these people and integrate them into our society" (Q & A 20/03/06). The use of such words as "deal with" and "manage" reflect these groups as problems, which need to be solved and contended with. These narratives are centred on an argument of a "good" migrant, who has been "incorporated" into Irish society, and is counterpoised against migrants who do not conform. It sends a message that those who stay in the country should only be allowed to do so if they have "integrated". Narratives pertaining to immigration have led to a consistent insinuation of the illegality of migrants, with relation to the methods used to enter and remain in the country. Deportation was legitimised across many of the programmes, as narratives centred on the demonisation of immigrants through the use of words associated with criminality and delinquent activity. The exercising of markers such as "bogus asylum seeker" and "illegal immigrant" are simplistic scare mongering tactics that lead to the discrimination of immigrants. Over the total corpus, 11 programmes discussed this topic; the notion of "illegal migrants" was used 23 times, while debates referring to "bogus" asylum seekers were noted on four programmes.

The frame of outsider threat also played a significant role in discussions about the Travelling Community. For instance, the Managing Director of Irish International News agency, Diarmuid McDermott, stated that Travellers have not "accepted their responsibility as Irish citizens" (Q&A 21/11/05). The lifestyle and traditions of the Traveller Community were problematised, with panellists calling for Travellers to conform to the "Irish" way of life. The journalist Ian O'Doherty argued on *The Late Late Show* that "we're all Irish" yet went on to recommend to the Traveller Community that "either you adapt or you die" (LLS 17/11/06). The insinuation that Travellers are failing the state, and not playing by the rules of the national consciousness, solidifies notions of both difference and deviance. The predominance of the frame of criminality moreover appears both overtly and covertly in all programmes discussing the Travelling Community. Two major topics were deliberated, the direct involvement of Travellers in criminal activity, and the discussion of the high profile Nally/Ward case. Over six programmes the word "criminal" was used 43 times, along with reference to violence (9) and terror (3). Padraig Walsh from the Irish Farmers Association, when discussing the Nally/Ward incident and the Travelling Community in general, argued that "there's criminal elements in our society today that are, are [sic] preying on elderly people living alone in our community" (PT 14/12/06). The journalist and author Eamon Dillon also claimed that "criminality has become part and parcel of the…not the minority obviously but certainly a large minority" (LLS 17/11/06).

A *Prime Time Investigates*, broadcast on the 15th of November 2005, examined this case. This programme became one of the most lauded for the show, as it later won the Law Society Justice Media Award, the Society's top media prize, in 2006. The judges reached a unanimous decision on what they deemed to be a "masterful piece of televisual work" (LawSociety, 2006: p.14). Mary Wilson, the programme presenter, continually interrogated the victim's son and family during the programme, constructing the murdered John Ward as a criminal schizophrenic. She vigorously questioned the dead man's son asking "were you the getaway driver? Did he hurt himself, was this part of the illness, did he hurt himself? Was your father into fighting?" (PT 15/11/05). John Ward's character, health, and past were outlined for the viewers, depicting the victim as a troubled criminal. Mary Wilson went on to announce that

> It emerged in court that John Ward did have violent tendencies, there were voices in his head commanding him to kill. He'd been injured in sword fights and was feuding and he wanted to kill a man who'd attacked him with a Stanley knife.

Yet, in contrast, she treated the farmer, Nally, as a victim, articulating that he was a "man under pressure…the stress was becoming intolerable". This approach explicitly values the settled, Nally, over the Traveller, Ward. The programme was viewed by 48% of Ireland's television viewers that night, precipitating much debate. Misrepresentation such as this leads to "symbolic annihilation", and may feed into notions of powerlessness and denunciation of the minority, by the institutions of the state (Ross and Byerly, 2004).

Conclusion

Televised narratives have revealed a darker side to the Irish public discourses pertaining to ethnic minorities, adding to sentiments of trepidation with respect to ethnic minorities. One organisation survey respondent stressed that

> These programmes have an obligation to reflect issues of concern to the whole community. They could give leadership and address issues rather than what seems to happen is that debates are opened and stirred to the

> max-without much concern about raising and discussing issues (Organisation 2).

With repetition, metaphor and semantic choice, minorities' identities are socially constructed, emphasising the power of televised narrative and reinforcing negative stereotypes. Minorities were extensively under-represented, under-scoring further their alienated position in Irish society. The lack of ethnic minority speakers does not facilitate an equal and impartial discussion. The céad mile fáilte can no longer be accepted as a true representation of a nation whose national broadcaster has been shown to consistently broadcast sound bites of demonisation, over more detailed, balanced and reasoned debate. In-depth analysis over a two year period allowed for a focused and exhaustive study of the programme corpus. RTÉ is a definer of the discursive field of thought. This research unearthed many subtle and unassuming devices, which when seen as a whole, illuminated a surreptitious body of evidence, revealing many discriminatory practices. The broadcaster was shown to flout its commitments to a balanced and equitable arena for the discussion of "ethnicity". The NAPR's recommendations have not been achieved. Now as the recession tightens its noose these discriminatory perspectives are becoming more pronounced. During the Immigrant Council of Ireland's 10 year anniversary seminar in December 2011 Sr Stan Kennedy stressed that racism and racist abuse are increasing in Ireland, and directly linked this to misconceptions, most especially those linked to societal and employment threat. Overt exclusionary state practices may be visible when one encounters deportation, exile and forced segregation, but the more covert procedures of marginalisation, ostracism and discrimination may have greater far reaching and longer lasting effects.

Bibliography

Aniagolu, C. "Being Black in Ireland" in *Under the Belly of the Tiger* edited by E. Crowley and J. McLaughlin Dublin: Irish Reporter Publications, 1997.

Barthes, R. *Image, Music, Text.* London, Fontana Press, 1977.

Charteris-Black, J. "Britain as a container: immigration metaphors in the 2005 election campaign". *Discourse & Society,* 17, (2006) 563-581.

Dept. Of Justice, Equality & Reform, L. Planning for Diversity-The National Action Plan Against Racism Equal Status Division, Dept. of Justice, Equality & Law Reform. 2004.

Dittmer, J. "Captain America's Empire: Reflections on Identity, Popular Culture, and Post-9/11 Geopolitics". *Annals of the Association of American Geographers,* 95, (2005) 626-643.

Gillespie, M. *Television, ethnicity and cultural change,* London, Routledge, 1995.

Haldrup, M., Koefoed, L. & Simonsen, K. "Practical Orientalism-Bodies, Everyday Life and the Construction of Otherness" *Geografiska Annaler: Series B* 88: 2, (2006) 173–184

Hartley, J. "Invisible Fictions". *Textual Practice* 1, 1978, 121-38.

Hurwitz, R. "Ireland: From Emigrant Nation to Asylum-Seeker Destination" *Perspectives on Business & Economics,* 19. 2001.

Lawsociety. "Padraig Nally takes top honours". *Law Society Gazette 12.* 2006.

Lentin, R. "Racialising the other, racialising the 'us': Emerging Irish Identities as processes of racialisation" in *Emerging Irish Identities,* edited by R. Lentin, Trinity College Dublin 4-16. 1999.

Leudar, I. & Nekvapil, J. "Presentations of Romanies in the Czech media: on category work in television debates". *Discourse & Society,* 11, (2000) 487-513.

Livingstone, D. "Reproduction, Representation and Authenticity: a rereading" *Transactions of the Institute of British Geographers,* 23, (1998) 13-19.

Luibhéid, E. "Childbearing against the state? Asylum seeker women in the Irish republic". *Women's Studies International Forum* 27, (2004) 335-349.

Mac an Ghaill, M. "Beyond a Black-White Dualism: Racialisation and Racism in the Republic of Ireland and the Irish Diaspora Experience" *Irish Journal of Sociology* 11, (2002) 99-122.

Mahtani, M. "Representing Minorities: Canadian Media and Minority Identities". *Canadian Ethnic Studies.* http://canada.metropolis.net/events/ethnocultural/publications/mahtani_e.pdf. 2001.

Maneri, M. & Ter Wal, J. "The Criminalisation of Ethnic Groups: An issue for Media Analysis". *Forum: Qualitative Social Research,* 6. 2005.

Mastro, D. E. & Robinson, "A. L. Cops and crooks images of minorities on primetime television". *Journal of Criminal Justice,* 28, 385-396. 2000.

Patrona, M. "Conversationalization and media empowerment in Greek television discussion programmes" *Discourse & Society,* 17, (2006) 5-27.

Penet, J.-C.. "From Idealised Moral Community to Real Tiger Society. The Catholic Church in Secular Ireland" *Estudios Irlandeses,* 3, (2008) 143-153.

Ross, K. & Byerly, C. M. (eds.) *Women and Media,* United Kingdom Blackwell, 2004.

Share, P., Tovey, H. & Corcoran, M. P. (eds.). *A Sociology of Ireland,* Dublin: Gill & MacMillan, 2007.

Spencer, S. *Race and Ethnicity: Culture, Identity and Representation,* London & New York, Routledge, 2006.

Stares, P. B. & Yacoubian, M. Terrorism as a Disease: An Epidemiological model for countering Islamist Extremism *Matthew B. Ridgway Center.* University of Pittsburgh. 2007.

Stupples, P. Visual Culture, "Synthetic Memory and the Construction of National Identity". *Third Text,* 17, (2003) 127-139.

Van Dijk, T. A. "Elite discourse and racism" in *Approaches to Discourse Poetics and Psychiatry: Papers from the 1985 Utrecht Summer School of Critical Theory* edited by I. M. Zavala, M. Diaz-Diocaretz, and T. A. V. Dijk, Amsterdam John Benjamins Publishing Company, 1988.

White, E. J. "Forging African diaspora places in Dublin's retro-global spaces; Minority making in a global city". *City,* 6, (2002) 251-270.

CHAPTER NINE

ÉIRÍGÍ: CHANGING NARRATIVES IN IRISH REPUBLICAN ACTIVISM

ROBERT BUSBY AND PADDY HOEY

The use of the virtual sphere to advance political messages is commonplace for small political parties or fringe political movements in seeking to challenge prevailing political wisdom. In Northern Ireland, a range of republican activists have populated the Internet accommodating a range of radical messages and means of disseminating their message. This demonstrated the range of diverse opinion that evolved in the evolution of republican understandings of how to address a divided Ireland. At the centre point of republican dissent in the years of the Troubles was Sinn Féin. However, in the aftermath of the Peace Process the political scenario changed. Sinn Féin changed from a body that communicated primarily with loyal and dedicated followers, to a party that tried to reach out across the political spectrum and legitimise itself as a mainstream organisation. With the advent of new media and changes in the perception of propaganda and how it might be distributed, there existed an environmental backdrop that necessitated a revision of the republican message and the means of its dispersal.

This chapter identifies how modern political agendas, such as those of éirígí, are rooted in understandings of new media, the virtual sphere and lessons learned from other radical and fringe political movements. éirígí, meaning arise in Irish[1] represents a modern radical republican movement that maintains an on-going opposition to the direction of the Peace Process. It entertains many values similar to those held by Sinn Féin

[1] Arise comes from the French revolutionary slogan of Camille Desmoulins, "The great appear great because we are on our knees: Let us rise." It was a rallying cry of 1916 Rising leader James Connolly and appears on the statue commemorating his fellow trade union leader James Larkin on O'Connell Street in Dublin.

before the onset of the peace initiatives. It employs a range of strategies to advance its own distinctive interpretation of republican thought, and maintains an electoral presence underpinned strongly by street activism and online participation. In this context it mirrors other movements but carries forward the evolution of the integration of fringe politics and the exploitation of online sources.

The Internet: platform for dissent

The emergence of the Internet as a means through which to communicate on an equal platform to that entertained by mainstream political parties has been important to the development of minor political parties and fringe movements. Bypassing mainstream news outlets and advancing alternate political views via the web has become common practice for fringe movements intent on communicating radical platforms and for the creation of like-minded virtual communities. The Internet offers a space where existing political communities can be restructured and redefined and allows a form of "self-determination and control 'from below'" (Kahn and Kellner, 2005: 77). Accordingly, the web has become a field in which alternative political positions can vie for influence. Internet communication has inspired protests in one state to be replicated in others and suggests online activism is particularly important for fringe political groups. Commonly the struggles of the Zapatista movement in Central America, and its use of the Internet to propagate its messages is pinpointed as the template from which other leftist movements drew inspiration. With the advent of blogs and social networking, the route through which narratives have, and can be, developed has immense power to access virtual communities and link local and global identities. Kahn and Kellner identify this as the emergence of interlinked "smart mobs" whereby computer based activism has helped to create "highly-informed, autonomous communities" removed from the traditional mainstream party based hierarchical organizations (Kahn and Kellner, 2004: 89).

The alternative public spheres in which radical political groups operate serve to underline how emergent political groups can create their own realms of discussion and establish new political narratives and online discourses. The web allows for the fracturing of conventional and orthodox political understanding and fragments internal interpretations of political movements, as happened with splinter groups from Sinn Féin. It also acts as a forum through which to engage virtually with what is on-going in the real political world, including street protest, organization, intra-party debate and a bonding between on and off-line relationships

(Atton, 2002: 11). In alignment with the demise in consumption of hard copy print based political materials, the rise of cyber discussion has changed the foundation from which constructed narratives arise. It has moved from being one largely in the hands of editors and guiding managerial or party influence to one where the consumer becomes the producer of the narrative, capturing emergent political themes and creating a constantly evolving narrative. In Northern Irish politics, which has undergone rapid change in recent years, this has provided a realm in which divergent communities can understand and contextualise not only their own local experiences, but root them in a wider globalized construct of protest and dissent.

The use of the web for radical or non-conformist movements, particularly in the aftermath of the peace process in Northern Ireland, is important as it serves as a forum for dissidents to have inclusivity and intra-group acceptance in a realm where more overt displays of support might be questioned. The splintering of republican thought in the aftermath of the peace process is testament, in part, to the democratization of the republican movement alongside the exploitation of the web as a means of re-ordering and reinventing what the on-going narrative of struggle means to communities of divergent persuasion. As pinpointed by Wolfsfeld, there is good reason for minority and splinter groups in politics to desire access to political communication via new media (Wolsfeld, 2011: 17). In simple terms they are forced to take this route on account of their being unable to access the conventional news framework. Wolfsfeld identifies several reasons why minor political movements or "backdoor" challengers utilise new media as a political interface. They seek to mobilize potential voters to their cause; pressurise mainstream media into covering the impact of groups on alternate media forums; to generate widespread sympathy with minor movements and the challenges they face and, finally, to have a meaningful influence on politics. The reasons for and use of new media however doesn't necessarily translate into real political influence. The political participants within a new media political network can be imbued with a "false sense of empowerment" that over-emphasises the influence of their politics, in a saturated realm of diverse political messages (Papacharissi, 2002: 17). This creates a virtual narrative of politics which stands alongside a political reality which may be fundamentally different to that presented online.

Sinn Féin had realised the potential of the Internet as a place to disseminate its message to its members and the wider community before many other political parties and groups in Ireland. It made *An Phoblacht*, its main print outlet, the first Irish newspaper to have a parallel online publication, initiating its web presence in the mid-1990s. It also utilised the web when both a radical fringe party and after its accommodation into mainstream politics. Circulation of *An Phoblacht* was estimated to have reached a high of about 30,000 copies weekly during the late 1970s and early 1980s (An Phoblact, "About"), but declined to a weekly average of 15,000 by the late 2000s before moving to a reduced monthly publication in 2011. Reflecting the importance of new media as an emergent communications forum, it had 100,000 unique online users weekly, living up to its own billing as "Ireland's Biggest Selling Political Weekly". More recently Sinn Féin had also been quick to recognise the marketing potential of social networking sites like Bebo, mySpace, Facebook and, latterly, Twitter.

éirígí: a virtual republican cause

By the later 1990s activist groups across the world had embraced the empowering new technologies of forums, message boards and blogs that gave platforms for their causes yet distanced them from the mainstream corporate media. Irish republican bulletin boards like *Irish Republican.net*, *Republican Socialist Forum* and *Irish Nationalism.net* had attracted large numbers of republicans. Similarly, "secular" forums and blog sites like *debate-central.com* and *Sluggerotoole.com* also became places where Republicans could air their views and articulate their arguments without the "controlling" hand of Sinn Féin leadership in the aftermath of the peace process. Mark McGregor, a former Sinn Féin activist who blogged regularly on republicanism at Slugger O'Toole, says that it was in these new spaces of social media interaction that activists first felt safe to articulate differing approaches to mainstream republican ideology, particularly dissenting anti-Peace Process sentiments (Interview, 2010). The repositioning of Sinn Féin allowed for the emergence of new republican movements, which remained opposed to a British presence in the North, and argued against Sinn Féin's accommodation of the peace process and its involvement in discussions with mainstream Northern Irish political parties.

When republican splinter group éirígí launched in April 2006 it did so with a dynamic website, a constitution adopted in 2007, but without a conventional hard copy party newspaper. In interviews its general secretary Breandán MacCionnaith discussed the reasons for the embrace of new media. Most senior éirígí activists had a background in Sinn Féin and had sold *An Phoblacht* during the paper's years of declining circulation. The experience of having to sell a newspaper in decline had partly informed their decision to embrace a primarily digital media policy. This would be augmented with film and video content as well as one-off information sheets and newsletters which harked back to the earliest days of the roots of republican activist media in the North (Interview, 2009). Writing in the Irish Times, Dan Keenan said, for éirígí, there was "little point in broad-based membership if activism is limited to selling ballots and circulating *An Phoblacht*" (Keenan, 2009). éirígí, to reach and recruit disaffected, yet committed, activists from across the republican spectrum, did so with a brand of republican socialism that Sinn Féin had been drifting from since the mid-1990s. éirígí advanced its political mandate via multi-dimensional activism to gain wider attention than it would within the often narrowly defined boundaries of republicanism. This built on prior strategies of republican activity as practiced by Sinn Féin when seeking to give a minority movement a hold on the political agenda setting forum (Miller, 1994: 114).

éirígí advanced itself as a political movement of both local and global concern. It supported a diverse spread of issues from the Shell to Sea Corrib gas protests in the West of Ireland, to pro-Palestinian/anti-Zionist causes. This was placed within a framework of media interaction that eschewed traditional print media products. This allowed the party to accommodate new ideas at short notice, to prompt debate, and to associate itself with other leftist movements prominent on the Internet. éirígí created spectacles to accentuate its presence in the political framework and backed this up with its virtual political presence. éirígí's publicity director Pádraig Mackel explained that éirígí's day-to-day external media policy is coordinated by a central team of senior activists planning "spectacles" or "stunts" aimed at aggressively setting the media agenda, drafting press releases for the news desks of national newspapers and broadcasters while local "ciorcals"[2] re-package these for local media (Interview, Mackle, 2010). Publicity stunts were conceived for maximum impact within the digital media environment with éirígí utilising the dissemination of self-shot video in the online environment. The scaling of the Mansion House in Dublin in January 2009 by activists, and their anti-NAMA protests in May 2010, captured on video and distributed on YouTube and on www. éirígí.org are examples of how the group sought to expand its media activism beyond established republican propaganda practices and replicate the practices of anti-globalisation activist networks.

[2] As Sinn Féin calls local groups of activists cummans, éirígí uses the Irish word for circle "ciorcal" for its branch meetings.

éirígí: alternative political narratives

éirígí, from both a political and propaganda standpoint, has sought to recapture the radical left agenda which Sinn Féin had followed throughout the late 1980s and 1990s and which it had marginalised since the Good Friday Agreement. Bean argues that Sinn Féin's narratives of transformation and progress have seen it move from a brand of identity politics which aligned it with the post-1968 New European Left and identified with national liberation struggles, feminism, gay rights and other social justice issues as central organising principles, to the mainstream and the "cherished centre ground" of post GFA Northern Ireland (Bean, 2008: 155). Maillot argues that in the process of transformation from political wing of the IRA to political party, Sinn Féin pursued a range of social justice issues which emphasised direct action outside of the institutions of the state, and the experience of being a campaign group saw the party begin to occupy a political space in Ireland that has been unfilled for many decades-a party involved in direct participatory democracy yet deliberately placed outside of the auspices of the state (Maillot, 2004: 89). Just as Sinn Féin identified directly with global liberation struggles of the 1970s and 80s, éirígí have identified issues, and sold them to activists both disillusioned with the role of republicans within Northern Ireland peace process and with wider interests in social justice and ecology.

éirígí advocates a form of republican socialism aligned to that advocated by 1916 Easter Rising leader James Connolly. In this it clearly places republican struggle within the ambit of class and labour struggle and sees the Irish republican project as fitting within a wider global context rather than the narrow confines of Irish national liberation espoused by older strains of republicanism. At the centre of the éirígí project is the confluence of nationalism, language and culture, international struggle and women's liberation. In this the party has published work by Mary Wollstonecroft, Simone de Beauvoir and Rosa Luxemburg as well as more conventional Irish nationalist figures like Connolly, Pearse and James Fintan Lawlor (éirígí, Archives Index). This is clearly in line with what Sinn Féin activist Eoin O'Broin identifies as a type of republicanism that appeals to a "broad range of constituencies who want meaningful social and economic change" (Ó'Broin, 2009: 302). This mirrored the radicalism of the "new European and Scandinavian left whose organising principles centred on anti-imperialism, feminism, ecologism and other popular movements" (Bean, 2010: 139). While there may be ideological overlaps between éirígí and Sinn Féin on some issues, for example, opposition to the Corrib Gas pipeline, Lisbon Treaty, Orange

Parades and sympathy for Palestinian causes, éirígí's wider agenda has seen it try to reclaim the radical left from Sinn Féin, particularly in its virtual message. General Secretary of éirígí, Breandán MacCionnaith, observed:

> Instead of reverting to armed struggle we look to South Africa and the popular movements which achieved shifts in power, Venezuela for example. Where we would have previously looked towards South America for armed struggle we now see populist movements coming to power without a shot being fired and Republicans should recognise that. ...Whether we are talking Marx or Connolly, Ireland cannot be divorced from struggles elsewhere in the world, there are similarities and it is only right that we show global solidarity (MacCionnaith, Interview).

Among the many issues that éirígí campaigned on in its first three years, approximately 25% of its press statements focussed on the Shell to Sea Corrib gas pipeline protests, another 10% approximately focused on support of news on popular left wing régimes in Venezuela, Cuba and Latin America while opposition to policing and justice reform proposals in Northern Ireland, supported by Sinn Féin, were also highly prominent. At key times in the Northern Irish calendar, the party also campaigned against Orange Order parades and highlighted instances of racism and homophobia in Ireland. Through the use of the virtual narrative the party could make the local international and take international reflections of minority struggle to make them tangible to local activists.

éirígí's communications strategy fits with the global networks of activist journalism that emerged in the era of the Internet. Its approach is influenced by global activist networks that converge across the Internet and their resulting shared experience of trying to set the agenda of the mainstream media which these groups see as largely "antagonistic" to their message. De Jong, Shaw and Stammers state:

> In order to subvert this existing source hierarchy and conform to contemporary news styles, activist groups organise events and pseudo events or spectacular actions to draw at the attention of news producers (De Jong, Shaw and Stammers, 2005: 7).

Mackel stated that its initial impetus was to utilise media strategies which place emphasis on events with a capacity to spread to a wider audience either virally through activist networks, wider online networks, or are taken up by the mainstream media as a result of their supposed newsworthiness. Mackel observed:

> When we first sat down strategically to plan press and publicity we knew the capitalist media was not impartial and we had the mind-set that we were going to have to battle on every single issue. We knew that we were going to have to try and set the news agenda, we were going to have to force our way into the news (Mackel, Interview).

éirígí, to a certain extent, fits with the existing models of activist media communication. Atton cites Melucci's assertion that these new forms of activism, "tend away from the traditional hierarchical and bureaucratic forms of social organisation," and that new protest groups "eschew existing channels of resistance" (Atton, 2002: 83). éirígí's decision to use its website and engage in an online media campaign which utilises video, blogs and social media is born of Mackel's acknowledgement of the difficulties of achieving a high profile in mainstream media channels. It may be out of necessity rather than virtue, but it has been successful in organising and growing membership and promoting its own agenda in the online world. Melucci also identifies the fluid nature of membership within activist media groups where there are few criteria for membership and jobs often rotate around active members (Atton, 2002: 83). It is however difficult to situate éirígí wholly within the global activist media, replete with its utilization of the web to disseminate its cause and attract members; it is clear that it also orbits the republican mainstream which remains dominated by Sinn Féin, with its successful, hierarchical and centralised media operation (Spencer, 2006: 380). In this case, its resistance can be perceived as being sublimated to Sinn Féin's gravitational pull. Secondly, as large numbers of its senior activists come from a Sinn Féin background, the power structures of the bigger party are largely replicated in éirígí. Communications strategy is largely concentrated into the hands of senior activists and there is no sense of fluidity in éirígí's membership, which is tightly controlled. All new members serve a probationary period in which they also go through an education programme which emphasises key moments in left wing republican history. The ad hoc and diverse nature of activist media organisations witnessed in other political theatres is not replicated in éirígí, which controls its membership and media agenda closely.

Communication Strategies

The philosophical underpinnings of éirígí's media strategy is illustrative of the ideological influences which have afforded a level of flexibility to republicanism. As Wolfe Tone looked to revolutionary France, the Fenians to mid-19th Century Marxist movements in Europe, and Sinn Féin to South Africa and South American revolutionary groups, republicanism has been open to influences which have helped frame their narratives, discourses and political practices. éirígí displays the same kind of ideological promiscuousness, embracing ideas from diverse areas of the activist sphere as well as the 200 years of Irish republicanism. As a nascent political party, éirígí has learned much from the Internet sphere which has become a home for many leftist pressure groups which make a diverse and diffuse coalition of anti-neo-liberal, anti-globalisation movements. These groups embraced the opportunities of the Internet quickly and saw not just its potential for bringing people together over vast geographical spaces but also its flexibility for disseminating its message through new technologies. In one particular strand of the anti-neo liberal agenda, the Culture Jammers, sought to undermine the rhetoric, ideology and hegemony of global corporations by subverting the iconography of advertising and branding, particularly within the corporate environment itself, to which it is particularly hostile. For example, Nike billboards in the USA would be defaced to illustrate the problems with workers' rights in Free Trade Zones in the Far East.

Culture Jammers, borrowing from the work of the French Situationist movement, fought what they saw as the detrimental influence of big corporations and consumerism and addressed the effect that the production of consumer goods was having in the third world where they were being manufactured. Beyond the manipulation of the symbolism of the modern consumer age, the Situationist influence also extends to the flash mobs and sit-ins designed to draw attention to the effects of modern capitalism in the urban environment. In London, the Space Hijackers, a group of "anarchitects" who are "dedicated to battling the constant oppressive encroachment onto public spaces of institutions, corporations and urban planners", targeted Starbucks as one of the corporations that were colonising the high streets of Britain (Albert, 2002). éirígí was involved in a similar event in 2008, rebranding shops in Dublin and Belfast, although its campaign was erroneously instigated on the basis of the corporation's alleged support for Zionist causes (Politics.ie, 2009). In the Situationist sense, Culture Jammers sought to seize the spectacle of modern advertising and consumerism back from the corporations, Kalle Lasn, founder of the Ad Busters Media Foundation says this impulse was, "literally turning around, détournement, re-routing spectacular images, environments, ambiances and events to reverse or subvert their meaning and thus reclaiming them" (Lasn, 2000: 103).

éirígí's media campaigns reflect the influence of this global movement with often ironic and postmodern posters that self-consciously destabilise the iconography and images of popular culture, Ireland, and republicanism. In December 2008, in response to the television talent show X Factor releasing the song "Hero" in support of a British Armed Forces charity, éirígí released its own version which showed the British army on the streets of Northern Ireland, describing it as "an alternative video highlighting the true nature of modern day imperialism" (éirígí, "X Factor Heroes?"). This rapid exploitation of contemporary popular culture aligned with an exploitation of the platform of the web, has given éirígí the ability to conduct eye catching visual campaigns and illustrates the kind of intellectual flexibility with propaganda tools that republicanism is seldom given credit for.

A prime example of éirígí's inventive re-presentation of the narrative of republicanism was a set of posters that it produced for the Lisbon Treaty referenda of 2008 and 2009. The first campaign saw the party appropriate the iconography of the United States' Uncle Sam character for both a poster and physical campaign. The second Lisbon vote saw éirígí appropriate the aesthetic of old Guinness adverts at a time when the company was prominently celebrating its 250th anniversary, while another used the pop art iconography of the punk band the Sex Pistols. éirígí's opposition to the Lisbon Treaty did not radically diverge from any of the other groups campaigning for a No vote. Like Sinn Féin, it opposed the neo-liberal agenda perceived as spreading across the continent with greater emphasis on privatisation, closer association with multi-national globalised corporations and the effects of the erosion of nation state sovereignty. Louise Minihan, éirígí's former Sinn Féin councillor in Dublin, outlined éirígí's opposition to the treaty:

> The Lisbon Treaty is designed to bring us one step closer to a federal united states of Europe. A Europe based on a foundation of neo-liberal capitalism. NAMA, savage cutbacks, the privatisation of healthcare and education and the introduction of water charges are just a few examples of what we can expect if the Lisbon Treaty is passed (éirígí, "Republican Councillors Against the Lisbon Treaty,").

However, it is in the poster campaigns of éirígí and Sinn Féin that illustrates how the two parties diverge in propagandist approaches. Sinn Féin's 2008 poster campaign saw it focus firstly on an inevitable diminution of Ireland's power in the European super state and upon the threat to the Republic's farming community, but its posters lacked the inventiveness and dynamism of those of éirígí (Sinn Féin, "No 2 Lisbon"). éirígí's posters saw "Uncle EU", with his urgent, stern face and pointing hand, ironically call to the voters "I want you for a United States of

Europe," with the party's calling for electorate to "Vote No to Lisbon" (éirígí, "éirígí say no to the Lisbon Treaty"). Demonstrating a willingness to take innovative approaches to campaigning, éirígí took to street activism to challenge Irish political leaders on their support for the Treaty. An éirígí activist, dressed as Uncle EU, ambushed Fine Gael leader (and current Taoiseach) Enda Kenny, Labour leader Eamon Gilmore and Fianna Fáil minister Barry Andrews in Dublin city centre, ironically shouting through a megaphone: "Vote yes to Lisbon for a militarised Europe," "Vote yes for more battle groups," "Vote yes for a European defence agency," and "Vote yes for a United States of Europe" (éirígí, "Tackling the liars on Lisbon). éirígí's inventive activist media strategies saw it impact upon the mainstream media agenda as the stunt was reported by both television news and by the Irish Independent, a large circulation national newspaper with a recent history of hostility to Republican groups (Kerr, 2008).

Its 2009 campaign followed a similar inventive template. This time, the posters used the classic designs of John Gilroy's Guinness posters of the 1930s and 40s (éirígí, Say No to the Lisbon Treaty). The trademark Toucans fly across the first poster with pints of beer on their beaks but with the drink's famous slogan was changed to "Lisbon is bad for you: Vote No". On the second poster the same message appears with "Vote No" branded on a pint glass. The party's spokesman Daithí Mac an Mháistír told the Irish Times,

> The eyes of the world are on the Guinness celebrations and we decided to inject a bit of seriousness into it. Guinness has been great for Ireland but there's little about Lisbon that's any good for us (Carroll, 2009).

The second campaign borrowed further from the Situationist influences on anti-globalisation movements originating, as it did, with the commandeering of a classic pop cultural reference and launching with a piece of street theatre aimed at attracting popular and media attention. It took the famous 1977 Sex Pistols album sleeve, replacing the title with the slogan "Never mind the bollocks: It IS the same treaty. No to Lisbon 2". Clearly, éirígí is situated within the ideological confines of Irish republicanism and its left influences, but it has a deeper connection, in its activism, with the emerging global left than many of the other groups in Ireland and this allows it to frame its discourses more dynamically.

Conclusion

In the local elections in Northern Ireland in 2011, éirígí ran two candidates in council wards in West Belfast in direct opposition to the dominant Sinn Féin incumbents. It polled a respectable 2,000 votes in total, about 10% of the votes cast. Barry Monteith, an independent republican candidate and former Sinn Féin councillor, but aligned with éirígí, was returned in Dungannon in County Tyrone. The vote was perhaps illustrative of the support the party had gained in a short time, partly through its use of new online media channels. Employing and exploiting the Internet as a means of activist engagement, éirígí has attempted to make its political narrative global and capitalise on global issues relevant to its local struggle. With an eclectic set of activist media and the exploitation of popular cultural references, it has developed the republican narrative by embracing contemporary practices and global activist movements. As Sinn Féin used wider left media strategies prior to its integration into the political mainstream, éirígí has innately drawn on a new activism centred on the coalescence of the global left on the Internet to present a new version of radical republicanism which counters the orthodox narratives of the Peace Process, partition and gravitational pull of Sinn Féin. Moreover, the changing backdrop of Irish politics, combined with an understanding of the decreasing significance of print media, has offered éirígí the opportunity to engage with new variants of republican dissent and promote a new narrative which draws on the past but which also places it in a modern globalised present and future.

Bibliography

Albert, Saul. "Graffitiing the Brain Space", *Mute Magazine*, 9 May, 2002. Available at: http://www.spacehijackers.org/html/history.html

"An Phoblact–A History", *An Phoblacht*. Available at: http://www.anphoblacht.com/about

Atton, Chris. *Alternative Media*. London: Sage, 2002.

Bean, Kevin. *New Politics of Sinn Féin*. Liverpool: Liverpool University Press, 2009.

—. "Book Review", *Irish Political Studies*, 25(1), 2010

Carroll, Stephen, "Lisbon outtakes: Borrowing from Arthur," *Irish Times*, September 26, 2009.

De Jong, Wilma, Shaw, Martin and Stammers, Neil. *Global Activism, Global Media*. London: Pluto Press, 2005.

éirígí, "X Factor Heroes?"Available at: http://www.eirigi.org/latest/latest141208.html
—. Say No to the Lisbon Treaty." Available at: http://www.eirigi.org/campaigns/no_to_Lisbon.html
—. "Republican Councillors Against the Lisbon Treaty." Available at: http://www.eirigi.org/latest/latest240909.html
—. "Tackling the liars on Lisbon," http://www.eirigi.org/latest/latest050608(02).html
Kahn, Richard, Kellner, Douglas. "Oppositional Politics and the Internet", *Cultural Politics*, 1(1), 2005.
—. "New media and internet activism: from the 'Battle of Seattle' to blogging", *New Media and Society*, 6 (1) (2004): 89
Keenan, Dan. "Radical group seek republican ground lost by Sinn Féin," *Irish Times*, July 27, 2009.
Kerr, Aine, "Uncle Sam makes splash on cross-party city canvass," *Irish Independent*, 6, June 2008. Available at: http://www.independent.ie/national-news/uncle-sam-makes-splash-on-crossparty-city-canvass-1399598.html
Lasn, Kalle. *Culture Jam*. New York: Harper Collins, 2000.
MacCionnaith, Breandán. Interview, April 2009.
McGregor, Mark. Interview, January 2010.
Mackel, Pádraig. Interview, April 2010.
Maillot, Agnés. *New Sinn Féin: Irish Republicanism in the 21st Century*. Abingdon: Routledge, 2004.
Miller, David. *Don't Mention the War: Northern Ireland, Propaganda and the Media*. London: Pluto Press, 1994.
Ó'Broin, Eoin. *Sinn Féin and the Politics of Left Republicanism.* London: Pluto Press, 2009
Papacharissi, Zizi. "The Virual Sphere", *New Media and Society*, 4(1), 2002.
"Éirígí activists rebrand Starbucks," *Politics.ie*, 17 January, 2009. Available at: http://www.politics.ie/northern-ireland/40529-Éirígí-activists-rebrand-starbucks.html
Sinn Féin, "No 2 Lisbon."Available at: http://www.sinnFéin.ie/no-2-lisbon
Spencer, Graham. "Sinn Féin and the Media in Northern Ireland: The New Terrain of Policy Articulation", *Irish Political Studies*. 21(3), 2006
Wolfsfeld, Gadi. *Making Sense of Media and Politics*. Abingdon: Routledge, 2011.

CHAPTER TEN

PUBLIC GRIEF IN CONTEMPORARY MEDIATISED IRELAND

FIONA FEARON

What is the difference between "grief" and "mourning"? To "mourn" is "to grieve over, to lament, to express grief; to wear mourning". It is a verb, a doing word which implies an action, "wearing black or dark coloured clothing as a sign of grief" (OED). It is a semiotic message, communicating publicly the inward experience of grief. "Grief" by definition is a feeling, "deep sorrow; pain; distress of mind", it is the opposite of joy, hilarity and ecstasy or exultation (OED). Psychologist, Catherine Sanders, defines grief as the "particular reactions one experiences" while in a state of bereavement, which might include "anger, guilt, physical complaints and illnesses, despair and sadness" (1999: 4). Therefore to talk of "public grief" is to articulate the public display or performance of this interior feeling. Mourning in the majority of Western European and American cultures is a restrained, mostly controlled ritual process, where the physical loss of a human being is marked by a religious or secular ceremony that allows family and friends to publicly celebrate the life of the person lost and marks a stage in their grieving process. Sanders describes "mourning" as "the culturally defined acts that are usually performed after a death" (1999: 5). The performance of such "culturally defined acts" allows the family and friends of the deceased to process their loss publicly and to move on into the next stage of their grieving, which most psychologists recognise as a long and complex human experience which varies from one person to another and depends greatly on the type of death being grieved over (Sanders, 1999: 17-37; Keane, 1995: 15-25). The initial public stage has a very important function in allowing the grieving person to "perform" their love, respect, duty for the person lost; but also allows for the very public support of their friends and family, and even the wider community, to be "performed".

Richard Schechner and Victor Turner have clearly outlined the link between performance and ritual, and there has been much scholarly analysis of the origins of theatre in the ritual performances of early civilized cultures (Schechner, 1998, 2002; Turner, 1986, 1995; Zarilli, et al, 2006). Schechner defines performance as "Ritualized behavior [sic] conditioned/permeated by play". He continues:

> Rituals are a way people remember. Rituals are memories in action, encoded into actions. Rituals also help people (and animals) deal with difficult transitions, ambivalent relationships, hierarchies, and desires that trouble, exceed, or violate the norms of daily life (Schechner, 2002: 45)

Frequently death does "violate the norms of daily life" when it is unexpected and unprepared for. Even when it is expected it is still a time of difficult transition where grieving provides a liminal space for families and community to process the loss of a person, and the rituals of religious and civic practice enable that process. However, the historic and traditional cultural practices around funerals in the West in general, and Ireland in particular, seem to be undergoing change.

Increasingly death is performed not only publicly in funeral services but on television and the Internet, and this Western phenomenon is having an impact on how we understand and perform the rituals around death in contemporary Ireland. Carolyn Kitch and Janice Hume's observation of British culture post the death of Princess Diana suggests that what Ariès called "the romantic, rhetorical treatment of death" is reserved for those who have any tangential public importance, and "public mourning has returned to an almost Victorian level of ritual" (2008: xii). Kitch and Hume argue that news media has "become the primary forum for the conveyance and construction of public grief today" (2008, xiv). Visibility in the news media is diffused through the use of blogs, YouTube and Facebook, which according to Buchan, Gibson, and Ellison complicate the boundaries between the private and public experiences of death:

> The boundary between public and private life is increasingly blurred and contested as a false dichotomy in an age where technological mediation of life and death is ubiquitous. [...] The deprivatisation of death and dying in a technologically mediated, entertainment-based news culture is part of a broader historical condition of deprivatisation that is celebrity, YouTube broadcasting and social networking culture (2011: 13)

The impact of the public performance of grief in a deprivatised "technologically mediated, entertainment based culture" is the confusion of performance with real grief, as in the mourners at Stephen Gately's funeral who clapped as the body was processed through the street, or the criticisms of the Queen for her lack of a performance of grief at the death of Princess Diana (YouTube, 2009: Kear and Steinberg, 1999). This chapter will contextualise the cultural practices most commonly used in Ireland today in the process of public grieving, and will analyse the impact of some aspects of the media on their performance. This will be analysed through three case studies; the death of five school girls in a bus crash in Co Meath in 2005, the death in 2009 of Steven Gately, singer and member of Irish boy band, Boyzone and the death of Irish radio and television personality, Gerry Ryan, in 2010.

Death in Ireland

Since the late nineteenth century across the Western world the treatment of death has become increasingly "cellular, private, curtained, individualised and obscured" (Buchan et.al., 2011: 4). Funerals, at least in Britain and America, have adopted a similar tone, becoming as Sanders observes, "small scale, private and personal" (1999: 5). However, funerals in Ireland have a very different character. Professor Anthony Clare suggests that:

> One of the more attractive aspects of life in Ireland is how as a culture we accept and acknowledge death. Anyone caught as I have so often been in a Dublin traffic jam around 5:30 in the evening as a funeral cortège winds its way across rush-hour traffic will be struck at the importance still publicly granted to private grieving, the priority afforded to the rituals of death in the very midst of the hard, mercenary activities of earning a living [...] Death in Ireland still commands curiosity, interest, explicit reference. (Keane, 1995: 15)

In contemporary Ireland cultural traditions which emerged from the religious observations of mainly Catholic funeral services allow for clearly marked stages of grieving which are frequently public: The wake and laying out of the body in the house, the procession of the body through the street or village before the service, the procession of objects representing the lost person during the funeral service, the speech or speeches about the dead during the funeral service or at the grave side, the process of paying respect to the members of the family at the grave side, the gathering for food and drink after the funeral, and the "month's mind" (Taylor, 1989; Ó Sùilleabháin, 1976; Ó Crualaoich, 1998; Keane, 1995). Lawrence Taylor suggests that the cultural practices around funerals in Ireland emerge from the historic development of Catholicism in Ireland, and that the independence of the Irish Church from mainland Europe led to the persistence of many practices right up to the present day, that were eradicated elsewhere in Europe. The infamous excesses of Irish wakes in the nineteenth century, which included liminal practices of excessive drinking, violence and sexuality, were eventually tamed by the Church, but Taylor suggests there still exists a tension "between the wake and the highly charged ritual events surrounding burial"(1989: 182).

The Merry Wake and rural funerary practices exhibited an inherent understanding of the value of the performance of grief in the ritual process, however the political performance of grief was recognised in the nineteenth century with the funerals of important political figures like O'Connell, Parnell and O'Donovan Rossa attracting thousands and being stage managed by republican political forces to their advantage. Rossa's funeral in Glasnevin Cemetery was famous for Padraig Pearse's oration over the graveside, but also highlights one of the possible reasons for the importance of secular wakes and funeral practices in Ireland (Killeen, 2003: 86). From the Reformation onwards, Catholic burials generally took place in Church of Ireland graveyards, and therefore without the religious rituals of the Catholic Church. The intervention of a priest or the reciting of Catholic prayers was at the discretion of the Protestant minister, and if they chose to be intolerant, as Archbishop William Magee famously did in the 1820s, then the Catholic forms of burial were denied (Murphy and Murphy, 2004/2005: 126). Cultural practices around mass for the dead being said in the house before the funeral, or even a month later–the "month's mind"–and speeches and Catholic prayers at the graveside were resistant strategies developed by a repressed people trying to maintain their religious belief. The excesses of the Merry Wake might have had their origins in pagan practices, but they are also part of that resistance to oppression. Magee's evangelical bigotry contributed greatly to Daniel O'Connell's intervention and the eventual establishment of independent graveyards in Goldenbridge and Glasnevin, which were open to all (Murphy and Murphy, 2004/2005: 126). The religious freedoms obtained by O'Connell and others throughout the nineteenth century precipitated a process of general integration of Catholic religious practice into both institutional and everyday life. Taylor argues that:

> The Irish Catholic Church was establishing its cultural hegemony by means of transitions in ritual and general religious conduct designed to bring about psychological as well as social transformations. A key element

> in these transformations was death–as it was ritualized, felt, and imagined (Taylor, 1989: 182).

The Church sought to establish control over the populous by suppressing the excesses of the more pagan approaches to grief of the Merry Wakes and political funerals, and institutionalising the practices that we now recognise. This control may have led to a more heavily ritualised and formal performance of grief but, as Anthony Clare suggests, Irish culture in the late twentieth century had resisted the general invisibility of death in modern affluent societies, and maintained the prominence of both religious and secular traditions surrounding funereal practice (Keane, 1995: 15).

However, Clare's observations predate the death of Princess Diana, the 9/11 attacks on the World Trade Centre in New York and the on-going "War on Terror", which catapulted private grief and the public performance of rituals around grief into the media age. British media arguments and public pressure on the Queen to display or perform her personal grief have been played out in academic articles as well as films like *The Queen* (Kear and Steinberg, 1999; Gibson, 2007). The aftermath of the mass outpouring of grief expressed at the death of Princess Diana has left its mark on British culture, and the public performance of grief has become more common place. Wootton Bassett has gained international attention and Royal recognition for what were initially impromptu public receptions of repatriated deceased British soldiers that passed through the town having been flown in to RAF Brize Norton, and became public performances of grief (*Telegraph,* 2009). But this example is noteworthy exactly because such public performances were unusual in modern Britain. Diana's death and the shock of 9/11 opened a floodgate of emotion and more importantly a need to feel part of the performance of national grief. Gibson suggests that in the twenty first century "we live in both a postemotional and a hyperemotional society regarding how we react to and experience the deaths of others" (2011: 917). The thousands who physically laid flowers outside Buckingham Palace, or who logged on to the 9/11 Memorial website, are displaying that "hyperemotional society" engaged in an act of trying to touch authenticity. There is also some evidence to suggest that the use of technological media is contributing to that hyperemotional state, as we become overly engaged in the grief and pain of strangers, and attached emotionally to celebrities (Gibson, 2011: 148). In Ireland, even for non-celebrities, public sharing of grief has moved from newspaper announcements or memorials to websites like "RIP.ie" or "In Loving Memory.ie". Contemporary Ireland is not immune to the effect of this mediatised hyperemotional performance of grief.

A "terrible grief"

In May 2005 the tragic death occurred of five school girls from County Meath killed in a bus crash on their way home from school. By six o'clock that evening news reporters stood outside the schools involved, at the gates of hospitals in Drogheda and Navan, and by the site of the crash in Kentstown. Their job was to analyse and describe the events as they were understood to have occurred at that time, to look for causes and explanations for the five who had died, and the 46 who were injured. However, what they also observed was the arrival of shocked and distraught students, parents and teachers at the school or outside the hospitals. Carl O'Brien's *Irish Times* description is typical:

> Parents and school friends gathered in shocked silence, waiting for news of the condition of loved ones. Some hugged each other when they heard an update of a child's condition, while others stood silently, still waiting for news. (24 May 2005)

Local people, and particularly young people who had either known the children that died, or had some connection with the school, were interviewed both on television, radio and in newspapers; their authentic experience somehow giving weight to the obvious devastation of the local community. Because the bus was returning children from Navan to their local areas of Beauparc and Yellow Furse, the dead and injured all came from the same localities, and had attended national school and local sports clubs together, so that eventually counselling was offered "not just for the relatives and friends of the deceased but for the survivors and their classmates in St Patrick's Classical School, Beaufort College, Mercy Convent and Loreto Convent" (*Irish Times*, 24 May 2005). Children and young people who would have been more likely to joke and "perform" antics in the background of news reporters were now being sought as witnesses not only to the accident, but to the grief of the community. Over the following days newspaper and television coverage observed the performance of the grief of the young survivors and friends of those killed in the crash, and the rituals of funerals practiced by very young children at both National and Secondary School. Michael O'Regan described scenes of "terrible grief" as the news filtered out and children went to the Loreto School to find out information (*Irish Times*, 24 May 2005). The classmates were obviously shocked and upset, and whether because their parents had suggested it or they felt the need instinctively, they congregated around the school. But they also "performed" grief. With little experience of how to behave, except that gleaned from media, they cried openly, luxuriously, in a manner more reminiscent of the aftermath of Princess Diana's death than might be expected. This was grief unbounded by the ritual practices of the Church, or in many cases the restraints to social definitions of excess enforced by parents or teachers. These children in the 12-18 age group had gained awareness in the post Diana, post 9/11 era, and were among the first generation in Ireland to be more likely to distrust the rituals of the Church than the excesses of the media. The presence of so many cameras and observers leant the scene an aspect of performance that was quite unexpected. These young mourners knew they could be seen, and even heard, and yet did not practice the reserve that older mourners might have done, keeping their tears for privacy. Perhaps this was their age, but I would suggest it is the result of their inherent experience of the performative, as described by Abercrombie and Longhurst; "a kind of activity in which the person performing accentuates his or her behaviour under the scrutiny of others. That accentuation is deliberate, even if unconscious" (1998: 40). We all experience ourselves as performers and audience all the time, and never more so than when caught up in a real tragedy which attracts the attention of the media. Instead of imagining ourselves to be looked at, we know we are being observed in the act of mourning; when that mourning is mediatised, that sense of performance is magnified.

The funerals of the five school girls took on the status of media events, with priests, families and communities recognising that television cameras and reporters would be there. RTE announced the funeral arrangements on the 24 May, the day after the crash, and reported with video and audio footage available on their website. It also confirmed that over 4000 messages of support had been received by the Diocese of Meath website (RTE, 26 May 2005). Four funerals took place on the same day in two separate parish churches, and although the video news coverage is discrete in its distance from the mourners, there are eight video and audio clips available on the RTE website. Editorial teams have removed any sense of a media presence at the funerals, but the reality is that cameras were there and those present at the funerals must have felt that sense of being observed. Abercrombie and Longhurst suggest "the notion of a narcissistic society embodies the idea that people act as if they are being looked at, as if they are at the centre of the attention of a real or imaginary audience" (1998: 88). The reality of the situation was that mourners were the centre of attention and must have been performing, even at a subconscious level. Abercrombie and Longhurst continue:

> People are presenting themselves to others and, in doing so, are imagining how the others will see them. They are, in other words, performing for an

> imagined audience. […] More of the events in everyday life are performances for which there is an audience. At the same time, more people see themselves as performers being watched by others; narcissism is the treatment of the self as spectacle (1998: 95-96).

Although the events were clearly a real tragedy for the families and the community, the media attention constructed the event as a spectacle. The initial shocked reaction of the young mourners became formalised and controlled by the ritual process of the funerals, so that the editorial reporting of the events, returns the funerals to dignified and controlled mourning, rather than performing grief.

A "friend and brother": Celebrity, Fandom and Death

Abercrombie and Longhurst theorise the blurring between "real" performance in either "simple" or "mass" audience contexts, and the performativity of everyday life. The death of Stephen Gately in October 2009 is an exemplar of this blurring, as the death of a celebrity, a real performer, became a news and media event that shows some of the ways death in Ireland is becoming mediatised. Stephen Gately was 33 when he was found dead in his villa in Majorca. News filtered out through radio, television and newspapers on Sunday 11 October, but was quickly confirmed by the band on the official Boyzone website: "We are completely devastated by the loss of our friend and brother, Stephen" (*RTE News*, 11 October, 2009). Initially, there was some controversy surrounding his death, as the cause was unclear, leading to considerable media speculation that drugs may have been the cause of death. When the coroner in Majorca confirmed death by natural causes, the mourning became more conventionalised with less potential for hysteria, with the exception of Jan Moir's homophobic *Daily Mail* article suggesting his death was caused by his lifestyle (Brooker, 2009).

However, as Gately was both Irish and an international celebrity singer, the funeral became a media event, with pop stars and politicians paying tributes alongside the ordinary fans at the funeral in Sheriff Street, Dublin. The surviving members of Boyzone acted like brothers, escorting the coffin back from Majorca and spending the night with Gately's body in the inner city Dublin church. This performance of the traditional "wake" was presented as extraordinary evidence of the devotion of the members of Boyzone, and was commented on by both national and international press and media (BBC, RTE, Sky News, *Irish Times*, *Daily Mail,* 19 October 2009). The funeral service itself was not open to the media, but camera crews and news reporters interviewed celebrities and photographed famous mourners as they entered the church, and the service was relayed by loud speaker to the thousands standing outside the church (Sky News, *Daily Mail* 19 October 2009). This practice of relaying the performance through loud speakers has become common at large funerals, and was part of the mourners' experience at the funerals of the five school girls in Meath. However, unlike the sombre behaviour at those funerals, the audience outside the church at Stephen Gately's funeral applauded as members of the band arrived, perhaps to show their support, but also echoing more normal fan behaviour at concerts or red carpet events (RTE News, BBC 19 October 2009). The arrival of the coffin at the church for the wake was greeted with applause and camera flashes like an Oscar night. During the actual funeral service, mourners, inside and outside the church experienced the first public performance of Boyzone without Stephen Gately, as they sang a song as part of the service, which the audience responded to with applause (Sky News, YouTube). The practice of applause after church music has become quite common after special services like Christmas or for a wedding, but it less practiced at a funeral.

As the coffin left the church, the mourners walked in silence and stood behind the coffin, but the audience of fans and public mourners watching, broke into a spontaneous round of applause. This oddly incongruous action emphasised the extent to which the whole event had become a performance, which would be endlessly re-run on news coverage and downloaded on YouTube. The Boyzone Official Website also has a separate Forum page where fans can leave tributes to Stephen Gately, and a number of other Stephen Gately memorial websites have also emerged. The whole event blurred the performance of rituals around death with fan behaviour and a diffused audience experience. Fans took photos of the funeral to prove that they had been there, as evidence of their authentic experience as "true" fans, and then put them on the website or watched themselves performing as mourners in the television coverage of the funeral. Reporters interviewed fans, took pictures of their elaborate tributes, and tried to find "human interest" stories, like the fan that spent £1000 travelling from Taiwan (BBC News, 19 October 2009). Louis Walsh, impresario and Boyzone manager, emphasised that Gately was an ordinary inner city Dublin "lad" and it was the ordinary people of inner city Dublin who had come to pay him tribute that day (BBC News, 19 October 2009). However, the behaviour of the crowd at the funeral was more like the audience at a pop concert than the restrained mourning that would normally be expected at a funeral. This is not to say that those present outside the church were not upset and deeply moved at the loss of the singer, but Gately's position as a pop star, the celebrity of both himself and other mourners, and the presence of television cameras and other media created a highly mediatised environment. The role of fans themselves as producers and consumers of that media environment cannot be underestimated also.

This relationship between fans and celebrity was on display again in 2010 when the RTE's long established day time radio host and television personality, Gerry Ryan, died suddenly of drug related heart failure. Ryan's morning chat show had been among one of the most listened to shows in Ireland and was effectively an institution, running for three hours each morning on RTE 2fm from 1988 to 2010 when he died (RTE News, 30 April 2010). The Gerry Ryan Show regularly achieved a listenership of 300,000 people, the majority women, and his humour, honesty and advice were a valued part of many ordinary Irish people's lives (irishtimes.com, RTE News, 30 April 2010). Even if they did not consider themselves a fan of Gerry Ryan, his voice and show were a backdrop to their lives as they went around shops, travelled in the car or bus, or went to work. News of his death filtered out in whispers and text messages. He did not arrive for work, and a substitute DJ, Fiona Looney, filled in for his show merely informing the audience that he was ill. At 1pm his partner entered his apartment in Leeson Street, and found Ryan's body. An ambulance and doctor were called, and by 3pm he was confirmed dead.

However, a media war ensued. A text was allegedly circulated from an unknown source that said Gerry Ryan was dead, and although RTE were aware of what had happened they made no formal announcement till the family were notified. However, in the meantime www.boards.ie had a post at 2.35pm which asked if anyone "had heard the rumours" about Gerry Ryan (http://www.boards.ie, "Gerry Ryan", 30 April 2010). By 2.40 "Twitter had gone nuts", and at 2.44pm Miriam O'Callaghan confirmed the story by Twitter. She then removed the Tweet because not all of the Ryan family had been informed of his death. Una Mullally of the *Sunday Tribune* and *Sunday Business Post* technology editor Adrian Weckler both discussed the breaking news on-line before it had been officially confirmed by RTE or the family (Linehan, *Irish Times*, 3 May 2010). Hugh Linehan points out how social media like Twitter do not have editors or set rules for the release of such news, and the medium itself creates a feeling of shared intimacy which negates the public nature of the act. The Gerry Ryan stream on www.boards.ie quickly took on the nature of a memorial page, but also suffered from the lack of an editor in that there were a number of negative posts, and even pages set up which were aggressive in their attacks on Ryan.

The public performance of grief moved from the on-line discussion to the public arena as soon as the news was confirmed. Journalists and presenters at RTE and other radio and TV stations frantically prepared obituaries for the early evening newspapers and prime-time news slots. RTE Radio 1 cut short its early evening Drivetime show to host a tribute to Gerry Ryan, while RTE 2FM just played music. The Six One evening news programme had reports and an emotional interview with Ryan's colleague and friend Joe Duffy. The *Late Late Show*, another long running Irish media institution, swiftly put together a tribute show for that evening celebrating Ryan's life, with veteran broadcasters and friends, like Gay Byrne, Joe Duffy and Dave Fanning invited to regale the audience with stories and memories of Ryan. Marian Finucane hosted a tribute show the following morning which received over 6000 texts. The Ryan show email address continued to receive a stream of Tweets and texts after the Friday, and by the Monday 4000 people had signed the book of condolence set up in the RTE studios in Donnybrook (RTE Media Advisory, "Gerry Ryan 1956-2010", 3 May 2010). The cream of Irish media annotated their grief, which was both personal and professional, in front of TV screens and on radio stations, and their tributes were available to be watched and listened to repeatedly through the RTE website.

The funeral itself became a media event broadcast live on 2FM and streamed on the RTE website so that audiences could listen and watch at home on their computers ("Preparations made for Gerry Ryan's funeral", RTE *Ten,* Wednesday 5 May 2010). The picture quality on the camera was not much better than a webcam, and was in a fixed position throughout and after the ceremony, so it had a sense of artificiality, almost like CCTV footage, unlike the normal filmed events broadcast on the television. The camera was probably placed discreetly in the church in Clontarf so as not to interfere too much with the dignity of the funeral; however there was no escaping the mediatised nature of the event. Politicians, broadcasters and entertainers made up the audience in the Church, and the musical accompaniment came from Bono and Westlife. The mourners outside broke into spontaneous applause as the coffin arrived at the Church, and came prepared as fans, with copies of Ryan's book in hand, ready to be interviewed. Fans/mourners who were interviewed described Ryan as their "friend" or "brother" who made them feel like he was talking to them personally in their own kitchen. Those interviewed by RTE news were invariably women. Sinead Crowley, RTE's Arts and Media correspondent, described the audience reaction as "dignified", but there was still a sense of the performative about the whole event (RTE News, 6 May 2010). Gibson suggests that "empathy and sorrow between strangers is something that the modern, mediated subject is familiar with seeing publicly enacted and reflected back via news media camera, social networking sites and the digital archive" (March 2011: 148). The audience of fans/mourners came to the funeral certainly to perform their respect and to celebrate their affection for Ryan, but there is also the possibility that some came to be seen, potentially to be interviewed.

Conclusion

Anthony Clare's observations on the importance of the rituals of death in Irish society are still relevant, "Death in Ireland still commands curiosity, interest, explicit reference" (Keane, 1995: 15). From the funerals of local teachers or GAA players, to the political funerals of figures like Michael Collins or De Valera, the importance of the ritual performance of grief in Ireland is evident. However, since the mid-2000s there is increasing evidence that in common with much of the rest of the Western world, our understanding and experience of death has become sensitised to the influence of the media, either consciously or unconsciously. There are a number of distinct aspects to the influence of the media. The first is in the diffused audience experience which predicates all encounters with the media now, so that it is only the very naïve person who is not aware that once the media is involved in the reporting of a news event even the most tragic of human experience and the most formal ritual environments take on a heightened layered performativity, as we saw with the funeral of the five Meath school girls in 2005. The second is the influence of social media networks and fandom. Grief for people we barely know, the "hyperemotional society" described by Gibson, is linked to the availability and access of celebrities to their fans, and the deeply personal relationships fans build with their object of affection. The funerals of Steven Gately and Gerry Ryan show how the rituals of funerary practice were blended with the online performance of grief, distribution of information about their deaths, and the performance of fan behaviour in the most inappropriate of circumstances. There is perhaps a point when the needs of the audience to have access to celebrity at all times, even in death, perhaps exceed the expectations of the families of the deceased.

Bibliography

Abercrombie, Nicholas and Brian Longhurst. *Audiences: A Sociological Theory of Performance and Imagination*. London: Sage, 1998.

Bial, Henry. *Performance Studies Reader*. New York and London: Routledge, 2004.

Brophy, Thomas. "On Church Grounds: Political Funerals and the Contest to Lead Catholic Ireland", *Catholic Historical Review*, 95: 3, (2009) 491-514.

Buchan, Bruce. Ellison, David, and Margaret Gibson, "Reflection on the Death Scene", special issue, "The Death Scene: Perspectives on Mortality", *Cultural Studies Review*, Issue 17, No. 1, (2011) 3-15.

Butler, Judith, *Precarious Life: The Power of Mourning and Violence*. London and New York: Verso, 2004.

Donnelly, Jr., James S. and Kerby A Miller, ed., *Irish Popular Culture, 1650-1850*, Dublin and Portland: Irish Academic Press, 1998.

Gibson, Margaret, "Death and mourning in technologically mediated culture" Special issue "Death, Dying and Loss in the 21st Century", Health Sociology Review: *International Journal of Health Sociology: Policy, Promotion, Equity and Practice*, 16 (5), (2007) 415-24.

—. "Memorials and the public culture of grief", special issue, "The Death Scene: Perspectives on Mortality", *Cultural Studies Review*, Issue 17, No. 1, (2011) 141-161.

—. "Real Life Death: Between public and private, interior and exterior, the real and the fictional" special issue, *South Atlantic Quarterly*, Duke University Press 917-932. Fall 2011.

Keane, Colm, *Death and Dying*, Dublin: Mercier, 1995.

Kear, Adrian and Deborah Lynn Steinberg, eds., *Mourning Diana: Nation, Culture and the Performance of Grief*, New York and London: Routledge, 1999.

Killeen, Richard, *Short History of Modern Ireland*, (Montreal: McGill-Queen's University Press, 2003)

Kitch, Carolyn and Janice Hume, eds., *Journalism in a Culture of Grief*, New York and London: Routledge, 2008.

Mooney, James, "The Funeral Customs of Ireland", *Proceedings of the American Philosophical Society*, Vol 25, No. 128, (1888) 243-296

Murphy, John A. and Clíona Murphy, "Burials and Bigotry in Early Nineteenth-Century Ireland" *Studia Hibernica*, No. 33, (2004/2005) 125-146.

Ó Crualaoich , Gearóid, "The 'Merry Wake'", *Irish Popular Culture, 1650-1850*, edited by James S. Donnelly, Jr. and Kerby A Miller, Dublin and Portland: Irish Academic Press, 173-200. 1998.

Ó Sùilleabháin, Seán, *Irish Wake Amusements*, Dublin: Mercier, 1976

Sanders, Catherine M. Sanders, *Grief: The Mourning After–Dealing with Adult Bereavement*, Second Edition, New York: John Wiley & Sons, 1999

Schechner, Richard, *Performance Studies: an introduction*, New York and London: Routledge, 2002.

—. *Performance Theory*, New York: Routledge, 1988

Schor, Esther, *Bearing the Dead: The British Culture of Mourning from the Enlightenment to Victoria*, Ewing, J: Princeton University Press, 1994.

Sontag, Susan, *Regarding the Pain of Others*, London: Hamish Hamilton, 2003

Taylor, Lawrence J., "Bás InEirinn: Cultural Constructions of Death in Ireland", *Anthropological Quarterly,* 62:4, (1989) 175-186.

Turner, Victor, *The Ritual Process: Structure and Anti-Structure*, New York: Aldine Publishing Company, repr. 1995

—. *The Anthropology of Performance*, New York: PAJ Publications, 1986.

Zarrilli, Phillip B., Bruce McConachie, Gary Jay Williams, Carol Fisher Sorgenfrei, *Theatre Histories: An Introduction,* New York and London: Routledge, 2006.

Web references

9/11 Memorial Website, http://makehistory.national911memorial.org/ (accessed 30 May 2012)

Enda Brady, "Top Irish Broadcaster Found Dead at Home", Sky News, http://news.sky.com/home/world-news/article/15623205, (accessed 30 May 2012)

BBC News, "Gately's Coffin Arrives in Dublin", http://news.bbc.co.uk/2/hi/entertainment/8311892.stm (accessed 19 April 2010)

—. "Tributes Paid at Gately's Funeral", http://news.bbc.co.uk/2/hi/8311894.stm, (accessed 19 April 2010)

—. "Louis Walsh: We have to Celebrate his Life" http://news.bbc.co.uk/2/hi/entertainment/8312155.stm, (accessed 19 April 2010)

www.boards.ie. Discussion thread 'Memorial Website', 20/7/10, 20.49pm, http://www.boards.ie/vbulletin/showthread.php?t=2055974980, (accessed 30 May 2012)

www.boards.ie discussion thread 'Gerry Ryan, 'Has anyone heard the rumours?' 30/4/10, 14.35pm, http://www.boards.ie/vbulletin/showthread.php?p=65662834 (accessed 30 May 2012)

Brooker, Charlie, "Mail columnist provokes homophobia storm over Stephen Gately's death", Greenslade Blog, *The Guardian,* http://www.guardian.co.uk/media/greenslade/2009/oct/16/dailymail-stephen-gately (accessed 19 April 2010)

Daily Mail Reporter, "Stephen Gately Funeral: Farewell to our brother, Farewell to our son", *Daily Mail*, 19 October 2009, http://www.dailymail.co.uk/tvshowbiz/article-1221030/Stephen-Gately-funeral-Ronan-Keating-breaks-tears-pays-tribute-Boyzone-star.html (accessed 19 April 2010)

Irish Times. Linehan, Hugh, "Journalistic ethics, Twitter and the reporting of Gerry Ryan's death", irishtimes.com, Posted: May 4, 2010 @ 6:21 pm http://www.irishtimes.com/blogs/mechanicalturk/2010/05/04/journalistic-ethics-twitter-and-the-reporting-of- gerry-ryans-death/ (accessed 30 May 2012)

O'Brien, Carl, "They were really nice, always cheerful, full of life", *Irish Times*, 24 May 2005, http://www.irishtimes.com/newspaper/frontpage/2005/0524/1116025820399.html (accessed 30 May 2012)

O'Regan, Michael "Families arrive to identify children in hospital", *Irish Times* 24th May 2005, http://www.irishtimes.com/newspaper/ireland/2005/0524/1116025820375.html (accessed 30 May 2012)

In Loving Memory.ie, http://www.inlovingmemory.ie/ (accessed 30 May 2012)

RTE. RTE News, "Funeral arrangements finalised after bus crash", 24 May 2005, http://www.rte.ie/news/2005/0524/navan.html (accessed 19 April 2010)

RTE News, "School girls funerals in County Meath", http://www.rte.ie/news/2005/0526/navan.html, (accessed 19 April 2010)

RTE News, "Singer Stephen Gately dies aged 33", 11 October 2009,

"Boyzone singer died of natural causes", 13 October 2009,

"Hundreds pay respect to Boyzone singer", 16 October 2009,

"Thousands attend Gately funeral', 17 October 2009 http://www.rte.ie/news/2009/1017/gatelys.html (accessed 19 April)

"Preparations made for Gerry Ryan's funeral", RTE *Ten,* Wednesday 5 May 2010 http://www.rte.ie/ten/2010/0505/ryang.html, (accessed 30 May 2012)

"Hundreds attend Ryan Funeral", RTE *Ten*, Thursday 6 May 2010, http://www.rte.ie/ten/2010/0506/ryang.html (accessed 30 May 2012)

"Broadcaster Gerry Ryan laid to rest", Thursday, 6 May 2010 http://www.rte.ie/news/2010/0506/ryang.html, (accessed 30 May 2012)

RTE Media Advisory, "Gerry Ryan 1956-2010", 3 May 2010, http://www.rte.ie/about/pressreleases/2010/0503/gerryryan03052010.ht ml , (accessed 30 May 2012)

RTE News, "Tributes flood in for the late Gerry Ryan", 30 April 2010 http://www.rte.ie/ten/2010/0430/ryang2.html, (accessed 30 May 2012)

RIP.ie, End of Life Matters, http://www.rip.ie/index.asp asp (accessed 30 May 2012)

Telegraph, "Hundreds pay respects as soldiers bodies return from Afghanistan", 13 August 2009, http://www.telegraph.co.uk/news/newstopics/onthefrontline/6022805/ Hundreds-pay-respect-as-soldiers-bodies-return-from-Afghanistan.html (accessed 16 April 2010)

Youtube, Stephen Gately's Funeral:
http://www.youtube.com/watch?v=73bAr1T5nr0&feature=PlayList&p =FF3996E5E8F365F8&playnext_from= PL&index=0 (accessed 16 April 2010)
http://www.youtube.com/watch?v=0k9oQ6mvZDc&feature=PlayList &p=FF3996E5E8F365F8&playnext_from=PL&index=1 (accessed 16 April 2010)
http://www.youtube.com/watch?v=ITOQOTYSSJA&feature=PlayList &p=FF3996E5E8F365F8&playnext_fro m=PL&index=2 (accessed 16 April 2010)
http://www.youtube.com/watch?v=CONK8gO0qQw&feature=PlayList &p=FF3996E5E8F365F8&playnext_fro m=PL&index=3 (accessed 16 April 2010)

CHAPTER ELEVEN

RE-ENVISIONING THE TROUBLES: NORTHERN IRISH FILM IN TRANSITION, 1990-2010

FIONA COFFEY

Since the 1990s, Northern Ireland has been marked by a gradual but significant transition from sectarian violence to a delicate but steady peace. Today, this "new Northern Ireland" has begun a process of not only envisioning a better and brighter future but also of redefining and re-presenting its past. Today's post-conflict[1] and peace-focused North is actively engaged in altering perceptions about many of the old binaries, stereotypes, and assumptions about the Troubles. Representations of the conflict are being rewritten with new nuance and complexity, afforded by the luxury of time and a newly stable state. This dramatic shift of relationship to and presentation of the past can be seen most clearly through the country's cultural and artistic output, most significantly with Northern cinema. Since 1990, there have been more than forty feature films addressing some aspect of the sectarian conflict[2]. As the country has

[1] While the height of the conflict is certainly past and the North is working hard towards peace and reconcilliation, the term "post-conflict" can be misleading as it implies that the conflict is over or in the past. I would like to acknowledge that the transition towards a post-conflict state is a slow and on-going process, and one that possibly is never truly finished.

[2] While by no means an exhaustive list, these films include *Fools of Fortune* (1990); *Hidden Agenda* (1990); *The Crying Game* (1992); *December Bride* (1993); *In the Name of the Father* (1993); *The Railway Station Man* (1993); *Patriots* (1994); *Nothing Personal* (1995); *Some Mother's Son* (1996); *The Boxer* (1997); *The Devil's Own* (1997); *The Informant* (1997); *Crossmaheart* (1997); *The Break* (1997); *Resurrection Man* (1997); *This Is the Sea* (1997); *My Brother's War* (1998); *Titanic Town* (1998); *Divorcing Jack* (1998); *Ronin* (1998); *Titanic Town* (1998); *Borstal Boy* (2000); *Silent Grace* (2000); *An Everlasting Piece* (2000); *The Last September* (2000); *The Most Fertile Man in Ireland* (2001); *Silent Grace*

transitioned from violence to peace, Northern Irish film has likewise gone through an important transformation, capturing and reflecting back the political, social, and cultural changes occurring in the North over the past twenty years.

An examination of films made between the 1990s to present-day reveals a distinct tonal shift which mirrors the country's own changing relationship to and perception of the conflict. Feature films about the Troubles made during the 1990s generally reflect a more pessimistic, narrow, and *closed* view of the North while later films made during the 2000s tend to present a more optimistic, nuanced, and *open* vision for the country[3]. This chapter does not intend to attach value judgments on "closed versus open" and "pessimistic versus optimistic" qualities of Northern cinema but rather aims to show that these films are a significant reflection of Northern Ireland's changing relationship to its past. This chapter will refer to the majority of films made in the 1990s as "Troubles films" and those made in the 2000s as "Peace Process films". However, these terms do not necessarily reflect a temporal definition but rather are associated with certain themes and tones which can be attributed to a conflict versus post-conflict outlook[4]. A comparison of key characteristics of Troubles films against two recent Peace Process films, *Five Minutes of*

(2001); *Boxed* (2002); *Sunset Heights* (2002); *Bloody Sunday* (2002); *Omagh* (2004); *Mickeybo & Me* (2004); *Breakfast on Pluto* (2005); *48 Angels* (2006); *Johnny Was* (2006); *50 Dead Men Walking* (2008); *Peacefire* (2008); *Hunger* (2008); *Five Minutes of Heaven* (2009).

[3] There are exceptions to every trend, and this paper does not argue that *all* feature films made during this twenty-year period fit within this pattern; however, it does argue that enough of the films being produced do fall within these general guidelines and thus demonstrate a distinct shift. In addition, it is important to note that an inherent limitation to this analysis is created by the fact that the majority of films about the Troubles tend to promote the Catholic perspective. Therefore, the Troubles films that this chapter examines tend to be from the Catholic Nationalist perspective whereas the Peace Process films tend to include multiple viewpoints and sympathies from both traditions.

[4] It is important to note that in the late 1990s/early 2000s, when the peace process was still in its infant stages, there are several films made during this period which are more representative of the Troubles film genre than the Peace Process genre. This is most notably seen with *H3* in 2001 and *Peacefire* in 2008. Each of these films operates within a closed-text system of interpretation, clearly delineating between the innocent Irish and the sadistic British and creating a strong storyline promoting British injustice that leaves little interpretation up to the audience. Thus, like any transition, there is a period in which films are part of a lingering ideology coming out of the Troubles and thus, I would argue, belong in the category of Troubles films even though they were made post-Belfast agreement.

Heaven (Oliver Hirschbiegel, 2009) and *Omagh* (Pete Travis, 2004), reveals this marked transition occurring in Northern cinema and in Northern society at large.

The first important shift from Troubles to Peace Process cinema is from a closed to an open text. In his seminal work, *The Role of the Reader: Explorations in the Semiotics of Texts* (1979), Umberto Eco posits the idea that semiotics can create either an "open" or "closed" interpretation of a text. According to Eco, an open text is one which creates ambiguity, asks more questions than provides answers, and allows the reader/viewer to engage his own ideas and thoughts as he is interacting with the text. In contrast, a closed text dictates to the reader/viewer exactly what ideas, emotions, or sympathies should be experienced. It typically only allows one specific interpretation and provides definitive answers. Thus the reader/viewer is not required to actively engage in a closed text but can be a passive recipient of that text's argument or viewpoint.

There has been a lot of critical and scholarly analysis of Troubles films, and scholars such as Martin McLoone, John Hill, Ruth Barton, Kevin Rocket, Mathew Brown and others have identified several typical characteristics of Troubles films that, I would argue, fit Eco's *closed-text* approach. The first closed-text characteristic of Troubles cinema is the often simplistic and one-sided representation of the films' heroes and villains which dictates to the viewer where their sympathies should lie. The most common example of this binary is "the Irishman who is good but misguided" versus "the Irishman who is bad and innately violent". Ruth Barton in her book *Jim Sheridan* (2002) identifies this trend, stating:

> ...most indigenous filmmakers have been constrained by the imperative of achieving a balanced view, whilst condemning acts of violence. Thus, paramilitaries have been consistently depicted as psychopaths acting without the consent of their community (a view that is inconsistent with history) or good people unwillingly trapped in a conflict for which there is no exit other than death (Barton, 2002: 100).

John Hill also identifies this binary as a distinct feature of Troubles cinema as far back as *The Odd Man Out* (1947) (Hill, 2006: 2), and Hill and Martin McLoone both trace the origins of the atavistic IRA man back to British colonialism which actively promoted the Irish as drunk, violent, and subhuman in order to justify imperialism and the suppression of Irish uprises (Hill, 1987; McLoone, 2000). This colonial caricature has also been used by Irish filmmakers to create a firm distinction between the fundamentally good/peaceful Irishman and the evil/violent IRA man. This can been seen in countless Troubles films including the pacifist Giuseppe

Conlon versus the sadistic IRA man Joe McAndrew in *In the Name of the Father* (Jim Sheridan, 1993) and reformed boxer Danny Flynn versus the militant, anti-cease fire IRA man Harry in *The Boxer* (Jim Sheridan, 1997). Other Troubles films develop this binary further in order to distinguish between the good and just Irish versus the corrupt and immoral British. This is best exemplified through *Some Mother's Son* (Terry George, 1996) which contrasts the loving Irish mothers, Kathleen and Annie, against the unfeeling and ruthless British government represented by Margaret Thatcher and her political aide Farnsworth.

In contrast to the closed texts of Troubles films which tend to show narrow and essentialist representations of heroes and villains, the open texts of Peace Process films lend themselves to multiple, overlapping, and sometimes conflicting interpretations of its protagonists. Instead of directing the viewer toward one inevitable conclusion, they actively encourage the audience to delve into the complex history of the protagonists, creating sympathy and compassion for all characters and ultimately blurring the lines between victim and perpetrator.

Based on a true story, *Five Minutes of Heaven* explores the attempted reconciliation between Alistair Little, a former Ulster Volunteer Force member, and Joe Griffin, a Catholic whose older brother was killed by Little during the height of the Troubles. The film, which is set decades after the killing and several years into the peace process, explores the question of whether reconciliation is possible-both on an individual level between Little and Griffin and also on a larger scale, implicating the entire North. The premise of the film surrounds a television program which intends to bring Little and Griffin together and publically broadcast their confrontation and efforts at reconciliation. Unlike Troubles cinema which tends to dictate a clear argument to their viewers within the first few minutes of their films, the opening moments of *Five Minutes of Heaven* disrupt the viewer's understanding of the past and of the traditional enemy-figure, negating any expectation the viewer might have that this film will direct their sympathies towards one specific interpretation of the film. The film opens with a voiceover by Alistair Little, the would-be villain of the film:

> For me to talk about the man I've become, you need to know about the man I was. I was fourteen when I joined the Tartan gangs, and I was fifteen when I joined the UVF-the Ulster Volunteer Force. At that time, don't forget, there were riots on the streets every week, petrol bombs every day, and that was just in our town. And when you got home and switched on the TV, you could see it was happening in every other town as well, and it was like we were under siege. Fathers and brothers of friends were being killed

> in the streets and the feeling was-we all have to do something. We're all in this together, and we all have to do something.

With its opening scene, *Five Minutes of Heaven* immediately upends the traditional Troubles binary of "the man of peace" versus "the man of violence". Instead, the film complicates the image of the standard malicious paramilitary member by giving the historical context which led this young man to kill, thus refusing to allow the film's viewer to make quick value judgments about Little's integrity or character. Instead of reinforcing old perceptions of innate Irish violence, the film suggests that a person's past and the experiences of his youth all contribute to his adult identity. Directly contradicting Troubles films, *Five Minutes of Heaven* proposes that a person is not *born* violent; one is not naturally atavistic; instead, one *becomes* something due to formative experiences in one's life. Little's opening dialogue is layered over archival footage of violence, bombings, and shootings in the streets of Northern Ireland, adding weight and profundity to his words. Through this opening sequence, the film suggests that society might bear some responsibility for Little's actions. As Little says:

> What I want to tell people, what society must do is stop people getting to the point where they join the group. 'Cause when you get to that point, it's too late; no one is going to stop you. No one is going to change your mind. And once you are in, you will do anything. You will kill anyone on the other side. Once your man has joined the group, society has lost him. And what he needs to hear is voices on his own side stopping him before he goes in. There were no voices on my side. None on my side of the town. Not on my estate. No one was telling me anything other than killing is right. It was only in prison that I heard that other voice.

In stark contrast to Troubles films, *Five Minutes of Heaven* suggests that the community, which raised these young men, may share responsibility for their violence. The film essentially intimates that a society engaged in warfare will turn its young people into criminals. In this way, the film asks the viewer to possibly implicate himself in Little's actions and to question what role the viewer himself has played in condoning or ignoring violence in his own neighbourhood.

Furthermore, by outlining the historical and cultural context of Little's past (and thus creating a nuanced picture of him), the viewer is asked to withhold judgment and instead delve into the complexity of what can turn a young man into a killer. The first twenty minutes of the film flash back to the night of the murder. The film spends ample time humanizing Little, showing him as a teenager in his boyhood room replete with posters of

Bruce Lee and childhood toys, following his ordinary, working-class parents as they eat dinner and watch television, and demonstrating his close friendships with local youths from the neighbourhood. All this signals to the viewer that this is an average young man rather than a sadistic killer. These elements of the opening sequence move directly away from Troubles representations of a one-dimensional vicious murderer and instead ask the viewer to place himself in Little's position and question what circumstances would bring the viewer to commit a similar crime. By engaging in this exercise, the viewer experiences compassion for Little and engages with the historical and political context that led to the murder. The film is also noteworthy in the equal time it gives to providing depth and complexity to both the Catholic victim, Griffin, as well as to the Protestant perpetrator, Little, signalling a distinct desire to show the intricacies of sectarian conflict. By showing how easily an ordinary young man can slip into paramilitary culture, this is one of the first films to humanize the perpetrator and controversially suggest that Little might be just as much of a victim as the man he gunned down.

Another important characteristic of the open-text quality of Peace Process films can be seen through a blurring of the line between victim and perpetrator. Perpetrators in Peace Process films are often riddled with guilt, contradictions, and shame for their actions, and the films ask the viewer to approach these characters with compassion[5]. *Five Minutes of Heaven* carefully charts Little's anguish as an adult, creating a nuanced portrait of a killer who is complex, pained, and feels deep remorse. The grownup Little sums up his life saying, "Guilty if I laugh, guilty if I drink, guilty if I forget, how you get through a day?" Conversely, the film shows an anguished and revenge-driven Joe Griffin who can barely contain his desire to kill Little. Indeed, the film's title even refers to the euphoria Griffin will experience in the five minutes it would take him to kill Little. While Little is the murderer who has been reformed, Griffin is now the victim turned into a potential killer. In addition, the cross-casting of Liam Neeson, a Catholic, in the Protestant role and James Nesbitt, a Protestant, in the Catholic role disrupts the traditional character that a sectarian audience would naturally gravitate towards. The viewer must sort through the complex characters, their backgrounds, and the actors playing them in order to figure out where their sympathies lie. In doing so, they actively

[5] This is also demonstrated in the Peace Process films *Hunger* (Steve McQueen, 2008) which creates a nuanced portrait of a Protestant prison guard on his duties in Long Kesh as well as in *Bloody Sunday* (Greengrass, 2002) which highlights at least two conflicted British military members who question the military's actions that day.

engage in the film and must also simultaneously question their own assumptions and expectations about the conflict[6].

Another strong example of the open-text quality of Peace Process films can be seen through Pete Travis' *Omagh,* which includes multiple, conflicting voices and also asks the viewer to imagine himself within the events depicted on screen. Like *Five Minutes of Heaven*, *Omagh* is a fictionalized account of true events, this time surrounding the 1998 Omagh bombing[7]. The film follows the Gallagher family in the aftermath of their son's death and during the formation of the Omagh Support and Self Help Group (comprised of the families of the victims). Like *Five Minutes of Heaven*, *Omagh* is noteworthy in its representation of both the Protestant and Catholic perspectives. The film makes a concerted effort to depict the painful experiences that Catholics and Protestants shared during the bombing, complicating the notion that the communities are inherently at odds with each other. As Brian McIlroy argues, *Omagh* "is not directly tied to nationalist and republican mythologies, but focuses on civilian victims and their families who hail from various traditions and backgrounds" (McIlroy, 2007: 446). Towards the beginning of the film, the protagonist, Michael Gallagher, waits at the local recreation centre for news about his injured son's condition. He runs into a Protestant friend who is waiting to hear about his own wife. Gallagher introduces his local priest to his neighbour's pastor. This subtle scene, which shows Catholics and Protestants, priests and pastors, coming together and comforting each other in crisis, dispels the notion that all of Northern Ireland is defined by sectarian division. The production notes from the making of the film include a quotation from the real-life Michael Gallagher who says, "I would like to think *Omagh* shows that in the midst of evil and wickedness, ordinary people from a wide variety of backgrounds have come together in the fight for truth and justice" (Travis, 2004).

---

[6] Inclusive representation of Protestants and Catholics and showing the traditional enemy with empathy can be seen in many of the Peace Process films including *Bloody Sunday*, which focuses on the efforts of Protestant MP Ivan Cooper during the Bloody Sunday massacre (complicating the notion that Protestants and Catholics are inherently at odds) and *Hunger* which shows with great compassion the stress and anguish involved with being a Protestant prison guard. The prison guard, one of the most traditionally vilified characters in Troubles films, is thus humanized and complicated through *Hunger*'s depiction of him as another potential victim of the system.

[7] This bombing is especially important in Troubles history because of the high number of casualties (twenty-nine killed and more than two hundred and twenty injured) and also its timing right before the historic 1998 Belfast/Good Friday agreement.

The film's commitment to this inclusive vision is also reflected in its production aspects. The producers consciously made an effort to include production staff and actors from the North, the Republic, and England. Producer Ed Guiney stated,

> From the very start, it was recognized that a film which tells the story of a tragedy which impacted hugely on the minds and consciousness of Ireland and the UK should be a collaboration between British and Irish filmmakers, producers, and broadcasters. It was felt that only by drawing on a shared experience and perspective could the production team hope to help develop and produce a film which would set out to tell the story of the Omagh Support and Self Help Group" (Travis, 2004).

While Troubles films tend to only represent one position on the conflict (often an overwhelmingly Catholic viewpoint[8]), *Omagh*, like *Five Minutes of Heaven*, purposefully shows multiple viewpoints, making it difficult for the viewer to latch onto only one perspective. This is exemplified in a scene which depicts a community meeting shortly after the bombing with victims from both communities arguing about how to proceed and who is responsible. This inclusion of multiple perspectives also shows a widening of the frame from a specific, sectarian position that represents the Nationalist perspective (typical of Troubles films) to an inclusion of both communities with conflicting and overlapping viewpoints. Voices from the community meeting express such varying points as:

> "My daughter had to strip to show her injuries to the compensation board. I can't believe that people would make her do that."
> "I'll tell you what this has to do with the RUC. 38 people have been arrested and 38 people have been released."
> "I've written to Tony Blair…he is the prime minister for God's sake."
> "As long as the bombs stay out of London, they don't give a damn. They don't care."
> "Please don't sit there and try and tell me this is somehow all the fault of the British."
> "When are the Irish going to take responsibility for what happens in Ireland?"
> "The Nationalist community? What about the Unionist community?"

[8] For more information on this, please see: David McKittrick's, "Why are all the Troubles films about Republicans?", *The Belfast Telegraph*, October 31, 2008.

The cacophony of competing views and voices shows a nuanced and complex representation of the multiple ideas and interests surrounding the aftermath of the bombing. The film does not simplify or reduce them in order to show a more coherent narrative or in order to promote a unified argument. Furthermore, while Michael Gallagher (a Catholic) becomes the leader of the Omagh Support and Self Help Group, he continues to represent all viewpoints. McIlroy remarks, "Gallagher is forced to voice the dissent, the feelings, and the concerns of the community affected, often at the expense of his own personal grief. It is as if Michael Gallagher is the repository of a collective memory and collective grief" (McIlroy, 2007: 452). Gallagher thus comes to embody the enormity of pain and anger from the diverse community, creating a much more complex and multi-dimensional protagonist than is typical of Troubles films.

Another important characteristic of the closed-text quality of Troubles films is their tendency to end with a demand for justice and punishment, directing the viewer to conclude that a peaceful Northern Ireland cannot exist unless those responsible for the injustices are punished. This can be seen clearly in *In the Name of the Father* which ends with the release of Gerry Conlon from prison. Gerry pushes his way through the crowds to the front of the courthouse, where he announces to the press and the people gathered that they all must continue to fight for justice and truth. As the film fades to black, a post-script tallies up the continued injustices perpetrated by the British judicial system since Gerry's release and asking that the viewer continue the fight to see justice done. Similarly, *Some Mother's Son* also concludes with a call for justice for the hunger strikers and for the British government to accept responsibility for its actions.

In contrast to Troubles films' mandate for redress and punishment, Peace Process films tend to pose questions (rather than provide answers) about how justice and reconciliation can be achieved. *Omagh* poses the question of whether it is possible for the country to forgive and heal *without* receiving justice or revenge, a fundamental debate in today's continuing peace process. In a meeting to discuss the IRA's role in the Omagh bombings, Gerry Adams tells Gallagher, "Look what we have got to do now is make sure the peace process keeps moving forward. Put the past behind us. That's the only way we are going to deal with this". Gallagher responds, "The war is supposed to be over. You say you want to build a new Northern Ireland, a peaceful Northern Ireland. But how can we build a peaceful Northern Ireland unless you help us to bring these killers to justice?" The film raises these questions and provides multiple views on the subject while refusing to provide a definitive answer, enhancing its open-text quality. *Five Minutes of Heaven* poses a similar question. A producer who is prepping Griffin for his television confrontation with Little tells him, "This is the question we are wanting the answer to: truth and reconciliation-what's at stake? Is it possible?" This tension between whether society needs to move on from the past (forgive and forget) or whether the past must be confronted and justice performed in order for the country to heal is a reoccurring theme in Peace Process films. While Troubles cinema ultimately contends that one cannot build a peaceful Northern Ireland unless those responsible for the violence are brought to justice, Peace Process cinema asks: Is the past holding Northern Ireland back and preventing the country from healing? Can a community move beyond its own history? Can the perpetrators forgive themselves, pay their debt to society, and move on? Can the victims allow themselves to heal? Can reconciliation happen on a national level or must it be worked out between individuals? In this way, Peace Process films distinguish themselves from Troubles films by asking and exploring these questions rather than providing definitive answers. In doing so, Peace Process cinema acknowledges that an important part of the transition in the North is having individuals participate in articulating the goals and expectations of peace and reconciliation.

It is also important to note that this opening up of space for opinions, viewpoints, and ideas is also reflected in Peace Process films by the widening of the lens and the storyline to a more universal context. *Omagh* and *Five Minutes of Heaven* both emphasize the universality of their stories and ask the viewer to apply the film to any community engaged in sectarian conflict. Oliver Hirschbiegel, director of *Five Minutes of Heaven*, says, "It is a universal story. It could be set in Bosnia just as well as Lebanon or other places" (Hirschbiegel, 2009). Similarly, Liam Neeson, who plays Alistair Little in the film, says, "It is specific, of course, to Belfast and to Northern Ireland but the stories could be easily be applied to any Troubles spot in the world" (Hirschbiegel, 2009). Likewise, at the end of *Omagh*, Gallagher addresses the media saying, "We speak not just for ourselves. We speak for the victims of the Troubles of whatever tradition and all those victims of terror wherever it happens". This is in stark contrast to the endings of Troubles films such as *In the Name of the Father*, *The Boxer*, and *Some Mother's Son* which ground their arguments and calls for justice firmly within their specific Northern Irish context. As Daniel Day Lewis, who plays Gerry in *In the Name of the Father,* says about Troubles films, "It's so easy to focus on politics and religion when you are dealing with any story dealing with Ireland and particularly the North of Ireland, immediately your vision becomes myopic…" (Sheridan, 1997). In contrast to the "myopic" viewpoint of Troubles films, this broadening of the frame to a more international context mirrors a general widening of space and viewpoint that is typically found in Peace Process films. This opening up of the Northern Irish narrative to a more international perspective may also be influenced by the number of non-Irish filmmakers who have recently directed Peace Process films. The German director Oliver Hirschbiegel and the English artist Steve McQueen (*Hunger*, 2008) are two examples of filmmakers outside of Ireland who have recently created films about the conflict.

In addition to the transition from a closed to an open text, the second important shift in Northern cinema is from a broadly pessimistic outlook to a more optimistic one. Troubles films tend to operate under a fatalistic sense of doom, showing the destruction of family unit, Romeo and Juliet love divides, and escape from the North as the only means of survival. This pessimistic fatalism is first identified as a feature of Troubles films by John Hill in his 2006 book *Cinema and Northern Ireland*. Hill identifies *Odd Man Out* as the film which would set the aesthetic and tonal precedence for most Troubles films thereafter. Hill writes that *Odd Man Out* "may be seen to have cultivated a particular view of the 'troubles' based upon metaphysics (the pessimistic workings of fate) rather than politics...As in classical tragedy, the film's story is concerned with the irreversible consequences of an initial error" (Hill, 2006: 191).

This fatalistic persona of Troubles films is demonstrated in part through the breakdown of the family structure. In Troubles films such as *In the Name of the Father, Some Mother's Son* and *The Boxer,* father figures are absent or dead, single mothers abound, and children are killed, imprisoned, or must flee the North for their survival. In an interview about *In the Name of the Father,* Jim Sheridan has said, "The idea behind the film is that the father figure becomes a kind of decimated symbol when you have a crushed culture. Once you destroy the father figure, the figure of authority, then you haven't got a society" (Barton, 2002: 76). Similarly, in *The Boxer*, the young fatherless Liam rejects Danny as a new paternal figure and acts out by setting fire to the boxing club. The absence of the father figure in Troubles films usually signals a lack of paternal authority, leading to the incarceration or death of the son. In *Some Mother's Son,* where fathers are noticeably absent, Kathleen's son is imprisoned and Annie's son dies on hunger strike. In each of these films, the Troubles is directly implicated in the breakdown and destruction of the family unit, and a stark pessimism about the future health of the family structure pervades the tone of these films.

While Troubles films typically show a fatalistic sense of doom and a landscape characterized by limited and closed options, Peace Process films are defined by a staunch optimism. Peace Process films open up space for possibility and change, presenting the family unit as damaged but intact and the North as a potential place for positive growth and change. In both *Five Minutes of Heaven* as well as *Omagh*, Troubles violence puts the family unit under extraordinary stress; however, the family ultimately survives whole and resolute, indicating a newfound optimism that a positive future can be forged in the North.

In *Five Minutes of Heaven*, Griffin is initially shown to be consumed by a hatred that is tearing his family apart. His anger and guilt over his brother's death has made him depressed, despondent, anxious and potentially violent. When Little sends a message to his home, Griffin becomes enraged, arguing with his wife and throwing her to the ground in front of his two daughters. Griffin is at a crossroads where he must choose between allowing his anger to control his life or making his family a priority over his trauma. Clarity occurs for him only after a violent fight in which he fails to kill Little. Griffin returns home and sits with his daughters, watching television. Griffin's daughter smiles at him, creating a mental and emotional breakthrough which allows his priorities to shift from vengeance to peace. The film immediately cuts to Griffin in a group therapy session for victims of the Troubles-the first time he has ever sought help. He tells the group, "I want my daughters to have a da they can be proud of. That's it. That's it. That's it…". Griffin repeats this last sentence several times as he breaks down in tears, finally having the cathartic experience he needs in order to break the cycle of hate and to begin healing. Griffin then calls Little and tells him, "We're finished". This is the release Little has been waiting for, and he falls to his knees, overwhelmed by emotion. Thus, the breakthrough for Griffin is arguably his daughters and his desire to remain connected to his family in a positive way. Directly against Troubles tropes of the absent, impotent, or dead patriarchal figure, *Five Minutes of Heaven* shows a father who comes back from the edge to remain intact and committed to his family.

Similarly, in *Omagh,* Gallagher is shown to initially pull away from his family and abandon them during their period of mourning. His daughter, Kathy, angry that he is neglecting his family, tells him, "You're always at a meeting. Every time I've rung, you've been at a meeting. Or on TV…Aiden's dead. He's dead. You should be here, daddy, looking after us". However, the end of the film shows a strong family unit, rallying around Gallagher. Towards the end of the film, Gallagher's wife, Patsy, appears at the Ombudsmen meeting where the families of the victims have gathered to hear the police's report on the bombing investigation. Gallagher pushes his way through the media, ignoring their requests for interviews and pictures, and runs to embrace his wife. Throughout the film, the media is portrayed as interrupting the family's private mourning, and the film also suggests that Gallagher's obsession with using the media to help find the bombers estranges him from his family. Thus, Gallagher's pushing the media aside to embrace his wife is an important signal that he, like Griffin in *Five Minutes of Heaven,* is committed to reuniting and strengthening his family. Flanked by his wife and daughters, Gallagher ultimately tells the newspapers and television cameras at end of the film, "We will not go away. We will not be quiet. We will not be forgotten". These are the words of a strong and undefeated family who will continue the process of mourning but will not be entirely crushed by it. One of the last images of the film is of Gallagher, his wife, and daughters walking down the road together hand in hand. This sense that the family unit can remain intact, strong, and healthy, despite the great trials and violence experienced during the Troubles, signals a definitive and newfound optimism in Peace Process films.

The political, social and cultural landscape of the North has changed dramatically from the 1990s to today. Nowhere has this distinctive shift been reflected so clearly as through the country's cultural production with cinema at the lead. If Troubles films have traditionally presented a closed ideological universe of restricted space, rigid binaries, and one persuasive viewpoint that directs the viewer toward an inevitable conclusion, it is because this cinema emerged from a period in which an entrenched and staunchly conflict-centred ideology was the norm. In contrast, Peace Process cinema has had the luxury of creating more nuanced and complicated representations of the conflict, reflecting a new optimism about the future and a new acceptance of ambiguity in representations of the conflict. This is, in part, due to a new post-conflict ideology that is redefining the country's understanding of its past as a much more complex and nuanced tangle of socio-political issues that can no longer be defined by or resolved with rigid binaries or absolutist, single-minded points of view. Just as the past is being redefined, the present-day North is also being re-envisioned as a place for growth, positive change, and stability. With a confident peace now in place and the benefits of a more stable political atmosphere, Northern Irish cinema is not only reflecting back this redefinition and re-presentation of the country's past but is also playing an important role in asking Northern audiences to help imagine and shape the new North.

Bibliography

Films

Five Minutes of Heaven. DVD. Directed by Oliver Hirschbiegel. 2009; London: BBC2.

In the Name of the Father. DVD. Directed by Jim Sheridan. 1994; Universal City, CA: MCA Universal Home Video.

Omagh. DVD. Directed by Pete Travis. 2004; New York, NY: Sundance Channel Home Entertainment.

Some Mother's Son. VHS. Directed by Terry George. 1997; Burbank, CA: Warner Home Video.

The Boxer. DVD. Directed by Jim Sheridan. 1997; London, UK: Universal.

Critical Texts

Barton, Ruth. *Jim Sheridan: framing the nation.* Dublin: Liffey Press, 2002.

—. *Irish National Cinema.* London: Routledge, 2004.

Eco, Umberto. *The Role of the Reader: explorations in the semiotics of texts*. Bloomington: Indiana University Press, 1979.

Hill, John. *Cinema and Northern Ireland: film, culture and politics.* London: BFI Pub, 2006.

MacKillop, James. *Contemporary Irish Cinema: from the quiet man to Dancing at Lughnasa.* Syracuse, N.Y.: Syracuse University Press, 1999.

McKittrick, David. "Why are all the Troubles films about Republicans?" *The Belfast Telegraph*, October 31, 2008.

McIlroy, Brian. *Genre and Cinema: Ireland and transnationalism.* New York: Routledge, 2007.

McLoone, Martin. *Irish Film: the emergence of a contemporary cinema.* London: British Film Institute, 2000.

Rockett, Kevin, and John Hill. *National Cinema and Beyond.* Dublin: Four Courts, 2004.

Rockett, Kevin, Luke Gibbons, and John Hill. *Cinema and Ireland.* Syracuse, N.Y.: Syracuse University Press, 1988.

PART IV

DRAMA AND LITERATURE

CHAPTER TWELVE

PERFORMING NATIONHOOD IN MAC INTYRE'S *ONLY AN APPLE*: A PALEO-POSTMODERN READING

CATRIONA RYAN

Tom Mac Intyre's play *Only an Apple* marks a new direction in his theatrical work. Since the late seventies much of his theatre has been steeped in experimentation where a Grotowskiesque emphasis on the body took centre stage. In his previous work the author tended to avoid issues concerning politics preferring to focus on an archetypal Yeatsian aesthetic power of the unconscious: "Out of the argument with ourselves we create poetry out of the argument with others' politics" (Ryan, 2012: 227). Though Mac Intyre does explore a variety of Yeatsian dimensions in *Only an Apple* it is also possible to read the text as an allegory of the continuing transition of the Republic of Ireland's political identity from being a nationalist state to that of the European other. This transition is metaphorised in a paleo-postmodern context. I created the term paleo-postmodernsim to describe the uniqueness of Mac Intyre's aesthetic of balancing traditional themes with postmodern deconstruction. The play involves an analysis of a Yeatsian paleo-modernist representation of political identities which, in a Lacanian sense, are mirrored in language and are deconstructed. The drama is concerned with an Irish Taoiseach who is battling to save his leadership and is distracted by the supernatural apparition of two archetypal representations of Irish and British Nationalism, Grace O'Malley and Queen Elizabeth I.

The play was first performed at the Peacock Theatre in Dublin in 2009 and it had a mixed reception [...]. According to Patick Lonergan, "*Only an Apple* [...] is vacuous, crude, and infantile. [...] And because of all those things, it is a stunningly appropriate and stimulating portrait of our political system" (Lonergan, 2010: 316). Lonergan is referring to the Irish political scandals that erupted in the early nineties and resulted in two decades of tribunals. The sociological repercussions resulted in a deep distrust by the Irish electorate in the political system. Mac Intyre's drama is a farcical portrayal of the later life of the disgraced politician Charles J. Haughey, who was at the centre of those tribunals, and whose demise in 2006 marked the end of one of the most Machiavellian characters in 20th century Irish politics. Like the Taoiseach in the play Haughey's reputation went beyond political corruption as he also indulged in extra-marital affairs. However, rather than portraying an all-out political villain, Mac Intyre's Taoiseach is a tragic persona who is essentially searching for spiritual salvation. The play's archetypal "visitors," Grace O'Malley and Elizabeth I, are succubi who have taken human form and they use sex to manipulate their victims. According to Arkins, the Taoiseach's Cultural Attaché,

> Arkins: Succubus, singular, succubi, plural. They move,
> It seems, between the worlds. Voraciously! Upright, on
> All fours, missionary, sixty-nine, plain old welcome-home-sailor, marathon
> or quickie, infinite variety their signature and seal. (Mac Intyre, 2009: 25)

The succubi are mythical demonic figures who, through continual sexual intercourse with men, eventually kill their prey.

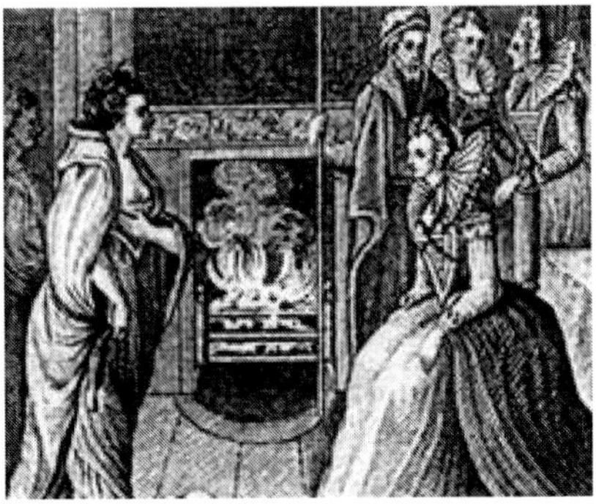

Fig 12.1, The meeting between Grace O'Malley and Queen Elizabeth 1 in 1593.

In *Only an Apple* they target the Taoiseach and adopt politically iconic identities which mirror the Taoiseach's historical sense of self, namely representations of the Irish and British colonial conflict. In Irish history the 16th century figure Grace O'Malley was the chieftain of the O'Malley clan who were the most powerful in Ireland. She developed a reputation as a pirate and won the respect of Elizabeth I whom she met in 1593. Queen

Elizabeth I ruled England for forty four years and her reign was considered to be the golden age for literature and trade. Their meeting was an unprecedented historical occasion where the two leaders of Britain and Ireland were female. In *Only an Apple* the political facades adopted by the succubi are designed to lure the politician through a familiar political narrative which mirrors his own ego to the unfamiliar supernatural borders of an unknown spiritual identity which is symbolised as the space of the European Goddess.

As already noted the methodology which will be used for discursive analysis is paleo-postmodernism. This is a term I previously developed to describe Mac Intyre's idiosyncratic aesthetics of balancing postmodern experimentation with traditional Yeatsian ideology. Paleo-postmodernism has three aspects: 1. Yeats's paleo-modernism which deals with Yeats's early modernist revivalist interest in the past, most particularly Celtic history and mythology. Frank Kermode first coined this term in the sixties to describe early modernism which, in the late nineteenth century, was characterized by "formal desperation and an apocalyptic vision" (Kermode, 1971: 40). Yeats's paleo-modernist vision in the late nineteenth century reflected the wider European *fin de siècle* anxieties about man's existence and his interest in Irish history and mythology has a major influence on Mac Intyre's work. 2. Carl Jung's ideas on the archetypal dimensions of the unconscious also influenced Mac Intyre who associates paleo-modernist symbolism of the Celtic past with Jungian archetypal representations of the anima. 3. Jacques Lacan's concept of language is relevant to Mac Intyre's work as it provides a useful framework for understanding Mac Intyre's deconstruction of language and how that relates to the psychological motives of the protagonists. Lacan's concept of the Real, the Imaginary and the Symbolic aspects of language is based on Freud's idea of the Oedipus complex. The Real is concerned with the child's absolute identification with the mother. Once the child leaves the space of the Real all its drives are directed towards re-attaining that original union with the maternal body; as the child matures the pre-linguistic space of the Imaginary is adopted in order to overcome the trauma of separation from the mother where the child maintains the fantasy of maternal identification. The Symbolic is where the child renounces his desire for identification with the maternal space of the Real through the adoption of the patriarchal code of language. According to Lacan it is the construct of Symbolic language that structures a subject's identity and in Mac Intyre's play the Taoiseach and the visitors mirror each other as their identities are structured by the language of English and

Irish which, in key parts of the play, dissolves to reveal a transcendent European feminine space; the Lacanian Real.

Performing Nationhood

The drama is set in Taraford which, in the play, is the Taoiseach's official residence. The Taoiseach is preparing to counter a challenge to his leadership by his main rival Mac Phrunty and part of his plan is to introduce the Irish nation to his recent visitors Elizabeth I and Grace O'Malley:

> Taoiseach: They are-to my impartial eye-well-furbished women of the world, *some* world; their credentials merit the closest scrutiny. Optimum reading? The greatest English sovereign ever-and our pirate of legendary prowess-select Taraford for pleasure-ground and the Irish Head of State for confidante. I can go with that. These women have a contribution to make, and I intend to give them scope. I know the citizens of this island, Hislop. They demand the hubbub of event. Without it, they looked starved, are *starved*. That, sir, is the insidiously abiding germ of blight in the soul of the Gael, and I, for one, will not be party to its propagation! (Mac Intyre, 2009: 24)

The Taoiseach is speaking of the supernatural visitors and the significance of their presence at his home. In other plays such as *The Great Hunger* and *Rise up Lovely Sweeney* Mac Intyre always uses the presence of women to represent the feminine side of the male characters in the context of the Jungian anima (Ryan, 2012: 223). According to Jung the anima is "a factor of the utmost importance in the psychology of man where emotions and affects are at work" (Jung, 1999: 70). Mac Intyre's conception of the anima in his drama was always associated with a revivalist-styled ideation of a female Celtic archetype, "In Yeats's view Ireland was only superficially Christian or modern. Underneath the provincial imperial-British surface he sensed the presence of ancient paganism and the half-remembered myths of antiquity" (Richards, 2004: 49).

Yeats often embodied that underlying power in feminine terms. In a *Pot of Broth* he refers to Grace O'Malley as an idealized image of Ireland:

> Her eyes are gray like morning dew,
> Her curling hair falls to her shoe,
> The swan is blacker than [Looks round
> for a simile, then at his kand.~\ my nail,
> Beside my queen, my Granuaile. (Yeats 2006)

"Granuaile" is the Irish translation of the name Grace O'Malley. In *Only an Apple* the Taoiseach is convinced that the supernatural appearance of the visitors is a miraculous event and believes it reflects his position as head of state. He doesn't realise Grace O'Malley and Elizabeth I represent an otherness of identity which is connected to his own anima nature. The Taoiseach's lack of knowledge reflects the fact that he can't see past his own political identity which is historically bound up in the colonial and post-colonial relationship between Britain and Ireland. He thinks that somehow the appearance of the visitors will immortalize him politically in the face of the leadership challenge from Mac Phrunty. When the Taoiseach states the manifestation of these characters will feed the Irish public's "starved" need for the "hubbub of event" he is talking about using the event to his political advantage. The term "hubbub" historically has some interesting connotations. According to Robin E. Bates the term "hubbub" was used by the British in the seventeenth century to refer to the "barbarous Irish" (Bates, 2008: 20). According to David Greene, "the history of the word 'hubbub'" is rooted in "an interjection of aversion or contempt" and abú, "the war cry of the ancient Irish" (Greene, 1971: 167). Therefore the word "hubbub" is rooted in the historical conflict between the British and the Irish.

The word "hubbub" is associated with "event" which the Taoiseach refers to as the imminent introduction of these characters to the Irish public; an introduction in which they would be used as propaganda. The term "event" also has postmodern connotations. According to Derrida the word "event" is the point where presence in language immediately recedes upon articulation. It is the idea that there is no central meaning in language and that meaning is always deferred. The word "event," in the play, is attributed to the word "hubbub" which also has postmodern connotations in that it refers to "a chaotic din" and therefore implies the disruption of a centered meaning in language (Oxford Dictionaries Online). According to Derrida language is in a constant state of chaos or "play" where a central signified meaning is always deferred.

The postmodern decentring quality in this instance is that it casts a further reflection on the other Irish and English linguistically politicized hermeneutical associations of the word '"hubbub" by exposing the deconstruction of meaning. Lacan says the subject is socially constructed by Symbolic language and in *Only an Apple* the deconstructive characteristic of the word "hubbub," which refers to the appearance of the visitors, reflects the falsity of the nationalist identity of the visitors themselves; since they use a language of Irish and English which has become de-familiarised via the word "hubbub". This conjunction of political identification and the unreal is reflected in recent critical discussions regarding twenty-first century post-nationalism in Ireland and Britain: according to Richard Kearney "The shibboleths of both Irish and British nationalism begin to become undone when exposed to the razor of contemporary change. Britain and Ireland are, in Benedict Anderson's resonant phrase, 'imagined communities'" (Kearney, 1997: 9). This idea of "imagined communities" in the word "hubbub" has an explosive paleo-postmodern impact on the play which conjoins a paleo-modernist Yeatsian vision with postmodernist deconstruction. This reinforces the idea that rather than being the actual characters of Grace O'Malley and Elizabeth I the visitors are performing these roles; they are essentially performing nationhood.

Judith Butler's ideas regarding the social performance of gender are very relevant here:

> If the body is not a 'being,' but a variable boundary, a surface whose permeability is politically regulated, […] I suggest that gendered bodies are so many 'styles of the flesh' […] consider gender, for instance, as a corporeal style, an act, as it were, which is both intentional and performative, where 'performative' suggests a dramatic and contingent construction of meaning (Butler, 1990: 139).

In a similar way Grace O'Malley and Elizabeth I undertake a political "corporeal style", based on the "contingent construction of meaning" which is mirrored in their Lacanian Symbolic use of language. This idea is also mirrored in the Taoiseach whose self-belief in his political identity is mirrored in the political identity of the visitors. But his status is one where he identifies with his political ego and is proud of the fact the visitors chose to pick "the Irish Head of State for confidante". His over-confidence also betrays a deep insecurity in his identity. On the level of the Lacanian Symbolic the visitors represent both the Taoiseach's languages of Irish and English, but in the context of the Lacanian Imaginary stage they are the mirror for the Taoiseach's fantasy of his idealized egoic self. According to Lacan the Imaginary stage is where the child creates an idealized mirrored self-reflection in order to cover up the realization of his own separation from the maternal body, in other words his own fragmentation. In the play this original union is portrayed as a feminine world that exists beneath the visitor's camouflaged nationalist personas. The appearance of O'Malley and the British queen represents the fact that the Taoiseach's political identity is about to fragment.

The Lacanian Real and the European Other

Understanding the function of language in Mac Intyre's work is central to understanding his drama. In my recently published monograph, *Border States in the Work of Tom Mac Intyre: A Paleo-Postmodern Perspective*, I argue that Mac Intyre uses the Irish language, in plays such as *The Great Hunger* and *Rise up Lovely Sweeney,* to deconstruct the colonial language of English in order to discover a primal unconscious Irish identity. In *Only an Apple* the author takes a different route in that the languages of English and Irish become political constructs which are disrupted by the powers of the European other. In Act 2, scene 5 of the play the Taoiseach discusses the significance of the visitors in terms of his fate, with Arkins, a gay character, who is portrayed as a wise poet:

> Taoiseach: Grace insists I've been howling for them for at least a decade. Is that possible? Always been taken by them-Grace O'Malley and Elizabeth, who wouldn't?-but *howling*-for at least a decade?
> …
> Arkins: Few of us know for what we howl. Our fate, some say.
> …
> Taoiseach: Our fate what the hell is that? Your fate. Explain, explain-
> Arkins: Three Goddesses out there, it's in all the stories. One releases you into the world, the next determines the nature of your life, the third snips the thread-gone! (Mac Intyre, 2009: 90-91)

In European mythology the three Goddesses who represent fate have different manifestations which are linked:

> the traditional representation of the three Goddesses as spinsters […] The 'Never-Nevers' are a combination of Clotho, 'the spinning fate.' Lachesis, 'the one who assigns to man his fate,' and Atropos, 'the fate that cannot be avoided' […]The 'European faces' of these *Parcae*-spiders evoke a grim vision of the destructive powers of Europe. (Bemorg, 2008: 85)

Beneath the political facade the visitors represent the three goddesses of fate who symbolise a transcendent European feminine power. They seek to possess the Taoiseach and take him beyond the borders of his familiar nationalist identity which is bound up with a complicated colonial history into the space of the European other. Richard Kearney notes that the challenge for the "imagined communities" of the British and Irish states in the twenty first century is maintaining a nationalist identity in the face of "the increasing momentum of European politics towards a postnationalist paradigm" (Kearney, 1997: 9). This is a reflection of the cultural tension in Ireland in the last twenty years in terms of dealing with an increasingly converging Europe where nations, through different treaties, have transferred powers to an increasingly more centralized European system. According to Tamar Mayer:

> Since Ireland joined the E.U. the paradigmatic links between Irish state and the Irish nation have weakened. Such weakening in correspondence between the symbolic content of the Irish nation and, particularly, the juridical content of the state, has resulted in the widespread perception in Ireland that the Irish nation itself is dissolving. […] As a result, since the mid-1980s national politics in Ireland have been largely dominated by highly gendered and sexualized political issues such as contraception, abortion and divorce-those issues which directly threaten the moral symbolic content of the Irish nation (Mayer, 2000: 71).

The moral debate regarding contraception, abortion and divorce and the impact of Europe was very much the dominant theme throughout the nineties in Ireland. The European court of Human Rights had the power to pressure the Irish government on the issue of women's issues, "pressure from Europe to conform to community legal standards regarding women's rights proved to be an important factor in forcing a reluctant Irish male political elite to address many of the economic and social policy issues" (Coulter, 1997: 265).

There is a proto feminist dimension to Mac Intyre's work as he is aware of the negative historical impact of the Catholic Church on women in Ireland:

> The truth we're talking about for me brought up in Gestapo Ireland of the thirties and forties […] where you were told you had no permission to think…and women don't exist by the way […] the Catholic Church was leading the Gestapo attack […] if you are interested in quality story-telling you have to […] shed everything you have and follow the star that is your star and you will come back to the Goddess really […] the aisling figure or put it another way to the conversation with the form interior (quoted in Ryan: 2012, 220)

In *Only an Apple* Mac Intyre presents an aesthetic attack on the Catholic Church's view of women by evoking a powerful archetypal feminine force. The visitors are sexualized entities, and as the European other they challenge a moral authority in an Irish society which has been dominated by Catholic conservatism. As Mac Intyre notes the goddess archetype is an important part of male creativity, she is the anima part of his identity, the source of which, for him, dwells in the unconscious. In the play the

European tripartite goddess, is embodied but hidden, in the visitor's performance of nationhood. The play conveys a sense that the journey the Taoiseach is about to take reflects a world, which is beyond traditional Irish/British political relations, and is associated with the mystical other. This mystical other is symbolic of an otherness of identity; a European identity, as the Taoiseach states the visitors represent "the turbulent landscape of the new" (Mac Intyre, 2009: 20).

Tamar Mayer's reference to an "Irish nation dissolving" is reflected in the fragmentation of the Taoiseach's political identity. His sense of the "landscape of the new" also refers to the Taoiseach's interior journey towards his anima nature. According to Jung the anima is often "hidden in the dominating power of the mother" (Jung, 1999: 71). In the context of the Lacanian space of the Real, Jung's association of the anima with the maternal is significant as the Lacanian Real represents an infant's total identification with the mother and, according to Lacan, the basis of the maturation process of separation into the Imaginary and the Symbolic is always the subject's unconscious drive to return to the space of the Real. As already noted, the dissolving of the mask of political identification, and its associated Lacanian Symbolic language, reflects the fact the Taoiseach is about to transcend the empirical boundaries of his familiar political identity into the interior landscape of the trans-linguistic Lacanian Real; which is maternally associated with the anima space of feminine power. In a paleo-postmodern sense the dissolution of the Lacanian Symbolic representation of language erodes Irish and British identities in the face of the growing power of the European other.

Spiritual Unity: The Vampiric Protestant Aesthetic

The supernatural power of the visitors is reinforced in the play through the symbol of the vampire:

> Taoiseach: she's off the leash! See that flitther of her fangs-and you're worse!
> Grace: should I bate me breast?
> Taoiseach: I prefer *her*, she's honest about her venom-but *you*, you'll soother and wheedle and jook, the you'lll sink the teeth!
> Grace: And, if I do, it's for mutual pleasure, as you should be the first to know. Suffrin' Christ, I had such faith in you. Now a hasky welt in the voice, and a *strainc* on the puss, but at least I know the *why* of it. [...]Mc Phrunty, God bless him, had a bit o' style! Did I not tell you, he had a *céad mile fáilte* loss o' consciousness?
> Taoiseach: is he still in it?

> [...]
> Grace: isn't he after b'in' looked after, a chroí? Wasn't I meself the one-as the three of us entered harbour-that gev him *The Mortal Kiss?*
> Taoiseach: *Mortal kiss?*
> Grace: Aye, it's one of the sweetest explorations-for the likes of us, y'know-a stillness to it-and a softness-it's a srtov a lishpeen of a pógeen-God in Heaven, I wish I could *express* meself–ever feel, Taoiseach, that your willowy tongue-that lovely green offal-is just an upstart insubordinate, a upsthart unshubordinate dissolvin' solvint! (Mac Intyre, 2009: 79)

In this scene the Taoiseach makes reference to the passionate natures of the visitors who enter and drain their lovers of energy. He uses vampire imagery such as "fangs" and "sink the teeth" to describe such all-consuming behaviour. Grace O'Malley defends their actions and associates the passion with "the mortal kiss". This is a reference to a famous painting called *The Mortal Kiss* by the Russian artist Dimitri Vrubel. The painting was a mural created when the Berlin wall fell and is an iconic symbol of that historical event. It consists of the communist politicians Leonid Brezhnev and Eric Honecker kissing.

The immediate impact of the fall of the Berlin wall was the reunification of Germany which had a major effect on the pace of expansion and integration of the European Union. In *Only an Apple* Grace's reference to "the mortal kiss" relates to collapsed borders and in the case of the play the collapsed borders is the familiar historical narrative of British/Irish relations which the Taoiseach identified with. It is a reference to what lies beneath Grace's constructed Irish identity, the tripartite Goddess of European power. What is very significant in this scene is when Grace tries to explain the mortal kiss her use of the languages of Irish and English become disrupted. She says to the Taoiseach, "I wish I could *express* meself–ever feel, Taoiseach, that your willowy tongue-that lovely green offal-is just an upstart insubordinate, a upsthart unshubordinate dissolvin' solvint!" (Mac Intyre, 2009: 79). She is referring to how her language, where she speaks both in Irish and English, is becoming disrupted and it happens at the point of referring to "the mortal kiss". She feels the language of Irish and English is "insubordinate" and disintegrates-like the Berlin wall-like a "dissolvin solvint" in the face of something more powerful, the European other. Grace as a Yeatsian revivalist ideal of the past becomes a paleo-postmodern vision of an idealized history that has dissolved via the Lacanian construct of Symbolic language. This speech echoes Tamar Mayer's statement that in the twenty first century, "the Irish nation itself is dissolving".

The sexualised association of "the mortal kiss" and vampire imagery is reminiscent of Bram Stoker's novel *Dracula* where female vampirism is linked with sexual promiscuity:

> The fair girl went on her knees, and bent over me, fairly gloating. There was a deliberate voluptuousness which was both thrilling and repulsive, and as she arched her neck she actually licked her lips like an animal, till I could see in the moonlight the moisture shining on the scarlet lips and on the red tongue as it lapped the white sharp teeth (Stoker, 1997: 42).

Jonathan Harker's experience of the vampire conveys a sense of alienation in the face of the supernatural creature. Alienation is a characteristic of the Irish protestant aesthetic (Dawe, 1984: 21-22). Stoker's and Yeats's sense of the alienated self was developed as a result of being part of a religious minority in the late nineteenth and early twentieth century Ireland. Mac Intyre's protestant alienated vision is situated within the unconscious and is concerned with male protagonists who are disconnected from their anima natures. For Jung the vampire is an archetype of the primitive, voracious amoral shadow side of the personality (Cheung, 2009: 326). In the play Mac Intyre presents this attribute as a necessary aspect of the anima goddess side of the male subject. When Grace O'Malley refers to the disruption of language as being like a "dissolvin' solvint," it is contrasted with the physical action of "the mortal kiss" which is associated with vampirism. The physical action of the vampire's "fangs" is connected to the deconstruction of political walls; political identities. It is a physical link to the language of the European other which transcends the borders of the empirical world and ruptures the Lacanian Symbolic language (English and Irish) of the political facade that is Grace O'Malley. *Dracula* has often been interpreted as a xenophobic novel which highlighted a fear of the European other. Hailing from Transylvania the spectre of Dracula symbolised the worst fears of Victorian Britain regarding the effects of immigration and reverse colonisation.

Yeats was aware of Stoker's novel and in his play *Cathleen Ní Houlihán* he included vampire imagery. Cathleen Ní Houlihán, in Yeats's play, is depicted as a homeless old woman who has been dispossessed of her land and she visits a family and charms them with tales of her loss and sings songs of old Irish heroes. She inspires a young man, who was about to marry, to join the 1798 Irish rebellion against the English. The boy dies and it is reported the old woman transforms into a young female. The boy's sacrifice rejuvenates the young woman who is a metaphor for Irish nationalism. The vampiric dimension to the play is in Cathleen's statement, "They that had red cheeks will have pale cheeks for my sake"

(Yeats, 2006). The idea of "pale faces" is a common expression used to describe vampires. They are the undead who survive through taking the blood of the living. Like a vampire Cathleen becomes rejuvenated through the blood sacrifice of the young man. Yeats's paleo-modernist vampiric image of Cathleen as the embodiment of nationhood is disrupted by the paleo-postmodern performance of nationhood in *Only an Apple.* In Yeats's play the image of vampirism reflects the desire for a fulfilled Irish nationalist identity. In *Only an Apple* vampirism becomes the physical language of the European other which deconstructs the political identities and languages of Irish and British nationalism.

At the end of the play the Taoiseach decides to travel with the visitors to the other world:

> *The atmosphere changes utterly. All stand. Elizabeth takes from her bosom a blood-red apple, studies it, kisses it, takes a large bite, slings it to Grace. Grace studies it, licks it lovingly, takes a large bite, slings it to the Taoiseach. Taoiseach studies it, holds it aloft as you'd raise a glass of wine. Deep breath, he takes a large bite, throws the remains over his left shoulder.*
> *Pause.[…]*
> *'activating the object'[…]the two embrace and, the snake writhing companionably about them, they stroll from the room, door opening to their advance and remaining open.*
> *The Taoiseach has witnessed, as in witnessed, all this.* […] *He rises and walks slowly through that open door. Slow fade. A modest spot contests the slow fade. Finally this spot is vivid and focused trimly on what's left of that apple. It brushes that apple* (Mac Intyre, 2009: 103-104).

The silence of the scene conveys the idea that the languages of Irish and English and the related political identities have been deconstructed. The focus is on the apple which links all three characters through the silent process of biting. This vampiric image represents the language of the other and the snake is also linked to the ancient European worship of the great Goddess (Haarman, 1995: 60-61). By walking through the door the Taoiseach's familiar political identity and language has dissolved as he embraces the mystic world of the European other.

Mac Intyre's *Only an Apple* marks a move away from his other drama which generally associates the mystical world with Irish identity. This play takes a more contemporary slant as it symbolises Ireland's transition from a nationalist to a European identity. Mac Intyre portrays the shift as a positive paleo-postmodern apocalyptic moment where the future has unlimited potential and the psychological chains of Irish political history is relegated to the dark corridors of Ireland's traumatic past.

Bibliography

Bates, Robin E. *Shakespeare and the Cultural Colonization of Ireland*. NY/Oxford: Routledge. 2008.

Bemong, Nele et al. *Re-Thinking Europe: Literature and (Trans) National Identity*. Amsterdam: Rodopi. 2008.

Butler, Judith. *Gender Trouble: Feminism and the Subversion of Identity*. NY/London: Routledge. 2009.

Cheung, Theresa Francis. *The Element Encyclopaedia of Vampires: The A-Z of the Undead*. London: Harper Collins. 2009.

Coulter, Carol. "'Hello Divorce, Goodbye Daddy': Women, Gender and the Divorce Debate." *Gender and Sexuality in Modern Ireland* (1997) 258-275.

Dawe, Gerard. "The Bleak Inspiration of a Protestant Imagination". *Fortnight* 203: (1984) 21-22.

Greene, David. "The Irish War Cry." *Éiru* 22: (1971)167-173.

Haarman, Harald. *Early Civilization and Literacy in Europe: An Inquiry into Cultural Continuity in the Mediterranean World*. NY/Berlin: Mouton De Gruyter. 1995.

Jung, Carl. *The Archetypes of the Collective Unconscious*. London: Routledge. 1999.

Kearney, Richard. *Postnationalist Ireland: Politics, Culture, Philosophy*. London: Routledge, 1997.

Kermode, Frank. *Modern Essays*. London: Collins, 1971.

Lonergan, Patrick. "Theatre Review: Only an Apple." In *The Theatre of Tom Mac Intyre: Strays from the Ether,* edited by Bernadette Sweeney and Marie Kelley, 314-316. Dublin: Carysfort Press. 2010.

Mac Intyre, Tom. *Only an Apple*. Dublin: Abbey Theatre/New Island Press. 2009.

Mayer, Tamar. *Gender Ironies of Nationalism: Sexing the Nation*. London: Routledge. 2000.

Meany, Helen. "Only an Apple." *The Guardian*. May 4, 2009 Accessed February 25, 2012.
http://www.guardian.co.uk/stage/2009/may/04/theatre-review-only-an-apple 2009.

Richards, Shaun. *The Cambridge Companion to Twentieth Century Irish Drama*. Cambridge: Cambridge University Press. 2004.

Ryan, Catriona Ryan. *Border States in the Work of Tom Mac Intyre: A Paleo-Postmodern Perspective*. Newcastle: Cambridge Scholars Publishing. 2012.

Stoker, Bram. *Dracula*. NY/London: Norton & Co. 1997.

Yeats, W.B. *Cathleen Ní Houlihán*. Accessed February 25, 2012. http://www.readbookonline.net/readOnLine/26361/ 2006.
—. *The pot of Broth*. Accessed February 25, 2012. http://archive.org/stream/hourglasscathlee00yeatuoft/hourglasscathlee00yeatuoft_djvu.txt 2006

CHAPTER THIRTEEN

IRISH WRITERS AND THE FEMALE DOUBLE: SOME PERSPECTIVES ON EXEMPLARY DOPPELGÄNGERINEN IN THE WORK OF ANNE ENRIGHT AND MARINA CARR

CARY A. SHAY

> "Something comes back because in some sense it was never properly there in the first place"
> —Nicholas Royle, *The Uncanny*.

In the introduction to his 1971 translation of Otto Rank's pioneering study of the Doppelgänger, Harry Tucker, Jr. refers to what he terms an "interesting feature" of the motif, namely that "the double does not appear in the female, but solely in the male form" (Rank, 1971: xxi). He reminds us that this point had been made previously by Otto Weininger and he suggests that an explanation is needed in order for teachers of literature to come to an understanding of the significance of the Doppelgänger in literary texts. Andrew Webber concurs with this assertion in the context of his study of the Doppelgänger in German literature. He claims the Doppelgänger is "the more or less exclusive property of the male gender" and "host and visitant are axiomatically gendered as male" (Webber, 1996: 4). Although Rank's and Webber's studies are generally confined to exclusively male cases, the double is virtually a universal phenomenon from Plato through to the present day and there are numerous examples of Doppelgängerinen (female doubles) in literature and film[1]. Hence, the apparent need to clarify the gender exclusivity of this device deserves

[1] See Plato's *Symposium*. Examples of the Doppelgängerin in literature and film which are relevant to the present discussion include the 2010 film *Black Swan*; the 1991 film *The Double Life of Veronique*; Anne Enright's *What Are You Like*; Marina Carr's *Woman and Scarecrow* and *Portia Coughlan*, to name just a few.

further scrutiny, as Tucker suggests. When appraised in view of feminist revisions of psychoanalytic theory, which stress the inherent exclusions of the feminine from language, culture and the possibility of subjectivity, the segregation of the feminine from the literary usage of the double in itself suggests potential insights into contemporary women writers' use of this device.

The postmodern crisis of subjectivity is central to the appearance of the double in contemporary literature and doubles, by their very design, suggest splitting and the fragmented nature of the human subject. Critics agree that the Doppelgänger is used to disrupt, destabilize and displace notions of static subjectivity. And yet, the appearances of the Doppelgängerin also point to the ongoing and ubiquitous crisis of feminine ontology in the face of social realities which, despite major and enduring upheaval, continue to efface women's voices, women's concerns, and even their very existence. In Irish women's writings the double is often used to examine and question familial, social, religious and psychological projections that continue to affect and even govern women's lives in Ireland and to begin the work of processing seemingly inescapable histories, the ugly truths of which continue to spill out into the public domain.

Doubles appear with striking regularity in the works of late 20th century Irish women authors. They are employed as a means of acknowledging and processing deep psychological traumas and dysfunctional histories characterized by suicide, incest, sexual and emotional abuse, gender trouble, problematic pregnancies and even racism. Despite the widespread changes and social upheaval of the Celtic tiger years, the continuing lack of provision of abortion,[2] adequate childcare and even the recent instances of educational discrimination against teen mothers[3] are

---

[2] Despite a 2010 ruling by the European Court of Human Rights that Irish Law breaches a woman's right to medical termination of pregnancy in certain circumstances, the Irish state has thus far neglected to clarify its position or to ensure the availability of such treatment. Adding to the numerous controversial cases where women have been denied abortion in Ireland is the recent case of Savita Halappanavar. On 28 October 2012 Halappanavar, a dentist who was originally from India, died in agony of septicaemia at University Hospital Galway after her repeated requests for a medical termination of the foetus she was miscarrying were refused. Halappanavar and her husband were allegedly told "this is a Catholic country".

[3] A recent case reported in the Irish media in the final week of April 2012 detailed a situation in which a school girl in Munster was refused a place at school on the grounds that she was pregnant. The principle of the school wrote to the girl's mother stating that the school did "not take in such girls" and to the Ombudsperson for Children stating that "the school has an uncompromising [Roman Catholic]

evidence that prescriptive definitions of women and motherhood in economic, religious, social and political discourses—article 41 of the Irish constitution for example—have not been effectively challenged. The pain surrounding what Nuala O'Faolain has termed the casual wrecking of people's lives in the last fifty or more years by the conservative, patriarchal influence of the Irish Catholic church and its implicit collusion with the Irish state often finds expression in the discourse of doubles in Irish women's writing (O'Faolain, 1996: 58). Central to this discourse is the unconscious drama surrounding the maternal, which both Luce Irigaray and Julia Kristeva have argued is fundamental to the formation of human identity and to the problems surrounding female subjectivity. The ongoing rise of Irish women's poetry, drama and fiction which directly address the major theme of the problematic nature of motherhood as it has been constructed by traditional forces amounts to almost a revolutionary movement which aims to confront the established, conservative maternal discourse in Ireland. The literary use of the Doppelgängerin is a key component to the feminist interventions in Irish culture which women writers have made and continue to make in order to call attention to the latent fear and loathing of the maternal in Ireland.

Playwright Marina Carr and novelist Anne Enright both address the problems surrounding the maternal role and interrogate extremely difficult, even taboo, social issues using the device of the female double. Enright garnered widespread acclaim in the early aftermath of the Celtic Tiger for her novels' unflinching explorations of current and pressing social ills. She is most well known for her 2007 Booker Prize winning novel *The Gathering*, which tackled the problem of childhood sexual abuse, and she continues to enjoy a reputation as one of Ireland's most important living authors. Her novel *What Are You Like* was written at the start of the economic boom and depicts the history that preceded it in which women's choices were severely restricted. One of Ireland's most well-known playwrights, Carr has also been extensively praised for her unwavering portrayals of sexual abuse, incest, sexism, racism and for her challenges to traditional gender role stereotypes. Carr's plays have been produced internationally and her depictions of such difficult subjects have coincided chronologically with the rise and fall of the Celtic tiger and with the on-going scandals rocking the Catholic Church and the Irish government. In Carr's *Portia Coughlan* the title character's haunting by

---

ethos and will not become a dumping ground for those rejected elsewhere". The ombudsperson's report can be accessed in full at:
http://www.oco.ie/assets/files/complaint/OCOInvestigationretheactionsofSchoolA.pdf

the nearly insurmountable loss of her twin through suicide is compounded by the acute torture she suffers under the weight of social and familial projections of her identity. Similarly, Enright's *What Are You Like* details a young woman's struggle to negotiate the confusion over her identity under the shadow of both social prescriptions and the unconscious presences of her dead mother and her twin who was given up for adoption. These characters cannot escape the simultaneous presences and absences of their doubles, for they are the revenants who relentlessly haunt their on-going existences and who embody the confusion over who they are or what they may potentially be.

These doppelgängerin tales are characterized by a crisis for the host surrounding questions of how they know themselves, how they exist in the world and whether they can do so at all given the extremely difficult traumas they experience. Every appearance of the double brings with it a threat to the host and every double is inextricably bound up with death in some way. Even though some of these scenarios are resolved to relatively benign conclusions the element of the uncanny is unavoidably present. Each narrative contains a problematic depiction of mothers in relation to their daughters. The mothers in these texts are themselves split into two and sometimes three or more separate personae. They are often undifferentiated from their offspring so that the uncanny horror of repetition characterizes virtually every exchange. Indeed, some of these characters are so threatened by what they see in their doubles that they view death as the only alternative to a life of uncertainty surrounding their identity, and this is one of the key characteristics of the double in literature which Rank discusses. What is important in these examples is that the host's concerns—her desires, her traumas and questions surrounding her identity and her fate—are voiced through the device of "othering". A crucial element here is what Irigaray has called the "explosive nucleus" of the mother-daughter relationship—thus far underrepresented in culture—which continues to move to the fore of Irish women's writing (Whitford, 2000: 50).

The tendency to view the double as an exclusively male motif in modern literature, therefore, is paradoxically accurate in one sense and a fallacy in another. It is a fallacy because of the numerous examples of Doppelgängerin whose concerns and crises centre around questions of subjectivity. Yet it is also accurate because, as Luce Irigaray has established, woman is in a state of *déréliction*; she is not properly installed within the symbolic order and is excluded from language. In order to speak she must confront her own absence; her own death, and such confrontations are constitutive of the use of the double. In these tales,

Doppelgängerin are uncanny reminders of the central characters' feelings of invisibility, of their difficulties with expressing themselves. As Elisabeth Bronfen has argued, "the form of speech conceded to women is in some sense always connected with death...to speak, she must [...] perform the position of absence, of the double, which is the rhetoric of death" (Bronfen, 1992: 404). In Carr's *Woman and Scarecrow* for example, the necessity of speaking is precipitated by the woman's impending death and she is both aided and tormented by her double, Scarecrow, until the two voices eventually run together. Kristeva also has noted the threat of death which the double constitutes, and she has stressed the need to face up to the other within ourselves (Kristeva, 1986: 210). It is also the case, then, that women writers use the Doppelgängerin as a strategy for confronting marginalization within language. Deliberate othering can be said to be an example of the disruptive mimesis suggested by Irigaray whereby women mimic their own estrangement in order to jam up the machinery of masculine hegemony. As with the (privileged, male) Doppelgänger itself, what is at stake is a fundamental ambiguity surrounding the notion of static subjectivity and the recognition that it is a chimera. As Bronfen has stated, such "texts compulsively repeat so as to disclose the point of non-existence beyond which a woman writing can't, as yet, move" (Bronfen, 1992: 407). Indeed what drives the doubling—or compulsion to repeat—is both the fear of death and the desire for it. A fundamental ambiguity toward life itself is at the heart of doubling.

Both Julia Kristeva and Luce Irigaray have argued that all of western culture relies upon the murder of the mother and that unconscious matricide is the *sine qua non* of individuation in both Freud's writings concerning object loss and Lacan's work surrounding a child's entry into language, which both ascribe a fundamental lack to the feminine. Women are in a continual state of *déréliction* in culture, argues Irigaray. In other words they are at the margins and in exile; abandoned in terms of religion, myth, culture and language. If the god of the Old Testament created Adam in its image and likeness, then Eve is the other of the other and from the very beginning her subjectivity has been in question. Kristeva maintains that women should therefore align with the marginal and use double language which subverts static and hegemonic notions of identity. Irigaray, on the other hand, suggests that women highlight the mother-daughter dyad and disruptively repeat their marginal position so that they "convert a form of subordination into an affirmation, and thus begin to thwart it" (Irigaray, 1985: 76).

Enright's *What Are You Like* enacts these very strategies for highlighting and challenging such marginalization. The novel is filled with the confusion, anger, desperation and fragmentation that result from a woman's uncertainty over her identity. The novel also addresses the suffocation of women within the sole scope of an impossibly rigid and unrealistic maternal which is underpinned by political and religious ideology wholly divorced from the realities faced by women in everyday life. Enright uses doubling to illustrate the pain of the divided, multiple, and invisible self. Her narrative opens with an ambivalent description of Maria, the (host) twin whose mother is denied the choice of treatment for brain cancer because of her pregnancy, and dies. She is never informed of her illness, which goes untreated so that Maria and her twin may live. Maria is raised by her father, Berts, and step mother, Evelyn, while her double, Rose, is given to an order of Catholic nuns who arrange her adoption. The maternal in *What Are You Like* is viewed from multiple angles in the narrative. The twins' mothers are separated out into a confusing quaternity of biological mother, temporary surrogate nurse, stepmother, and adoptive mother. At one point in the narrative Berts refers to the twins' dead mother as "my wife" and Evelyn has to remind him that *she* is his wife (Enright, 2001: 224). There is also the potent presence of the religious maternal, in this case, the Virgin Mary who haunts the psychological life of Sister Misericordia, who provides temporary care and oversees the adoption.

Even though Maria occupies the central position in the narrative she is nevertheless cast from the outset as an uncanny other. She is described in the first line as "small for a monster" and the remainder of the opening is unsettling and gruesome: "You could eat her, that's all, her bladder like a sweet onion and her softly sprouting brain" (Enright, 2001: 3). A few lines later, Maria's father, Berts even imagines killing the child: "What would happen if he dropped her on the floor? What would happen if he cracked her on the mantelpiece, or swung her by an arm against the wall? All her little sacs would burst and leak. He could feel the soft snap of her bones" (Enright, 2001: 4). Yet Enright also gives Maria an early hint of a self, a kind of impermissible autonomy and desire for differentiation from her parents although this, too, is cast in an uncanny light. Berts' sisters mistake Maria's first words for "Ma Ma" but Berts realizes what she is saying: "What could be more monstrous than her birth? Only this: that the first word to bubble in her throat was her own name-twice" (Enright, 2001: 9).

When the narrative shifts forward to New York, where a young adult Maria now lives, she is outside herself looking in and she sees herself as the other through the eyes of Anton, a man she is falling in love with. An initial anagnorisis comes for Maria when she searches through Anton's bag in an attempt to quell her fear of abandonment and discovers a picture of what appears to be herself, aged twelve, with Anton. "It was a small bag, but it was important. There were important things in it. If he left her now, he would not come back again". The hollowness of Maria's identity is palpable here as she compulsively empties the bag and examines the contents. Her response to what she discovers is to return to the mirror—an object which appears repeatedly in the novel and with which each of the female characters struggle—to "check if [her smile] was still there" (Enright, 2001: 25). The photograph causes a crisis for Maria and looking at it again she "want[s] to laugh. She had always felt like someone else. She had always felt like the wrong girl" (Enright, 2001: 37). She also feels a want, "the kind that could make you kill someone" (Enright, 2001: 39). She imagines pouring boiling water on Anton, but eventually turns this violence inward and cuts herself.

Enright uses the scenario of a Catholic first communion to demonstrate the early genesis of Maria's feeling of invisibility. As Evelyn makes the paper cut-out that will eventually be the communion dress Maria stands on the dining room table with fresh scrapes and bruises all over her legs from playing in the garden, Evelyn asks "What are you like?" (Enright, 2001: 27). Maria is not the picture of an innocent little girl making her first communion the next day. Maria awakens to find the finished dress and imagines it as "a white cut-out girl floating up the patterned wall. Maria tries to imagine being inside it" (Enright, 2001: 28). Here there is a conspicuous sense of disassociation; of not fitting with this dress or the image it engenders. There is even an uncanny sense of vacating the body. When Maria visits the zoo after the communion, she leaves the others and goes alone, first into the reptile house, and then into the lion house, "looking for the Virgin Mary in with the lions" (Enright, 2001: 30). Eventually she meets the eyes of the lioness and suddenly has to urinate so urgently that she must sit in a trough of plants to relieve herself. A man that Maria did not see "bends over her and says 'You're a dirty little thing aren't you?' He roots in his pocket for something that Maria is afraid of. But when he finds it, it is a two-shilling piece" (Enright, 2001: 31). The terror of this scene contains multiple layers. There is a sense in which Maria is being put into a communion costume and being made into an image of something she is not. Searching for the Virgin Mary—the impossible image of the chaste virgin mother with whom she is told to identify—among the lions is a search for a version of herself which can be negotiated in the context of what she is being asked to embody by her parents and society. The setting of the zoo establishes the scopic economy within which Maria is placed and with which she is forced to cope.

Maria's gazing into the lioness' eyes, losing control of her bladder, and being confronted by an adult man who "roots in his pockets for something Maria is afraid of"–a man who watches her and subsequently labels her as "dirty"–all demonstrate the terror and confusion over the sexual projections that Maria is being asked to assimilate. It is no surprise, then, that when the communion photographs arrive Maria, who knows nothing of her lost twin, thinks "this is the other girl" and proceeds to colour over the face with crayon. Finally Maria tears the photo and "puts the pieces under her mattress for later" (Enright, 2001: 35). In these scenes Maria is haunted by her missing twin: the Doppelgängerin is an unconscious presence which also suggests the lost self that is continuously eclipsed by the projections Maria is being asked to embody.

At age eleven Maria visits her dead mother's family in Donegal. A mention of her grandmother's delph, which Maria will inherit, the "one cracked reference [her mother's family] had made to the blood between them and her mother who had died" (Enright, 2001: 49), is the outward symbol of further projections of her identity. She is asked to step into her dead mother's shoes and is thus dislocated both psychologically and physically by unfamiliar surroundings. She is expected to stand in for her mother when her uncle John kisses her: "Maria knows that it is not her he is kissing but his big sister that died and she feels her mother flower inside her..." (Enright, 2001: 47-8).

Leaving Donegal, Maria's unconscious connection with her mother is exposed. Her grandfather who, until this point had not spoken to her at all, "lean[s] his face towards her [and says] 'You might have died inside her. You have your father to thank for that'" (Enright, 2001: 54). This cruel remark both reveals something of which Maria consciously knows little and suggests to her that Berts chose her life over her mother's. Maria's unconscious matricide, necessary for her to become an individual, is here made concrete and she is made to carry the "blame" for her very existence. Ultimately Maria is made into a double of her mother, and her sense of absence and confusion is painful. Maria reacts to the trauma of all of this after her return to Dublin with both anger and frustration. In response, Evelyn inexplicably prepares her for her first menstruation:

> When they get home, something unfair starts to happen to her. Her chest starts to go all stupid and so do her eyes. She has a feeling like there is someone always coming around the corner who never arrives, the sight of crockery makes her so mad, she would smash a dish sooner than wash it. 'No one said it was easy,' says Evelyn, who gives her a plastic bag full of meshed up cotton and safety pins for no reason at all (Enright, 2001: 54).

All of the women in the narrative are connected through their menstruation and the maternal because this is the only role permissible to them. Their emotional connection is also limited to the maternal and is therefore undifferentiated, fused and problematic. Maria's double, Rose, is unable to connect with her adoptive mother, who is nearly a stranger to her. Nor can Maria connect to her step mother: her co-workers always call out "mother alert" when Evelyn enters the shop where Maria works. Thus pregnancy in *What Are You Like* is virtually a repetition compulsion. As Irigaray has stated, women's confinement within the role of the maternal is central to their *déréliction* and the absence of healthy examples of the signification of the mother-daughter relationship in culture keeps them in that position.

The brief description of the nun who oversees Maria's twin Rose's adoption repeats the doubling scenario yet again and reinforces the conflict over the maternal within the context of Catholicism. There is confusion from the outset over her name which is split into multiple versions: "...never mind the name. Sr. Misericordia, Maura Reynolds, The Misery... Matron Maura Reynolds...Mater Misericordiæ. Mother of Mercy" (Enright, 2001: 81-3). She is as a fragmented and split being; she is a nun and yet she is "God-hating" (Enright, 2001: 90) and cannot reach out to god because it would "break her in two" (Enright, 2001: 84). She "doubted the God who made this symmetry [of twins]" (Enright, 2001: 88). Misericordia broods over the motherless twins: "they had no mother. No mother. It was like a gash on your soul and Misericordia prayed for the Virgin to protect them and the whole, motherless world" (Enright, 2001: 88). Misericordia's confusion over her own identity which she had relinquished along with her hopes when she changed her name is expressed as she names the motherless twins after these lost hopes and "not to honour the Virgin at all" (Enright, 2001: 89). The section concludes with her recognition that she is invisible and her identity is elided by the presence of Agatha, her superior, whom she loathes and who has overshadowed her for years.

Maria's twin, Rose, is raised in England with parents who also regularly foster troubled teenage boys. She describes herself to herself as a woman who was "born with a hole in her head, a hole in her life" (Enright, 2001: 140). Her confusion and anger at her circumstances manifests in the games she plays during "foster boy wars", the men she dates, and in her compulsive shoplifting. Rose wrestles with Anton when her parents take him in and she feels that "she would win. He could kill her if he wanted to–she would die winning", as if victory was a way to be seen, to be assured of her existence (Enright, 2001: 104). Rose steals constantly while "everyone [watches] her and no one actually [sees]. It was like escaping and being locked up, both at the same time". Rose is trying to be seen, trying to be noticed and shoplifting is an angry, defiant gesture, like the foster boys who stole "just because they could" (Enright, 2001: 123). Eventually Rose gets caught. She stands for half an hour outside the store from which she is ejected in a rage, wanting to catch the eye of "the bitch" who caught her, the one who finally recognized her. Her failure to catch the woman's eye; her inability to look back at the woman and see herself reflected precipitates almost a panic and Rose begins looking at all the women passing her on the pavement and thinking that any of them might be her mother.

Both Rose and Maria are saturated with suicide, death, and the inability to know who they are. They are haunted by these unknown, Doppelgängerin presences that they cannot consciously identify. Maria cuts herself on her way back to Dublin and ends up in hospital and Rose conjures a scenario whereby the woman across the street hangs herself before she can reach her to stop her. Rose becomes a probation officer and one of her charges commits suicide. She relishes the funeral and meeting with the family almost as one relishes a good meal. In this way death is identified as a refuge. Both Rose and Maria long for death as an escape from their invisibility, yet they also fear it.

The first word that Rose and Maria utter to each other when they finally meet accidentally in the dressing room of the shop where Maria works is "one" as if the subconscious desire for unity within their individual psyches and for an un-splintered sense of self was spilling out uncontrollably. Incredibly they do not cease the mundane exchange in order to explore the obvious, but Rose goes straight into the dressing room to try on a garment. Eventually the two meet in the mirror of the open dressing room, and the obvious is inescapable. The mirror as a symbol of trouble and splitting yields a reification of the split in the image of the two together. There is no resolution for Maria and Rose, who do not achieve the feelings of security that they sought in a singular, visible identity. Rather, they are led to accept that fact of their multiplicity and sempiternal ambiguity. "The fact that there were two of them made it somehow easy. They could be happy and sad at the same time" (Enright, 2001: 254). Rose takes this realization of Maria as an explanation for her very existence. "No wonder they had given her away. They had another one, just the same" (Enright, 2001: 253).

Just as Maria is cast as an uncanny other in Enright's novel, the title character in Marina Carr's *Portia Coughlan* is referred to as "cracked", a "poor haunted monster", "a changeling", "a demon" and "an evil goblin" among other crude epithets (Carr, 1999: 203-44). Portia is a thirty-year-old mother of three who is stuck in an unhappy marriage and haunted daily by her beloved but dead twin. Convinced by her father to forgo college in order to marry, she exists in alternating states of rage and drunken misery over her predicament. Virtually all of the other characters project their own ideas of what Portia is—or what they would like her to be—onto her, hence the seemingly endless appellations. Even Portia's Doppelgänger, her dead brother Gabriel who committed suicide when he was fifteen by drowning himself in the Belmont River, has such a strong hold on her that she constantly fears him pulling her deathward, "He's closing in on me. I hear his footfall crossing the worlds"· (Carr, 1999: 251). Portia feels so suffocated by the demands from outside herself that she drinks heavily, spends most of her time at the site of her brother's suicide, flies into fits of rage, and even resorts to physical violence in an attempt to rebel against her predicament. All the while she knows that she cannot escape these projections or her history which is a record of incest, xenophobia and not-so-quiet desperation. Ultimately Portia is at the mercy of her history, which keeps repeating, or doubling, with each generation of her family. Again the emphasis is on the maternal relationship which is highly problematic in each of the generations represented.

The play is set beside the Belmont River, named for a mythical character who, as Portia recounts, was not a "hoor" as she was labelled, but so "different" that the townspeople "impaled her on a stake and left her to die" (Carr, 1999: 219). The opening scene is the morning of Portia's birthday with her husband Raphael criticizing her care of the children. He gives her a gaudy diamond bracelet and reminds her of its price. From the outset the play reeks with Portia's dissatisfaction in her life and her relationships, her frustration with the demands that others, including her young children, make on her and her unwillingness to meet those demands. She even insists to one of her several lovers "I'm not yours or anyone else's" (Carr, 1999: 202). There is a strong sense of gender trouble in the play. Portia expresses dissatisfaction that there are no men in the town to her liking: "If there was e'er a bull or a ram around" (Carr, 1999: 197). Portia's dead twin Gabriel is remembered by several characters for his feminine voice and the fact that he "looked like a girl", (Carr, 1999: 224) as though his association with his sister contaminated any chance he had at masculinity.

Most striking of all are the problems in the play surrounding the maternal. There exists extreme hatred between Portia and her mother, Marianne, and between Marianne and Portia's father's mother, Blaize. Portia refuses to care for her own children, who are all under the age of twelve. She refers to them as "nearly men" as if to relieve herself of the responsibility for caring for them (Carr, 1999: 199). When Raphael confronts her on her neglect she frankly explains, saying "I never wanted sons nor daughters and I never pretended otherwise to ya; told ya from the start. But ya thought ya could woo me into motherhood" (Carr, 1999: 221). Portia also admits that she is "afraid of [her children]...what [she] may do to them" and that she simply "can't love them...I'm just not able" (Carr, 1999: 233, 221). She accuses her own mother of wanting one of Portia's sons to drown, just as Gabriel did, and she insists that by neglecting her children she is saving them from harm: "I leave them alone and no mark is better than a black one" (Carr, 1999: 216). Blaize also accuses Marianne of having killed Gabriel and calls her a tinker: "ya can kill a body just be lookin' at them if ya look long enough and ya look wrong enough. I know your dark auld fuckin' Joyce streak and what it does" (Carr, 1999: 216).

Portia's desire to escape the motherhood that she feels was forced upon her, and her hatred of her situation eventually comes to a boiling point. Portia physically attacks her mother, telling her "you have me suffocated so I can't breathe anymore" (Carr, 1999: 239). The play moves between worlds, travelling from depictions of the dead Gabriel to the half-life of Portia, to the death of Portia. Scenes depicting Portia's suicide and funeral reveal that some underlying secret, "where the rot began and how the rot began" is what is causing all the pain (Carr, 1999: 230). The next act moves back again in time and finally it is revealed that Portia's mother and father are brother and sister. The history of incest was repeated with the birth of Portia and Gabriel. Portia admits an incestuous relationship with her brother, who felt betrayed when she began to see other boys. Portia recalls feeling undifferentiated at times from Gabriel, of the confusion over her identity without him: "we don't know which one of us is the other and we don't want to" (Carr, 1999: 254). Portia felt that her only chance at survival was to be noticed, to be seen, just as Rose attempts to be seen by the one who catches her shoplifting, and yet she concedes that her one chance "to enter the world and stay in it, which has always been a battle for [her]" fails (Carr, 1999: 255).

For Portia, the Doppelgänger is deadly. Gabriel threatens Portia before he kills himself, telling her he will be back for her. Marianne recounts how, when he was alive, Gabriel "used start [Portia] choking just by looking at [her]. How he used draw blood when [she] tried to defy him" (Carr, 1999: 249). Portia cannot seize her one chance at life because she is caught in what she calls a fight to the death with her Doppelgänger. In this case the split self is fatal to Portia who was undifferentiated from her mother, relinquished her opportunity to individuate and remained in a state of déréliction until the day she died.

Both of these Doppelgängerin tales revolve around mother-daughter relationships which are severely strained, not just by problematic histories, but also by a lack of differentiation of identities. At the root of these stories we consistently find, not just the uncanny horror of repeating the past and a crisis of identity from which there seems to be no escape but also iterations of the uncanny otherness of characters that are caught in the gap between life and death. They are not fully alive because of the overpowering weight of projections from the outside. They desire death as an escape from the ambiguity and exile that they suffer, and yet they wish, above all else, to see themselves and to be seen rather than being forced to be a mirror. The persistent presences of doubles in Irish women authors' texts demonstrates an urgent need to deal with the nightmare of a history, not just in Irish culture, but worldwide. The changes in Ireland of the last 30 years have been significant and have precipitated the need to begin processing the injustices of the past. Doubles provide an imaginative means to do this as they offer a position from which to speak from the split. Although these characters are clearly asking difficult questions about who they are and how they can function in the world, they do not find resolution to their dissociative states. Doppelgängerin narratives do, however, accomplish the crucial tasks of giving voice to fragmentation and providing the imaginary ground from which to view, as Kristeva has said, the "truth itself about an otherwise repressed, nocturnal, secret and unconscious universe" (Kristeva, 198: 207).

Both Carr and Enright provide exemplary enactments of the split subject and her seemingly insurmountable struggle with individuation as a way of voicing the possibilities of breaking harmful cycles. Providing an unflinching exploration of unspeakable social ills, these writers offer a view onto the unconscious operations that reinforce women's position at the margins. The uncanny horror of the Doppelgängerin suggests an alternative to the notion that women must duplicate and reflect what is projected upon them. The presence of doubles and the pain of the ambiguity and dissociation that they evince counter the notions that women can or should fulfill prescriptive definitions of femininity, that they should enjoy motherhood and confine themselves to caring for their children, that the sole alternative to their invisibility is death. The contemporary use of the double in Irish women's texts is both indicative of the shifting cultural contexts in Ireland and crucial to the healing of the wounds of the past. The self-referentiality of the double and the ambiguous, life-or-death scenarios that Carr and Enright present indicate both the urgency and the possibility of transformation for the invisible female subject.

Bibliography

Bronfen, Elisabeth. *Over Her Dead Body: Death, femininity and the aesthetic*. Manchester: Manchester University Press, 1992.

Carr, Marina. *Marina Carr: Plays One*. London: Faber and Faber, 1999.

Enright, Anne. *What Are You Like*? London: Vintage, 2000.

Irigaray, Luce. *This Sex Which is Not One*. Ithaca: Cornell University Press, 1985.

Kristeva, Julia. *Strangers to Ourselves*. New York: Columbia University Press, 1991.

—. "Women's Time" in *The Kristeva Reader* edited by Toril Moi, Oxford: Blackwell, 1986.

O'Faolain, Nuala. *Are You Somebody?* Dublin: New Island, 1996.

Rank, Otto. *The Double A Psychoanalytic Study*, Tucker, Harry, trans. Chapel Hill: The University of North Carolina Press, 1971.

Royle, Nicholas. *The Uncanny*. Manchester: Manchester University Press, 2003.

Webber, Andrew. *The Doppelgänger: Double Visions in German Literature*. Oxford, Clarendon Press, 1996.

Whitford, Margaret. *Luce Irigaray Philosophy in the Feminine*. London: Routledge, 1995.

CHAPTER FOURTEEN

"THE KINGS OF ODD": FARCE AND DEPLETED MASCULINITIES IN *MARTIN MCDONAGH'S THE LONESOME WEST*

EAMONN JORDAN

Cosy homesteads

The disquieting dispiritedness of Martin McDonagh's male characters and the contributions that they make to their own destructiveness, added to the allegation that McDonagh does not adequately contextualise their marginalisation, has led to an array of charges being made against his body of work. McDonagh's male characters have been particularly critiqued, purportedly for how they replicate narrow, traditional colonial stereotypes (Merriman, 1999: 312). McDonagh has also been accused of doing little to either address or make sense of the "emotional scarification" of his characters (Murphy, 2006: 73), and indicted for exoticising rural figures, whereby "The characters have no society: no sense that work, institutions or social class inform forms of thinking, or criticism, and of emotion [.....] We do not find on the stage any representations of public or civic space" (Barry, 2001: 186).

In recent scholarly debate on masculinities and Irishness general discussions have focused on the ideological mechanisms of patriarchal dissemination, control and preservation, and on the need to contest the systemic reliance on and manipulation of "hegemonic, heteronormative masculinities" (R.W. Connell's much cited term) (See Magennis & Mullen, 2011: 1-10). In relation to theatre practices, Brian Singleton's recent work also considers how masculinity "not only lorded itself over women, but also subjected subordinated groups to its authority and control. Hegemonic masculinity, then, operated through a performance of patriarchy" (Singleton, 2011: 8). Singleton also emphasises, following on from Connell, the substances of subordinate, oppositional, "non-hegemonic masculinities", evident in illustrations of diverse sexualities, and in class, religion, race, ethnic and gender differentiations (Singleton 2011: 8). In their considerable non-embodiment of "hegemonic masculinities," McDonagh's characters generally appear to be a long away from forms of representational masculinities that are firm agents of patriarchy or significant benefactors of its dividends–including the "material", status and the "honour, prestige, and the right to command"–that Connell identifies (Connell, 2001: 40-3). Current scholarship is exceptionally effective in dealing with marginalization and subordination in terms of sexual orientation, but it less ambitious or assertive in dealing with aspects of class, particularly in relation to contemporary cultures. Paul Murphy's excellent recent work illustrates how marginalized, peasant or subaltern characters, both male and female, are "essentialized as a fantasy object which is symbolically central to dramatic and ideological representation", yet marginalized within society more generally (See Murphy 2008: 21).

My discussions will focus on *The Lonesome West*'s premiere (1997) (McDonagh, 1999) which was a Druid/Royal Court co-production, directed by Garry Hynes, has Maelíosa Stafford as Coleman, Brían F. O'Byrne as Valene, Dawn Bradfield as Girleen (Mary Kelleher), and Tom Murphy as Fr Welsh [1]. I will discuss the play's anarchic farcical form, its ambivalence about moral frameworks, and its particular spin on the funerary tradition (See Witoszek & Sheeran, 1998). McDonagh's play incites forms of contingent, routinized, competitive, abject, grotesque, non-empathetic and performative masculinities–as opposed to the more positively marked and less arbitrary femininity of the play's only female character, Girleen–that do not align with a "recoverable" masculinity, Gerardine Meaney's term when writing about John Ford's *The Quiet Man* (1952), which is often deemed to be central to a pastoral consciousness (Meaney, 2006: 256).

Additionally, I will contend that through this disavowal of any form of a redemptive or "recoverable" masculinity, and by subverting, through gross normalization, the politically incorrect misogyny, homophobia and racism which emanate from the language and actions of many of the play's characters, McDonagh's work does not simply lead to an attack on limitations of his male characters nor to an erasure of a broader social awareness of the dynamics. Instead the emphasis is on the less tangible forces such as religion and forms of popular culture that conspire to create

[1] My comments on this production are based on seeing the play in the summer of 2001 at the Gaiety Theatre in Dublin, with this cast, and on viewing a recording of that production made at the Town Hall Theatre, Galway in October 2001. This was made available for me by Druid Theatre Company's Ruth Gordon.

subordination, marginalization and subsistence living. Based on this production, I will argue for the contestation of a privileged heteronormativity, prompted by an anarchical, and farcical sensibility.

Domestic Gods

Jessica Milner Davis, who has done substantial work in the theorizing of farce, notes that "[f]arce favours direct, visual and physical jokes over rich lyrical dialogue (although words are not unimportant in farce and can be crucial to its quarrels, deceptions and misunderstandings), and it declares an open season for aggression, animal high spirits, self-indulgence and rudeness in general" (Milner Davis, 2003: 2-3). Additionally, in terms of comic techniques, Milner Davis contends that "farce like other forms of comedy makes ready use of things such as burlesque (referential mockery of characters and situations known to the audience from outside the play itself), and slapstick (physical but stylized beatings and the humiliation of agelastic targets), and improbable co-incidences (often based on a reduction ad absurdum of some initially realistic event); but the characteristic which distinguishes it from other comic styles, is, that it does so without seeking to point out any particular lesson for its audience" (Milner Davis, 2003: 3).

Furthermore, farce, according to Milner Davis, deals with "the inescapable facts that all human dignity is at the mercy of the human body and its appetites and needs" (Milner Davis, 2003: 3), meaning it is driven by basic desires for food, sex, territory, power, dominance and control. Nominally, in terms of sex, farce is often about attempts to seduce or to pursue illicit desires by those who are constrained by marriage or relationship commitments. In general, while there may be opportunities created for characters to be unfaithful, more often than not such desires remain un-fulfilled, suggesting, in part, that endings affirm a conservative dramaturgy of sorts.

Verbal aggressiveness or threats of physical destructiveness are commonplace in farce, motivated by sibling rivalries, excessive competiveness, petty jealousies, sheer self-absorption and self-indulgence. For Milner Davis "the comic spirit of farce is one which delights in taboo-violation, but which avoids implied moral comment or social criticism, and which tends to debar empathy for its victims" (Milner Davis, 2003: 141). Following on from this tradition, McDonagh similarly seemingly delights in taboo-transgression, and often critics fall for that tendency and overly focus on the nature of such violation only. (Others more sinisterly perhaps, align such contraventions, especially in terms of violence, with

McDonagh's notional Irishness, which, of course, is a far more problematic disposition).

In classic farce Milner Davis argues, although "violence is omnipresent," it is "often more sound and fury than actual harm, more symbolic gesture than potent action" (Milner Davis, 2003: 3). Violence in McDonagh's work is but one of the many ways in which McDonagh splinters away from that classical tradition, informed more by the licence and chaos that figures like Joe Orton provide, for example in *Loot* (1965). Milner Davis aptly contends that characters in farce are "[d]oomed to repetitiveness in both behaviour and mental processes... display exactly that aspect of '*du méchanique plaqué sure du vivant*' ('something mechanical plastered onto the living') which for [Henri] Bergson defined an event as being comic" (Milner Davis, 2003: 4). In *The Lonesome West*, the two brothers Valene and Coleman Connor are locked in a power struggle, yet are so disconnected from the outside world, so negatively interdependent, that their mechanical, imbedded, intuitive responses deny a more considered, humane reflex.

Their link to the world beyond their cottage is predominantly mediated by a spurious and misconstrued Catholic moral framework, sentiments formed by their interactions and responses to such things as female inflected, gendered narratives found women's magazines, and in popular culture more generally, the presence of the odd visitor and, most significantly by attendances at funerals, that are treated more like parties and not rituals of mourning. Sexual desire and intimacy are dominated by celibacy and its twisted affiliation with a Catholic ethos, whilst virginity is immaturely framed by them as evidence of homosexual desire. Their self-expression is driven mainly by rage, revenge, resentment, hatred, hostility, aggressive threats or deeds of violence. Yet, in their world view, violence and conflict are also expressions of care. It is a violence that always appears to be on the cusp of something more extreme.

Eric Bentley has tellingly emphasized the abstractness of the violence in farce whereby "Prongs or a rake in the backside are received as pin pricks. Bullets seem to pass right through people, sledge-hammer blows seem to produce only momentary irritations. The speeding up of movement contributes to the abstract effect" (Bentley, 1965: 222). Further, Bentley adds, farce is additionally "a question of the speeding up of human behaviour so that it becomes less human" (Bentley, 1965: 247). Moreover, Bentley goes so far as to claim that farce is "the theatre of the surrealist body" (Bentley, 1965: 252). Placed alongside Milner Davis's focus on mechanical repetitiveness, Bentley's identification of de-humanization and surrealism provide subtle considerations of the anarchic farce of *The Lonesome West* and in particular its focus on masculinity. That "abstract effect" both distances and de-contextualizes the violence in McDonagh's work. The dismembering of the dead paramilitaries in *The Lieutenant of Inishmore* or the smashing of the exhumed remains in *A Skull in Connemara* are also exemplary of this sort of abstraction, as the sensational and taboo breaking theatricality heightens the performative register of characterization, resulting in a fracturing of relationships with the notionally real. (Nothing on stage simply represents, and if that is the case, cannot be accused of misrepresenting.)

For the Druid/Royal Court co-production, Francis O'Connor creates a kitchen/living area of a cottage/farmhouse in Leenane, with a strong claustrophobic feel. The stage design looks exceptionally dingy, almost derelict, encrusted in grime due to the on-going negligence of the two bachelor and middle-aged brothers, Coleman and Valene, who don't cook, and seem to have a poor diet, comprising crisps, alcohol and whatever they can scavenge after funerals. Furnished with a table, chairs, and a single tattered armchair, the space also features prominently displayed on shelves Valene's fiberglass statues (figurines) of saints and popes. Over the stove, there is a double-barrelled shot gun and above that again is a crucifix. The letter "V" is embossed on most items in the space, indicating Valene's ownership of both the family home and of the objects resident therein. (Valene's branding is a further violation of the space itself. Later the arrival of a new, large orange stove does not escape Valene's compulsion to initial everything, without exception.)

Stafford's Coleman is slovenly in appearance, wearing a too tight brown shirt under an old three-quarter length leather jacket, looks under-dressed for his father's funeral, appears driven by a sadistic, provocative menace, and swaggers with a curious bravado that springs from a strangely cynical self-confidence, a pathology or a combination of both. In addition, there is neither substantial guilt nor traces of despair as he is excruciatingly assured that he will not face the forces of justice over his very recent killing of his father. Obliged to pour a drink of poteen for the priest, Father Welsh, who has presided over their father's funeral, Coleman aggressively rips off some sellotape that Valene has wrapped around a biscuit tin to seal it from him. Coleman's general disdain seems to have no particular individual target. Physically and emotionally, Stafford seldom pays much heed to any form of personal boundary. As Stafford performs him, Coleman is predominantly without sensitivity, while curiously and frequently vexed by the petty grievances he holds against his neighbours.

O'Byrne's Valene is regularly fanatical, fidgety, temperamental and petulant, but also obsessively compulsive in many ways. Valene appears to be the physically weaker of the two brothers, and is allegedly traumatized by Coleman's persistent negative behaviours towards him. Byrne's Valene also displays the demeanour of someone who has a newly acquired status, is strengthened by this misplaced confidence, and his verbal aggressiveness and challenges to Tom Murphy's out of his depth, exasperated Fr Welsh are brilliantly realized. On the day of their father's funeral, Valene and Coleman are pulled apart by a drunken Priest. In a way they are performing for him, affirming his anxieties, but also strangely expecting him to take individual sides. Fr. Welsh is dependent on them in so many ways, growing more and more distraught at their behaviour, and even at one stage, he starts to cry. However, for the brothers, Fr Welsh is the one that needs to grow up, cast aside his maudlin, vulnerable, sentimentality, because currently, he takes things "too much to heart" (McDonagh, 1999: 140). Out-manipulated and team-tagged by the brothers, Fr Welsh is then targeted for his apparent lack of compassion, prompting him to increase his self-questioning and self doubts. These anxieties are framed perversely by Valene as Fr Welsh's regular and notorious crises of faith. Tom Murphy brings a vulnerability to the role of Father Welsh, combining defenselessness, confusion, exasperation and distress, which mesh with a physicality that indicates low levels of self-esteem and self-awareness, while at the same time Murphy's Fr Welsh takes some re-assurance from his imprecise and erroneous understanding of the tenets of the Catholic faith.

Although Murphy's Fr Welsh may seem to be the polar opposite of the two brothers, yet in his quest for understanding and in his expressions of empathy and concern, he still sustains rather than undermines the sensibility of the overall *mise-en-scène*; he is never too much at odds with the play's dominant tonality, indeed, he perversely compliments it. This is an exceptionally difficult thing to achieve and Murphy does so especially well. In Hynes's production every miniscule transaction, every micro gesture the characters perform emphasize the fact that they believe fundamentally, whether accurately or not, that there is so much at stake in every instance, that levels of fear and threat are especially heightened in almost every encounter.

In this production encounters are transactional–based on money, indebtedness, threats, manipulation, and psychological ascendancy. Their notional present is distorted by the impact of previous slights, the petty snubs and vendettas that are essential to distrustful and revenge fuelled interactions. There is no centering or mindfulness, to use contemporary terminology. They are pained by each other's successes however minimal and are of similar mind only when they both have the same targets in their community. As Ben Brantley notes in his review of Hynes' New York production, these "two middle-aged brothers whacked away at each other like a liquored-up Punch and Judy" (Brantley, 2001).

"Querulous dyads" and a Funerary Tradition

Nina Witoszek and Pat Sheeran suggest that the Irish funerary tradition is central to the disparaging dynamic that exists between so many characters in Irish literature generally, arguing that literature and especially theatre has persisted with "Querulous dyads," relying on characters who "live in a state of negative symbiosis: while they trade insults they are yet dependent on one another". They also note how such a structure is "diametrically opposite" of the buddy system so pervasive in "American culture" (Witoszek and Sheeran, 1998:157-8). Such Irish dyads, Witoszek and Sheeran continue, "are part of a community of hatred which observes a 'taboo on tenderness'", a phrase coined by Ian D. Suttie (Witoszek and Sheeran, 1998:158). Consequently, Witoszek and Sheeran suggest:

> Vernacular hatred and its various verbal and behavioural manifestations (calumny, detraction, etc.) is a diffuse, low-voltage, insidious process of dealing with death.... At its most virulent–and Ireland is a pathogenic zone in this regard–it destroys personal identity and maims for life. It is in this sense that the manifold manifestations of the vernacular hatred may be treated as tropes of funerary culture, ways of willing and wishing death. Like the funerary tradition itself, vernacular hatred has a double aspect. It too provides a bond, but one that is scarcely worth having. It empowers literature, but blights life. It creates identity but one that is found, at bottom, on death (Witoszek and Sheeran, 1998:146).

As already outlined, very evident throughout McDonagh's play are the blighted, negative bonds and dispositions with which Coleman and Valene innately align, as well as the maiming, destructive qualities and the death wishing that Witoszek and Sheeran categorize within this tradition. Further, Witoszek and Sheeran contend that not only is it "hatred which energises the famous Irish wit: verbal assassinations, sneers, jeers, lampoons and venomous satires" (Witoszek and Sheeran, 1998: 142), but also it originates in religious belief, through its renunciation of the "world, the flesh and the devil: a requirement which inevitably refined the arts of self-hatred. Then it demanded the impossible: love one's neighbour as oneself. Most, it seems, resolved that contradiction by hating their neighbour as they hated themselves" (Witoszek and Sheeran, 1998: 149).

While I do agree with the way they connection religion, self-hatred and the funerary tradition, and indeed these are interlinked strands that this play confirms, I do not accept their overarching and unduly negative summary of Irish wit as it leaves little room for playfulness, subversiveness, irony or de-contextualization, and it does not address the role of either a reader or theatre audiences in resisting or contesting such destructive dispositions when they are on display. Also I think that across his work, McDonagh sets out to take this funerary tradition to task.

An Inglourious Sacrifice

The two suicides in the play do raise particular issues around masculinity, self-worth, self-hatred, religion and a curious belief in self-sacrifice. On another level these deaths draw attention to the major problem of male suicide in Irish society more generally. Early in the play Fr Welsh gets very upset by the fact that neither Valene nor Coleman could even "bat an eye" at the revelation that Tom Hanlon had just taken his own life (McDonagh, 1999: 150). There is a great moment when O'Byrne pretends to copy the Priest's gestures and to mirror his physicalization of grief. Fr Welsh drops his head on the table, spreads his arms across it, Valene mimics him, only to be initially distracted by a bag of Tayto crisps on the ground, which he sneakily raises with his feet to his hands. But despite his low-level efforts to feign empathy, O'Byrne's Valene cannot hold the pose for very long, as his recently arrived new stove keeps catching his eye.

Coleman's casual admission to the murder of his father over an insult about his hairstyle, which was compared to that of a drunken child's, Valene's confession to the cover up of the deed, and the spectacle of the two brothers wrestling on the floor for control of the bullets for the gun all leave Fr Welsh in a state of absolute consternation. Fr Welsh's impulsive response to such transgressions is to punish himself, plunging his hands into the liquefied fiberglass figurines that Coleman had destructively placed earlier in a hot oven in order to antagonize Valene. Welsh's gesture of self-sacrifice or of self-harm, a be-scalding of sorts, is intended to put a stop to what they are doing to each other. The gesture is however deeply comical in performance. In great pain, Fr Welsh is regardless exasperated by the fact that they persist in getting his name wrong. Pain is rightly abstracted in the way that Bentley talks about in terms of farce, and Tom

Murphy, as Fr Welsh, revels in the comic and downplays the traumatic implications of what he has just done to himself.

Yet, if Fr Welsh's self-harming is one form of bizarre, even surrealistic sacrifice on behalf of (an)other, then Fr Welsh's later suicide extends its significance further, as its gestural and symbolic relevance are de-substantiated and de-ritualized. In many ways the hold of this funerary tradition is both affirmed but also substantially undermined by these two key moments of apparent self-sacrifice. For Witoszek and Sheeran whether it is the figure of Cúchulainn or Cathleen Ní Houlihan, most if not "all of the traditional images and narratives of identity resort to the motifs of suffering and endurance. These are necro-static," as for Witoszek and Sheeran, most Irish writers "have been experts in brokenness and impotence, in diagnosing the symptoms of death-in-life" (Witoszek and Sheeran, 1998: 4). Tom Murphy's narration of his letter to the two brothers sustains a good deal of trauma that is not undermined by moments of irony.

In the Druid production, as the two brothers return from Fr Welsh's funeral they are dressed in suits. There is a great awkwardness between them when they shake hands. Interestingly, they swap their usual places around the kitchen table. To start, they share the food brought home from the funeral, and even Valene freely offers some poteen to Coleman. Indeed, when Valene pours two measured drinks, he gives Coleman the fuller glass. The admissions to destructive deeds in the past and the seeking of forgiveness appear to be on their agenda, prompted by Fr Welsh's wishes. As Valene, O'Byrne's mode of admission about the past seems almost genuine and the traumas associated with these incidents appear relatively grounded, but are not beyond suspicion. Stafford's approach as Coleman to apologizing is somewhat in earnest, but also involves a good degree of cynicism and calculation, soon seeing in the transactions further opportunities to transgress and to be disagreeable.

These exchanges create moments of great comedy in performance, but as the confessions to past deeds progress, they are prompted less and less by sincerity and remorse, and are increasingly guided by one-up-manship. The deluded belief that Catholicism's sacrament of confession effectively means you can do anything you want, once forgiveness is sought, soon emerges as Coleman's constricted world-view. So in the Connor household, their version of the sacrament of confession, the seeking forgiveness for one's sins, and the penance and absolution that follow becomes instead, and by degrees, a de-ritualized spectacle, a de-sacramentalized power play. This sensibility is confirmed by Coleman's comment: ".... Okay, it's my go. I'm winning" (McDonagh, 1999: 185). It is Valene's divulgence of his part in the injuring of Alison O'Hoolihan in school that led to the end to Coleman's friendship with her and her engagement with the doctor who treated her, which initially seems like something that could not be trumped, as it incites Coleman to sling sausage rolls at him.

Servants of Odd/Masters of (Getting) Even

Coleman admits that he harmed Valene's dog, Lassie, however Valene is inclined to believe the admission to be untrue, and affirms with some conviction that lying is not within the rules. Having slowly and theatrically placed the ears of the dog on O'Byrne's head, Valene leaves them there temporarily before easing them onto the table, at which point, Stafford offers him a marker so that he might take the opportunity to initial them. O'Byrne descends more and more into a hysterical rage, as the details begin to sink in, ensuring that the stand-off which follows, with Valene armed with a knife and Coleman with a gun, looks as if it is heading towards a violent climax, following the template of *Beauty Queen*, where daughter kills mother following a destructive revelation. But after all that competitive confessing, rage, and destruction of the final show down, Coleman invites Valene for a drink, just after having again apologized, with a bit more sincerity, for what he did to the dog, his second go at destroying Valene's figurines, their general fighting, and the killing of their father. This almost heart-felt invitation offers a sort of bizarre closure, as if he has discharged, literally and symbolically, all his needs for the day. Indeed, central to their shared value system seems to be the belief in the merits of conflict, which is evident in Coleman's remark that: "….And what's wrong with fighting anyways? I do like a good fight. It does show you care, fighting does…." (McDonagh, 1999: 194).

The guides and markers to their worlds are provided in the main, not so much by the moral framework of religion for which they have a surface affection and little understanding, but by the values of popular cultural, television series, women's magazines and comics–*Hill Street Blues*, *Alias Smith and Jones*, *Woman's Way*, *Take a Break*, *Bella* and *Spiderman*. The information and consumerist agenda that guides much of popular culture ensures the ideological dissemination of conservative values, which are humane and empathetic in identification and sentiment only, but have no inclination to illicit responses, thus not completing the empathy cycle. In addition one can recognize how popular culture can be self-validating in terms of personal values, as it regularly distinguishes between what is normal and abnormal. However, in the world of the brothers, dysfunctionality remains the norm, different to most narratives of supportive families and sacrifices made for friends or neighbours found in many women's magazines for instance, to which they are addicted. Attitudes to life can be seen in their responses to the attainments of the local Under Twelve's girl's Gaelic Football team, a team that causes mayhem whenever they play. Milner Davis notes that "Farce is comedy with *self-awareness* left out" (Milner Davis, 2003: 143), and, in many ways, that is the case for the characters in *The Lonesome West*.

I also think that there is room for farce to bring on board complex awarenesses, through its "primitive vitality" that Joan Fitzpatrick Dean identifies in her analysis of Orton's work (Fitzpatrick Dean, 1982: 482). The positioning of the work could be seen to place a greater onus on the spectator, through a complex form of evolved alienation, not fully in the manner of Brecht's usage, particularly in terms of a depleted or almost "zero-empathy" demonstrated by the characters and the responses it might initiate (See Baron-Cohen, 2011). The lack of empathy is one of the striking features of characters in farce as they pursue their own agendas, without consideration of the costs to anyone else they wound along the way.

However, the generally confused emotional landscape of all three males in *Lonesome* is complicated by the presence of the seventeen year old female Girleen, who on first appearance in the Druid production wears a school uniform. Somewhat like the youthful (Slippy) Helen McCormick in *The Cripple of Inishmaan*, but unlike the bored, frustrated, psychopathic Mairead in *The Lieutenant of Inishmore*, Girleen is consistently the challenge to male self-obsession and toxic thinking. She is in part their object of desire, but is also especially assertive, verbally aggressive, and funny. Girleen initially is also far more playful than any of the others and this is evident in her discussions about having sex for money, a proposition which leads in a circuitous way to a situation where she wonders whether or not Fr Welsh could afford to pay her for sexual services. Equally, Girleen is the more mobile, grounded and self-aware of the four characters. But that does not make her either the reality principle or the figure that simply compensates for the male void of empathy, that she gives access to or recognition of emotions and sensations that the male characters cannot find within or acknowledge as important for themselves. (At one point Coleman's lie that that Girleen paid him in drink for sex is exposed, but this detail says less about Girleen as a simplistically objectified figure, and more about the inappropriate fantasies and delusions maintained by the brothers more generally.)

Girleen's despair after Fr Welsh's death is the only grief of apparent substance in the play. While Valene reports that she close to a mental break down after the death that may be seen to be more about the male characters' unwillingness to embrace grief. They view trauma, not in terms of despair and loss, but more in terms of mental frailty. The only mention of their mother is in relation to a figurine given to her by an American, so in that sense woman is effectively an unmentionable, unfathomable absence. Girleen is someone who disciplines and challenges both brothers. Bradfield's performance as Girleen is dazzling in that she had both a foothold in that strange male world, insisting on a participative presence in it, on the one hand, but, on the other, she also maintains an easily distinguishable distance from it. In fact, Girleen is the most complex character in this play, and is realized in the affectionate, tactile, spontaneity of Bradfield's exceptionally engaging performance. Girleen's heightened levels of empathy and self-awareness, which when pitted against the rudimentary variations to the limited and inappropriate instincts of the male characters, creates a dialectically complex sensibility for the play's audiences. Girleen gives greater voice to non-hegemonic femininity and to subordination per se.

Equally, the contradictory attitudes of the brothers to women generally, whether they are neighbours, visiting nuns, or images of women from around the world is striking; there is fear, awe, desire, desperation and major anxieties about commitment and engulfment. Equally, their own virginal states, lead to accusations that are deeply homophobic: Coleman calls Valene "ya little virgin gayboy", and Valene calls Coleman the same thing later (McDonagh, 1999: 147). Coleman punctures the logic of Valene's ownership claims, suggesting that there is no way he could move around the space only by levitating, like "them darkies" (McDonagh, 1999: 142). This comment invites further inappropriate reflections on "darkies", "Pakies", and "whistling at the snakes" (McDonagh, 1999: 142).

Most of the misogyny, homophobia and racism seem grounded in fear and not in the experience of contact between those of different genders, sexual orientations or races. Catherine Rees argues that "the brothers live together in a pseudo-marriage with seemingly no female interaction. Welsh asks the brothers if 'there [are] no lasses on the horizon, for ye' to which Coleman recounts an experience of losing a girlfriend to a doctor, an image of a more successful and highly achieving male, whose predatory advances have left Coleman alone" (Rees, 2007: 243). Rees sees them like the "masculine pairing of Beckettian characters such as Vladimir and Estragon and Hamm and Clov, relationships of interdependence and frustrated ambitions" (Rees, 2007: 241-2). The relative stalemate at the end of *Lonesome*, suggests no bountiful future of plenty and abundance, and no hope of children. McDonagh does not counter the homophobia, racism and misogyny of his characters and the failures of Valene and Coleman to deal with their scars and wounds are less failures of dramaturgical imagination, and more perhaps to do with placing some onus of responsibility with the spectator, who is challenged to bring to a performance his or her own behaviours, values and dispositions.

Warring F(r)actions/ Acting White/ Or 'the dead end of whiteness'

By this play's end, there is neither an affirmation of the repetition compulsion that drives the characters nor does the work offer a form of closure that inspires optimism: the inconclusiveness is captured in Valene's attempt to structure something symbolic out of the crucifix, Fr Welsh's part-burned letter and Girleen's chain, purchased as an expression of affection for Fr Welsh, but also broken and discarded by her. Fr Welsh's last wishes initiate something different but they could never kick-start a fundamental shift in consciousness. Forgiveness and retribution are not possible and peace between them is as futile as the suggestion of superglue as a solution to the destruction that Coleman has caused during the play's final scene. Yet, there is a moment when they almost embrace each other in performance, yet it is Coleman's tendency to placate Valene after he has done something to harm him which seems like the pattern being exposed. They have numerous near death moments.

Through wide ranging discussions of visual cultures Richard Dyer argues that the fundamental drives behind many of the representations of normative male whiteness are never without "specific class, gender, or other socio-cultural inflections" (Dyer, 1997: xv). Dyer connects advantage, privilege, superiority, dominance, goodness, power and legitimacy to a normative male whiteness, seeing also its expression in religious iconography, objective neutrality, spiritual purity, in the subjugation of women and in imperial practices. For Dyer, whiteness is a by-product of "enterprise and imperialism"–enterprise in terms of adventure, application, problem solving, and wilfulness, and colonisation in terms of myths of civilisation and progress, predicated on racial difference, interaction and domination (Dyer, 1997: 13).Yet, following on from David Lloyd's work, Dyer argues that even more crucial is "the attainment of a position of disinterest–abstraction, distance, separation, objectivity–which creates a public sphere that is the mark of civilisation, itself the aim of human history" and this perspective underpins the "conception of white people...

as everything and nothing", in its realisation of a sense of "*dis*-embodiedness," for "to be without properties also suggests not being at all," which he explores as "pure spirit", which also hints at "non-existence or death" as "colourless" as "dissolving transcendence", as "narrative impotence" or "as death" itself as instability distorts its claims of universality (Dyer, 1997: 39-40).

But, Dyer argues "the way in which this superiority is conceived and expressed, with its emphasis on purity, cleanliness, virginity, in short, absence, inflects whiteness once again towards non-particularity, only this time in the sense of non-existence" (Dyer, 1997: 70). Further he suggests that "the invisibility of whiteness as a racial position in white (which is to say dominant) discourse is of a piece with its ubiquity" (Dyer, 1997: 3). On the other hand, non-whites are never afforded ordinariness, always marked as peculiar and exceptional, thus ensuring that whiteness this is threatened by non-whiteness, by women, by homosexuality, by class disparities in terms of abundance, difference and reproduction, which are central to the perpetuation of whiteness. Dyer claims that "Whites must reproduce themselves, yet they must also control and transcend their bodies. Only by (impossibly) doing both can they be white. Thus are produced some of the great narrative dilemmas of whiteness, notably romance, adultery, rape and pornography" (Dyer, 1997: 30).

Science fiction, the horror genre and zombie movies are, Dwyer notes, particular representations which make it "bearable for whites the exploration of the association of whiteness with death" (Dyer, 1997: 210), and to this we can add the pastoral and the funerary traditions of Irish culture. Equally, for Dyer, in science fiction, the vampire or the zombie genres, death and reproduction are particularly exposed, as in human terms there is "the sense of the dead-end, the death of whiteness, it is also suggested in relation to reproduction", and this inability to reproduce contrasts with the hyper-reproductivity and engulfment of alien figures (Dyer, 1997: 218). But McDonagh's "liminally white" characters, while generally lacking in "enterprise", are less the vampires of horror, the living dead of zombie movies, the automatons or androids of science fiction or the replicants of say Ridley Scott's *Blade Runner* (1982), instead they are performative dark clowns, who do not reproduce, and who over-invested in the failure of repetition, even in the performance of repetition. (It is to be noted that for his main characters none of them has a child or the possibility of a child in the future offering some possibility.)

Diane Negra also highlights how Irishness oscillates between "otherness" and "whiteness", but just as substantially suggests that Irishness has "become particularly performative" (Negra, 2006: 2). Amanda Third also stresses that Irishness "offers a way of *performing whiteness* with legitimacy" (my italics) (Third, 2006: 224). Performativity opens up so many possibilities, raising the notion of the performance of Irishness, but also the performance of both depleted and enriched forms of whiteness as well as ways of "performing whiteness" with illegitimacy. For Irishness, in this instance, one can indeed substitute "masculinity"; while McDonagh does offer a performative and othered masculinity with his characters, he also creates one that is performatively visible.

Through loneliness, jealousy, deviance, isolation, disempowered, enfeeblement, excessive interdependency, the absence of intimacy and subsistence living, the subordinate or subservient masculinities of all three male characters in this work are especially foregrounded, in ways that challenge hegemonic heteronormativity. Rees notes that "McDonagh's representation of males seems to deliberately subvert the narratives of normative representation associated with male behaviour, especially narratives constructed around violence, rurality and nationalism. In confronting these issues, McDonagh 'marks' masculinity as a political subject within the plays, but does not allow the audience to reach stable conventional conclusions about 'typical' or normative masculine behaviour" (Rees, 2007: 273). But just as crucial is the fact that while the focus is on masculinity, McDonagh also illustrates a subservient humanity that is not gender, religion, race and class specific.

Subordination, rather than equality, is the experience for the majority of the world's population, even amongst the relative privilege of first world cultures. Audiences perhaps acknowledge their own subservience, their own subordinate status in first world democratic societies that preach opportunity, choice, agency and the promise of equality, but true status and the appropriate "dividends", patriarchal or otherwise, will never accrue for the majority of people, whether male or female, apart from those who are relatively wealthy.

Conclusion

As Hynes directs her production, the performances are cartoon like, impish, defiant and what is amputated is a real sense of depth; truncated, then, is this third dimension associated with something that is notionally akin to the real, a dramatic world that bears the weight of excess and exaggeration, without seeming unnecessarily false, but that does not make it representative of something real. Morality is provocatively limited to a phrase like "against God" and personal awarenesses are apparently absent. Indeed, the farcical energy highlights a destructive funerary sensibility, but a considered playfulness destabilizes many of the negative implications of such a tradition as tabulated by Witoszek and Sheeran.

In McDonagh's work non-conformity to the traditional expectations of the farcical genre must be embraced. Equally, in the toxicity, ill-discipline and in the oddness of the characters there are major challenges to hegemonic ideological inscriptions and also a confrontation of the framing of Ireland in a positively naïve, "enriched" pastoral fashion. Therefore the combination of an inverted pastoral, a contestation of a funerary consciousness that is not simply just an Irish phenomenon, non-hegemonic masculinities and femininities, and a re-tabulating of "liminal whiteness" ensures the significance of subordination of McDonagh's disenfranchised, immutable, stigmatized characters, while always othering, but equally other to themselves, offer the potential of a transgressive, performative whiteness and not the consolation of a transformative, pastoral whiteness, nor the perversity of a funerary whiteness, obsessed by death and its consolations. But in the work's anarchic farce, there is something overwhelmingly positive about unrecoverable, depleted and demonstratively defiant identities, both male and female.

Bibliography

Baron-Cohen, S., *Zero Degrees of Empathy: A New Theory of Human Cruelty.* London: Allen Lane an imprint of Penguin Books, 2011.

Barry, K., "An end to representation", *Irish Review* 27, Summer (2001) 183-86.

Brantley, B., "Another Tempestuous Night in Leenane (Sure, It's Not a Morn in Spring)," *New York Times*, April 28, http://theater.nytimes.com/mem/theater/treview.html?html_title=&tols_title=LONESOME%20WEST,%20THE%20(PLAY)&pdate=19990428&byline=By%20BEN%20BRANTLEY&id=1077011432598 [Accessed 10/7/2010] 1999

Bentley, E., *The Life of the Drama* London: Methuen, 1965.

Connell, R.W., "The Social Organisation of Masculinity," in *The Masculinities Reader*, edited by Stephen M. Whitehead and Frank Barrett. Cambridge: Polity Press (30-50). 2001.

Dyer, R., *White*. London and New York: Routledge, 1997.

Fitzpatrick Dean, J., "Joe Orton and the Redefinition of Farce", *Theatre Journal*, 34.4. (1982) 481-492.

McDonagh, M. *The Lonesome West: Plays 1* London: Methuen, 1999.

Magennis, C. and R. Mullen, (eds.), *Irish Masculinities: Reflections on Literature and Culture* Dublin: Irish Academic Press, 2011.

Meaney, G., "Dead, White, Male: Irishness in *Buffy the Vampire Slayer* and *Angel*" in *The Irish in Us: Irishness, Performativity, and Popular Culture,* edited by Diane Negra, Duke University Press, Durham and London.254-281. 2006.

Merriman, V, "Decolonization Postponed: Theatre of Tiger Trash", *Irish University Review*, 29.2 (1999) 305-17.

Milner Davis, J., *Farce*, New Brunswick & London: Transaction Publishers, 2003.

Murphy, P., "The Stage Irish Are Dead, Long Live the Stage Irish: *The Lonesome West* and *A Skull in Connemara*" in *The Theatre of Martin McDonagh: World of Savage Stories*, eds. L. Chambers and E. Jordan Dublin, Carysfort Press, pp.60-78. 2006.

—. *Hegemony and Fantasy in Irish Drama, 1899-1949* Basingstoke: Palgrave, 2008.

Negra, D., "Introduction," *The Irish in Us: Irishness, Performativity, and Popular Culture,* edited by Diane
Negra Duke University Press, Durham and London, 2006.

Rees, C, "Martin McDonagh: Narratives of theatrical power and representation" PhD Thesis, Aberystwyth University, 2007

Singleton, B., *Masculinities and Contemporary Irish Theatre*. Basingstoke: Palgrave, 2011.

Third, Amanda, "'Does the Rug Match the Carpet?' Race, Gender and the Redheaded Woman" in *The Irish in Us: Irishness, Performativity, and Popular Culture,* edited by Diane Negra. Duke University Press, Durham and London, 220-253. 2006.

Witoszek, N. and P. Sheeran, *Talking to the Dead: A Study of the Irish Funerary Traditions.* Amsterdam-Atlanta, GA: Rodopi, 1998

CONTRIBUTORS

Shane Alcobia-Murphy is a senior lecturer at the University of Aberdeen. He has published three monographs on Northern Irish culture: *Governing the Tongue in Northern Ireland* (2005), *Sympathetic Ink* (2006) and *Medbh McGuckian: The Poetics of Exemplarity* (2012). He has also edited several collections of essays, including *The Poetry of Medbh McGuckian* (2010) and *Founder to Shore: Cross-currents in Irish and Scottish Studies* (2011).

Alan Bairner is Professor of Sport and Social Theory at Loughborough University. Before moving to England, he had lived in Belfast from 1978 until 2003. He has written extensively on the relationship between sport and national identity and is co-author of *Sport, Sectarianism and Society in a Divided Ireland* (1993) and author of *Sport, Nationalism and Globalization: European and North American Perspectives* (2001). He also edited *Sport and the Irish: Histories, Identities, Issues* (2005) and co-edited *Sport in Divided Societies* (1999), *The Bountiful Game? Football Identities and Finances* (2005) and *The Politics of the Olympics: a survey* (2010). He has advised both the Northern Ireland Assembly and the Irish Football Association on sport and community relations and is the founding editor of the *Asia Pacific Journal of Sport and Social Science*.

Robert Busby is Senior Lecturer in politics at Liverpool Hope University and his research is primarily in the field of political scandal and aspects of political communication. He has published three research monographs, two on political scandal and one on comparative political marketing.

Fiona Coffey is a PhD candidate in theatre history, literature, and criticism at Tufts University in Boston. She is a graduate of Stanford University and Trinity College, Dublin. Between her Masters and PhD, Fiona spent five years as a talent agent in New York City. Her research interests include Irish theatre and film, gender studies, and peace/conflict studies. She has been published in *The Irish Literary Supplement* and *Ecumenica Journal* and has taught at Tufts University, the University of Hartford and the University of Connecticut.

Joana Etchart is a lecturer in British/Irish History at the Paris-Sorbonne (Paris 4). She is a member of the SOFEIR (French Society of Irish Studies). Her current research interests are centred on the study of public policies and community initiatives in the field of peacebuilding in Northern Ireland. She recently published a chapter on loyalism and peacebuilding (Building Peace in Northern Ireland, 2011). She also studies urban regeneration projects in Irish and British cities. In her work, regeneration and peacebuilding projects serve as an entry point for analysing the policy-making process and the complex relationship binding statutory bodies, local communities and specialist groups (professionals, academics).

Fiona Fearon is a lecturer in Theatre Studies at Dundalk Institute of Technology, Ireland. Her principal areas of interest are audience and performance studies, and she has published on audience ethnography and the performance of grief in contemporary society, and in particular the intersection between audience, performance and new media. She is a member of the executive committee of the Irish Society for Theatre Research, and a member of the Performance Philosophy Working Group. She completed her PhD in December 2007 at the University of Sheffield, and is currently working on the revision of her thesis, *The Selection, Production and Reception of European Plays at the National Theatre of Great Britain, 1963-1997.*

Peter Guy is Assistant Professor in the Faculty of Policy Studies at Chuo University, Tokyo. His research interests lie in the area of Anglo-Irish literature, deconstructing ideologies and Church-State relations, with a focus on the exploration of the trauma narrative. He is also an active member of numerous literary societies promoting the study of Irish literature in Japan, in particular in the translation and production of the works of W.B. Yeats.

Kathleen Heininge is Associate Professor of English at George Fox University in Oregon. She has published on Frank McGuinness, W. B. Yeats, Eavan Boland, the Irish Renaissance, Gerard Stembridge, and Virginia Woolf, among other topics. Her book, *Buffoonery in Irish Drama: Staging 20th Century Post-Colonial Stereotypes*, was published in 2009. She is presently at work on a book about Virginia Woolf and her Quaker aunt, Caroline Stephen.

Paddy Hoey is a lecturer in media and communication at Liverpool Hope University and his research is focused in the area of Irish republicanism, new media, the public sphere and political communication.

Eamonn Jordan is Lecturer in Drama Studies at the School of English, Drama and Film, University College Dublin. His book *The Feast of Famine: The Plays of Frank McGuinness* (1997) is the first full-length study on McGuinness's work. In 2000, he edited *Theatre Stuff: Critical Essays on Contemporary Irish Theatre*. More recently, he co-edited with Lilian Chambers *The Theatre of Martin McDonagh: A World of Savage Stories* (2006) and *The Theatre of Conor McPherson: 'Right beside the Beyond'* (2012). His last monograph *Dissident Dramaturgies: Contemporary Irish Theatre* was published in 2010 by Irish Academic Press.

Sharon Leahy is a Post-doctoral fellow in the Department of Geography and SD at the University of St Andrews. She completed her PhD at NUIG in 2010, focusing on a critical study of televisual archives, providing an interrogation of the construction and transmission of discourses of "race" and "ethnicity" and their relations to "place", "belonging" and "Irishness" on Ireland's national broadcasting channel. She is currently working on the bio-political agendas inherent in sex trafficking policy.

Sarah Martindale completed her doctoral research at Aberystwyth University focusing on the relationship between film and the status of "Shakespeare" as a cultural phenomenon. Her study of Shakespeare as an icon of British culture within international contexts of film production and reception was the starting point for broader interest in the representation of cultural identity and cinema as a national/global medium. She is a Research Fellow at Horizon Digital Economy Research at the University of Nottingham and is contributing her knowledge of media texts and industries and audience research methodologies to interdisciplinary projects investigating the impact of technological innovations on television content and audience interactions with that content.

Catherine Rees is a lecturer in Drama at Loughborough University. She has a wide interest in all areas of Irish Studies, focusing primarily on Irish theatre, the subject of her doctoral thesis being playwright Martin McDonagh. She has published widely on his work, and has recently edited a new edition of *The Beauty Queen of Leenane*. She has also published on other areas of Irish national identity, theatre and performance. She is interested in the study of trauma and postmodernity, and has also published in other areas of contemporary British theatre, namely on the work of Sarah Kane and Harold Pinter.

Catriona Ryan is a lecturer and post-doctoral researcher at Swansea University and also lectures at Swansea Metropolitan University. Her research areas are Critical Theory, Irish and Global Literature. Her first monograph on the experimental drama and fiction of Tom Mac Intyre was published in 2012; the title being *Border Sates in the Work of Tom Mac Intyre: A Paleo-Postmodern Perspective*. She created the theory paleo-postmodernism to describe the uniqueness of Tom Mac Intyre's aesthetics and is planning to extend the paleo-postmodern framework into other areas of literature. She is currently editing a collection of essays on the Irish experimental short story entitled, *Writing from the Margins: The Aesthetics of Disruption in the Irish Short Story*. It will be published in late 2013.

Cary A. Shay holds degrees in Classical Studies, Anglo-Irish Literature and Drama and English Literature from universities in the U.S., Ireland and the U.K. Shay completed her doctoral dissertation, a critical study of the writing of Nuala Ní Dhomhnaill, at the University of Kent, Canterbury in 2009. Her research interests include Anglo-Irish and Irish language literature, psychoanalytic theory, and feminism and psychoanalysis. *Of Mermaids and Others: An Introduction to the Poetry of Nuala Ní Dhomhnaill* is forthcoming in 2013.

David Storey is Senior Lecturer in Geography at the University of Worcester. He has research interests in territory and identity, heritage and place promotion, and the geographies of sport. He has published various articles dealing with aspects of sport and national identity and is the author of *Territories. The Claiming of Space* (2nd edition, Routledge, 2012).

INDEX